Hanford Abram Edson

Contributions to the early history of the Presbyterian Church in Indiana : together with biographical notices of the pioneer ministers

Hanford Abram Edson

Contributions to the early history of the Presbyterian Church in Indiana : together with biographical notices of the pioneer ministers

ISBN/EAN: 9783337305123

Printed in Europe, USA, Canada, Australia, Japan

Cover: Foto ©Lupo / pixelio.de

More available books at **www.hansebooks.com**

CONTRIBUTIONS

TO

THE EARLY HISTORY

OF THE

PRESBYTERIAN CHURCH

IN INDIANA

*TOGETHER WITH BIOGRAPHICAL NOTICES
OF THE PIONEER MINISTERS*

BY

HANFORD A. EDSON

CINCINNATI, INDIANAPOLIS, AND CHICAGO
WINONA PUBLISHING COMPANY
1898

PREFATORY NOTE.

THESE pages seek to preserve materials which would soon have been beyond reach—diaries, letters, the reminiscences of pioneers. It will be a satisfaction if any one is prompted to put other such materials into a safe place.

Several years since I had occasion to make inquiries about the ministers who laid the foundations of our Indiana church. The study took me into an unknown land. I was surprised at every step. Courage, self-sacrifice, piety, were to be expected; but I found besides a beautiful social life, uncommon learning, undoubted genius for affairs, and gifts of utterance in every way memorable.

Such fathers leave for their children the best of all legacies. If in any degree I may have helped to perpetuate their memory and light up their example, I shall rejoice.

Indianapolis, May 1, 1898.

TABLE OF CONTENTS.

CHAPTER I.
BEGINNINGS AND SPREAD OF PRESBYTERIANISM IN AMERICA.

Genius of the Reformed Churches—Wide Extension of Presbyterianism—Earliest History of the Church in America—Presbyterians in New England, New York, New Jersey, Delaware, and Virginia—Francis Makemie, Old Hanover, and William Robinson—Samuel Davies—David Rice—Transylvania Presbytery 9

CHAPTER II.
THE SETTLEMENT OF INDIANA.

Discovery of the Great West—Spanish and French Explorers—La Salle and the Mississippi Valley—First White Man on Indiana Soil—Vincennes the Earliest Settlement—French succeeded by English Dominion—Northwestern Territory—Indiana Territory—Character of Early Settlers—A Large Presbyterian Element 20

CHAPTER III.
THE FIRST MISSIONARIES. 1800–1806.

Volunteers from Kentucky—Samuel Rannels—Samuel B. Robertson—James McGready—James Kemper—Thomas Cleland—Organization of First Church—Samuel Thornton Scott the First Settled Minister 30

CHAPTER IV.
HINDRANCES AND DISORDERS INCIDENT TO WAR. 1807–1814.

Palmyra Church—James H. Dickey—Lawrenceburgh—Samuel Baldridge—Charlestown—Joseph B. Lapsley—Matthew G. Wallace—Tour of Samuel J. Mills—William Robinson at Madison 45

v

CHAPTER V.

THE WAR OVER AND THE WORK ADVANCED. 1815.

More Missionaries—John McElroy Dickey—His Great Usefulness—Close of the Territorial Period 61

CHAPTER VI.

AID FROM NEW ENGLAND. 1816, 1817.

McGready, Cleland, and Lapsley Again—Samuel Shannon—First New England Missionaries—Nathan B. Derrow—Clement Hickman—William Dickey—Daniel C. Banks—John Todd at Charlestown—James Balch 81

CHAPTER VII.

A NOTABLE QUARTET. 1818.

William W. Martin at Livonia—Isaac Reed—Orin Fowler from the Connecticut Missionary Society—Ravaud K. Rodgers Commissioned by the General Assembly—Charles Stebbins Robinson on His Way to Missouri . 101

CHAPTER VIII.

BETTER ECCLESIASTICAL SUPERVISION. 1819-1821.

Lack of Settled Pastors—David Monfort—Thomas C. Searle—His Brilliant Promise and Early Death 131

CHAPTER IX.

INDIANAPOLIS. 1821.

Seat of Government Transferred from Corydon—First Settlement and First Settlers at the New Capital—Coe, Blake, Scudder, Ray—First Presbyterian Sermon—Ludwell G. Gaines—Church Organization Effected—David Choate Proctor 138

CHAPTER X.

EXTENSION TOWARD THE NORTH. 1822.

Fort Wayne—John Ross—His Unique History—Ezra H. Day at New Albany—William Goodell—Charles C. Beatty . . 148

CHAPTER XI.
THE SHADOW OF SLAVERY. 1823.

Joseph Trimble—The Madison Flock again without a Pastor —John Finley Crowe at Hanover—The Slavery Conflict . 156

CHAPTER XII.
THE FIRST PRESBYTERY. 1823, 1824.

Salem Presbytery Organized—Its Original Members—First Records—Tilly H. Brown the First Licentiate—John T. Hamilton 162

CHAPTER XIII.
HELP FROM PRINCETON. 1824.

Samuel Taylor Commissioned by General Assembly—George Bush at Indianapolis—Baynard R. Hall in the State Seminary at Bloomington—Alexander Williamson 169

CHAPTER XIV.
TWO FELLOW-TRAVELERS. 1824.

John Young's Brief Career—James Harvey Johnston 192

CHAPTER XV.
A PERIOD OF INCREASED MISSIONARY ZEAL. 1825.

Missions at Andover Seminary—Union of Missionary Societies—A. H. M. S.—Lucius Alden—Lewis McLeod—James Stewart—Samuel Gregg—William Nesbit—Stephen Bliss across the Wabash—Samuel G. Lowry in Decatur County 206

CHAPTER XVI.
ORGANIZATION OF THE SYNOD OF INDIANA. 1826.

Condition of Indiana—Truman Perrin—James Crawford—Samuel E. Blackburn—James Duncan—Isaac A. Ogden—Joseph Robinson—Synod Organized—First Records—Calvin Butler—Leander Cobb—William Lowry—William Henderson—James Thomson 214

CHAPTER V.

THE WAR OVER AND THE WORK ADVANCED. 1815.

More Missionaries—John McElroy Dickey—His Great Usefulness—Close of the Territorial Period 61

CHAPTER VI.

AID FROM NEW ENGLAND. 1816, 1817.

McGready, Cleland, and Lapsley Again—Samuel Shannon—First New England Missionaries—Nathan B. Derrow—Clement Hickman—William Dickey—Daniel C. Banks—John Todd at Charlestown—James Balch 81

CHAPTER VII.

A NOTABLE QUARTET. 1818.

William W. Martin at Livonia—Isaac Reed—Orin Fowler from the Connecticut Missionary Society—Ravaud K. Rodgers Commissioned by the General Assembly—Charles Stebbins Robinson on His Way to Missouri . 101

CHAPTER VIII.

BETTER ECCLESIASTICAL SUPERVISION. 1819–1821.

Lack of Settled Pastors—David Monfort—Thomas C. Searle—His Brilliant Promise and Early Death 131

CHAPTER IX.

INDIANAPOLIS. 1821.

Seat of Government Transferred from Corydon—First Settlement and First Settlers at the New Capital—Coe, Blake, Scudder, Ray—First Presbyterian Sermon—Ludwell G. Gaines—Church Organization Effected—David Choate Proctor 138

CHAPTER X.

EXTENSION TOWARD THE NORTH. 1822.

Fort Wayne—John Ross—His Unique History—Ezra H. Day at New Albany—William Goodell—Charles C. Beatty . . 148

CHAPTER XI.

THE SHADOW OF SLAVERY. 1823.

Joseph Trimble—The Madison Flock again without a Pastor
—John Finley Crowe at Hanover—The Slavery Conflict . 156

CHAPTER XII.

THE FIRST PRESBYTERY. 1823, 1824.

Salem Presbytery Organized—Its Original Members—First
Records—Tilly H. Brown the First Licentiate—John T.
Hamilton 162

CHAPTER XIII.

HELP FROM PRINCETON. 1824.

Samuel Taylor Commissioned by General Assembly—George
Bush at Indianapolis—Baynard R. Hall in the State Seminary at Bloomington—Alexander Williamson 169

CHAPTER XIV.

TWO FELLOW-TRAVELERS. 1824.

John Young's Brief Career—James Harvey Johnston 192

CHAPTER XV.

A PERIOD OF INCREASED MISSIONARY ZEAL. 1825.

Missions at Andover Seminary—Union of Missionary Societies—A. H. M. S.—Lucius Alden—Lewis McLeod—
James Stewart—Samuel Gregg—William Nesbit—Stephen
Bliss across the Wabash—Samuel G. Lowry in Decatur
County 206

CHAPTER XVI.

ORGANIZATION OF THE SYNOD OF INDIANA. 1826.

Condition of Indiana—Truman Perrin—James Crawford—
Samuel E. Blackburn—James Duncan—Isaac A. Ogden—
Joseph Robinson—Synod Organized—First Records—
Calvin Butler—Leander Cobb—William Lowry—William
Henderson—James Thomson 214

CHAPTER XVII.

INDIANA PRESBYTERIANS AND EDUCATION.

The First Schools—The State Seminary and College at Bloomington—Hanover Academy and College—Indiana Theological Seminary—Wabash College 228

APPENDIX.

I. Missionary Agencies at Work in Indiana previous to 1826 255
II. Ecclesiastical Relations of the Indiana Congregations previous to 1826 258
III. Bibliography 260

CONTRIBUTIONS TO THE EARLY HISTORY OF THE PRESBYTERIAN CHURCH IN INDIANA.

CHAPTER I.

BEGINNINGS AND SPREAD OF PRESBYTERIANISM IN AMERICA.

"Go ye into all the world" is a command suited to the genius of that community of Christians to which Presbyterians belong.

Nothing is more striking in a general view of the history of the Reformed Churches than the variety of countries into which we find their characteristic spirit, both in doctrine and polity, penetrating. Throughout Switzerland it was a grand popular movement. There is, first of all, Zwingle, the hero of Zurich, already in 1516 preaching against the idolatrous veneration of Mary, a man of generous culture and intrepid spirit, who at last laid down his life upon the field of battle. In Basle we find Œcolampadius, and also Bullinger, the chronicler of the Swiss reform. Farel arouses Geneva to iconoclasm by his inspiring eloquence. Thither comes in 1536, from the France which disowned him, Calvin, the mighty law-giver, great as a preacher, an expositor, a teacher, and a ruler; cold in exterior, but burning with internal fire; who produced at twenty-four years of age his unmatched "Institutes," and at thirty-five had made Geneva, under an almost theocratic government, the model city of Europe, with its inspiring motto, "Post tenebras lux." He was feared and opposed by the libertines of his day, as he is in our own. His errors were those of his own times; his greatness is of all times. Hooker calls him "incomparably the wisest man of the French Church"; he compares him to the "Master of Sentences," and says "that though thousands were debtors to him as touching divine knowledge, yet he was to none, only to God." Montesquieu declares that "the Genevese should ever bless the day of his birth." Jewel terms him "a reverend father, and worthy ornament of the church of God." "He that will not honor the memory of Calvin," says Mr. Bancroft, "knows but little of the origin of American liberty." Under his influence Geneva became the "fertile seed-plot" of reform for all Europe ; with Zurich and Strasbourg, it was the refuge of the oppressed from the British Isles, and thus indoctrinated England and ourselves with its own spirit.

The same form of faith was planted in the German Palatinate, modified by the influence of Melanchthon, receiving an admirable exposition in the Heidelberg Catechism and the writings of Ursinus, and forming the German Reformed Church. Holland accepted the same system of faith with the spirit of martyrdom ; against Charles and Philip, against Alba and the Inquisition, it fought heroically, under the Prince of Orange, of imperishable fame. In contending for freedom in religion it imbibed the love of civil freedom, which it brought also to our shores ; and though Guizot does not once name Holland in his "History of European Civilization," we can never name it but with honor and gratitude ; itself oppressed, it became the refuge of the oppressed. In England, God overruled the selfish policy of Henry VIII. to the furtherance of the gospel ; the persecution of Mary, 1553-8, sent forth the best of England's blood to Zurich and Geneva, there to imbibe more deeply the principles of the Reform and to bring back the seeds of Puritanism, which germinated in spite of the High Court of Commission and the Acts of Uniformity of 1559 and subsequent years. The universities were Calvinistic in their most vigorous period, when Bucer and Peter Martyr taught in them a pure faith. "The Reformation in England," says the *Christian Remembrancer* (1845), "ended by showing itself a decidedly Calvinistic movement." "The Reformation produced Calvinism ; this was its immediate offspring, its genuine matter-of-fact expression." And need I speak of Scotland, where the towering form of John Knox, also taught in Geneva, stands out severe in doctrine and morals, in vivid contrast with the loveliness of the frail and passionate Mary? Her chivalry could not stem the tide. Presbyterianism prevailed, never to lose its hold of the Scotch nation. Their "fervid genius" was well pleased with this strong theology. Tenacity like that of the Burghers and of the Anti-Burghers, both New and Old Light, and the indomitable spirit of religious independence go with them wherever they go. The Free Church battles in the nineteenth century for the principles of its sires. The Solemn League and Covenant reappear in our own land, transferred from religion to politics in the Mecklenburg Declaration.[1]

Upon the earliest history of the Presbyterian Church in America a degree of obscurity rests. The few feeble congregations on the new continent were scattered over an immense breadth of territory.[2] Probably the French Huguenots were the earliest Presbyterian immigrants. These came under the auspices of Admiral Coligny to the Carolinas in 1562 and to Florida in 1565. They were not successful however. Alexander Whitaker, "the self-denying apostle of Virginia,"[3] writes of his work in 1614. In New England a considerable number of Puritan Presbyterians were at work before the middle of the seventeenth century. Among those "inclined to Presbyterian views of church government" may be mentioned Thomas Parker and James Noyes, of Newbury, Mass., John Eliot, the Apostle to the Indians, and Peter Hobart, of Hingham.[4] At Southold, L. I., a church was organized October 21, 1640, by John Young, and not much later Pierson, Doughty, Fordham, and Denton were preaching in that neighborhood, Doughty being the first Presbyterian minister in New York City and Denton the second. The sufferings in Great Britain under James and Charles occasioned constant accessions to the Presbyterian community in America. After the battle of Dunbar, in 1650, many Scottish prisoners, Cromwell's Presbyterians, were shipped to the plantations beyond the seas to be sold. Upon the restoration of Charles II. there was a voluntary exodus from the persecuted parishes in Scotland. "Robert Liv-

[1] "Address before the Presbyterian Historical Society at St. Louis," 1855, by Dr. Henry B. Smith, pp. 13-5.

[2] See Sprague's "Annals," Vol. III., p. xi.

[3] Bancroft's "History," 1883 ed., Vol. I., p. 104.

[4] Briggs's "American Presbyterianism," p. 94. For a good *résumé* of the earliest history see Ency. Brit., Art. "Presbyterianism."

ingston came to New York in 1672 with his nephew. He was a son of the venerable minister of Ancrum who was banished to Holland, and whose name is linked in honorable remembrance with the signal refreshing at the Kirk of Shotts."[1] A Presbyterian settlement near Norfolk, Va., had a pastor from Ireland who died in 1683. Emigrants from Scotland and the north of Ireland multiplied in East Jersey, Del., along the York and Rappahannock Rivers, and in Charleston, S. C.

A congregational minister of London, one Henry Jacob, had removed in 1624 to Virginia, where he died. In 1642 an appeal was made to New England by seventy-one "inhabitants of the county of the Upper Norfolk in Virginia" for three ministers "faithful in pureness of doctrine and integrity of life." Knowles, Thompson, and James, who responded to this appeal, were successful in their labors, but were silenced by the Episcopal authorities, and in less than a year returned home. Through the continued intolerance of the government, aided by a plague and by Indian massacres, dissent was nearly rooted out of that region.[2]

The duty of sending the gospel to the colonies had been considered in Great Britain in 1641, Mr. Castell of Cortenhall parish devising a scheme for that purpose which was approved by seventy of the Westminster divines. The first formal application to the British churches for aid seems, however, to have been a letter from Colonel William Stevens. It was laid before the Irish Presbytery of Laggan in 1680, and Makemie, who yielded to the overture and soon after migrated to America, became one of the most useful pioneers of the church in this country.[3]

[1] Webster's "History," p. 66.
[2] Felt's "Ecclesiastical History," Vol I., pp. 216, 471-7, 487, 496, 515, 526-7. Vol. II., p. 7. (Referred to by Gillett, Vol. I., pp. 7-9.)
[3] "It is a fact not generally known that in the year 1636, soon after their establishment in Ulster, some of these emigrants [the Scotch-Irish Presbyterians] projected a settlement in New England. In the month of September of that year the *Eaglewing*

FRANCIS MAKEMIE, a native of county Donegal, Ireland, a student of the University of Glasgow, ordained by Laggan Presbytery, came in 1683 to "Maryland, beside Virginia." It has been thought that he first labored on the western shore of the Chesapeake,[1] as his name does not appear until 1690 in the records of Accomac County.[2] Not a mark of his pen is preserved with the exception of a half-dozen letters.[3] No contemporary sketch of his character is to be found. But he was evidently not only a pious, learned, and imposing minister, but also a remarkably resolute and persevering man.[4] Though he suffered imprisonment in New York for venturing to preach the gospel there, his defense of himself before the court both won respect and inspired fear. In 1704 he returned to Europe, coming back the year after with two more Presbyterian ministers, Hampton and McNish. It is probable that Samuel Davis also came to America under his persuasion; and Nathaniel Taylor, another of the pioneers, seems to have been connected with the Makemie family by marriage.[5] Only two of the seven[6] original members of

sailed from Loch Fergus for the Merrimac River with one hundred and forty passengers, including the celebrated preachers Robert Blair, John Livingston, James Hamilton, and John McClelland. The vessel was driven back by stress of weather, and the next year these ministers returned to Scotland, where they affiliated with the still more famous Johnston of Warriston and Alexander Henderson, and became prominent in the commotions, civil and religious, which led to the subversion of the English throne and the execution of its treacherous occupant.

"Two thirds of a century later, in consequence of persecution from a government which in some sense owed its existence to the heroism shown at the terrible siege of Londonderry, and the crowning victory of the Boyne, the emigration from Ulster to this country began in earnest, and from about the year 1720 swarm followed swarm from the great hive, some of the emigrants stopping in New England and New York, but the greater part passing into the upper regions of Pennsylvania, Virginia, and the Carolinas."
—A writer in the *New York Tribune*, January 13, 1877.

[1] Hodge's "History," p. 66.

[2] "This is the record of a suit brought by him to recover from one William Finney the amount due him for molasses sold."—Foote's "Sketches of Virginia," first series, p. 43.

[3] Briggs's "American Presbyterianism," appendix.

[4] Hodge's "History," p. 76.

[5] Webster's "History," p. 318.

[6] Hodge (p. 76), omitting the name of John Hampton, makes the number six.

the first Presbytery[1] could have been influenced by him in their resolution to preach the gospel in America. In 1708 Makemie died,[2] leaving for his family a considerable estate.

About the time of Makemie's decease began the settlement of that portion of Virginia west of the Blue Ridge, and it is interesting to observe how generally the prominent names of "the Valley" reappear in the later annals of the church upon newer ground. Lyle, Stuart, Crawford, Campbell, Moore, Wallace, Wilson, Cummins, McKee, belong not more to the "Potomoke" region than to Kentucky.

An austere, thoughtful race, they preferred the peaceful pursuits of agriculture to the wild license of the hunter's life and constituted a manly and virtuous yeomanry, of whom Washington is reported to have said, that should all his plans be crushed, and but a single standard left him, he would plant that standard on the Blue Ridge, make the mountain heights his barrier, and rallying round him the noblest patriots of the Valley, found, under better auspices, a new republic in the West.[3]

At their request, in 1719, "the people of Potomoke," near Martinsburgh, were supplied with a minister by the Synod of Philadelphia. Immigration to that region was rapidly increasing and several congregations maintained worship without interference from the prelatical authorities of the colony.

Besides the counties on the eastern shore, where the blessing of Makemie's labors remained, and the settlements in "the Valley," there were also remarkable religious developments in Hanover and the counties adjacent.

The established clergy were many of them notoriously profligate

---

[1] It is a familiar fact that the first leaf of the records is wanting. But the organization occurred in 1705 or 1706.

[2] "Spence's 'Letters' contain much information relating to Mr. Makemie. In Smith's 'History of New York' may be found an instructive account of his imprisonment and trial; and the most interesting portion of Dr. Hill's 'Sketches' relate to his character and labors."—Hodge, p. 76, foot-note.

[3] Davidson's "Kentucky," p. 21.

in their lives, and very few among them preached, or appeared to understand, the gospel of Christ. It was under these circumstances that some pious books, or fragments of books, which fell into the hands of a few individuals, were made the means of awakening them to a concern for their eternal interest, and of commencing a work of grace which was afterward most powerfully and happily extended.[1]

A few leaves of Boston's "Fourfold State," which had belonged to a good Scotchwoman, came into the possession of a wealthy planter, awakened his mind, and brought him to the truth. Another prominent citizen of Hanover, Mr. Samuel Morris, about the same time got hold of "Luther on the Galatians," and was deeply affected by it. In the spirit of genuine piety he at once became interested in his neighbors, and invited them to his house that they might together engage in the reading of religious books. Thus was established the famous "Morris' Reading House." The large number of people there frequently assembled soon attracted the notice of the government, but Mr. Morris and his friends declaring themselves "Lutherans" for a time escaped further annoyance.

It was now that William Robinson, son of an English Quaker, and a member of New Brunswick Presbytery, was making his memorable preaching tour through some of the remote counties of Virginia. A singular power accompanied him. Many conversions occurred. It happened that these results were witnessed by some of the young people of the "Reading-House" assemblies, and their report of the matter on their return home so interested these inquiring Dissenters that they despatched messengers to prevail with Mr. Robinson to visit them. On the 6th of July, 1743, he preached the first Presbyterian sermon heard in that region, and the interest it kindled rapidly increased during the four days he remained with them. "There is reason to believe," wrote Mr. Morris himself,

[1] Miller's "Life of Rodgers," p. 32.

"there was as much good done by these four sermons as by all the sermons preached in these parts before or since."[1] Upon Robinson's departure the people secretly conveyed into his saddle-bags, as a mark of their gratitude, a considerable sum of money, which he had before refused.

Discovering the benevolent artifice he no longer declined receiving the money, but informed his kind friends that he would appropriate it to the use of a young man of his acquaintance who was studying for the ministry, but embarrassed in his circumstances. "As soon as he is licensed," he added, "we will send him to visit you; it may be that you may now, by your liberality, be educating a minister for yourselves."[2]

Samuel Davies was the young student referred to, and thus occurs another distinguished name directly in that course of providence which, sixty years later, was to carry the gospel to the Indiana wilderness.

SAMUEL DAVIES, of Welsh parentage, was born in Newcastle County, Del., November 3, 1723, and seems to have been converted under the preaching of Gilbert Tennent. After his licensure, though affected with a threatening pulmonary disease, he went down to the eastern shore of Maryland, where, for two months, he preached by day, though delirious with fever at night. In the spring of 1747 he was sent, by Newcastle Presbytery, to Hanover, in Virginia, where "the people received him as an angel of God and earnestly urged him to settle among them." The following year he accepted the call, obtained from the General Court at Williamsburg permission to preach in the colony, and entered upon the work which was soon to secure, in 1755, the organization of Hanover Presbytery.[3]

---

[1] Gillies's "Historical Collections," Vol. II., p. 330.

[2] Gillett's "History," Vol. I., pp. 114, 115.

[3] Besides William Robinson, it is not to be forgotten that John Roan, the Blairs, and the Tennents had also preached the gospel in Virginia, assisting in laying "the foundation on which Davies builded." Foote's "Sketches of Virginia," first series, p. 146.

Though Davies afterward became a notable president of Princeton College and a preacher admired no less in Great Britain than at home, it is to be doubted whether anything he ever accomplished was more serviceable to Christ's kingdom than the modest beginnings in Virginia.

In 1750 Davies prevailed upon John Todd to come to his assistance. Settling in Louisa County, contiguous to Hanover, Todd soon opened a classical and theological school. In this academy James Waddell, Wirt's "blind preacher," became first a pupil and afterward an assistant instructor. It was here also that David Rice, a young man of Todd's congregation, received the inspiration and training which fitted him for his subsequent commanding position on the frontier, now to be moved westward to the hunting grounds of Daniel Boone, and to the very borders of the Indiana history.

The year 1783 opened with a prospect of peace with Great Britain, and of comparative quiet from savages ; while the abundance of the products of the soil promised to reward the labors of the husbandmen. New settlers poured [into Kentucky] by thousands, and the forest and the cane-brake rapidly disappeared beneath the axe and the plough. Among those who were attracted to this land of promise, flowing, as was represented, with milk and honey, was the Rev. David Rice, at that time pastor of a congregation at the Peaks of Otter. He came, not with the intention of becoming a resident, but solely with a view to make some provision for his numerous and dependent family ; but, being disgusted with the shameless spirit of speculation which was then rife, he returned without purchasing an acre. In vain were the broad rich lands of Kentucky spread in unrivaled beauty before him ; in vain did the cheapness of the price tempt him ; he valued his peace of mind too much to suspend it on the doubtful risks of inevitable litigation.

During his stay Mr. Rice preached as opportunity offered, and his appearance was hailed with joy by the Presbyterian settlers, some of whom had known him personally and all by reputation. They had learned by their long destitution and silent Sabbaths to appreciate the value of the stated ministry; and, like David in his exile, memory lingered with fond regret upon the lost pleasures of the sanctuary and the voice of joy and praise. Mr. Rice was warmly pressed to give them the benefit of his pastoral services; but he hesitated to take so important a step on a mere verbal invitation. He promised, however, that if a written invitation were drawn up, signed by such only as were permanent settlers and really desirous of constituting themselves into a church, he would take it into consideration. . . He removed to Kentucky in October; but owing to the impassable state of the roads, he was unable to travel, during the winter, beyond the neighborhood of Danville, and preached in private houses as he was invited. . . On the opening of spring (1784) Mr. Rice extended the sphere of his labors, and gathered three large congregations near Harrod's Station as a central point, Danville, Cane Run, and the Salt River settlement. Houses of worship were put up without delay, and the year following churches were regularly organized in them all.[1]

DAVID RICE, the father of Kentucky Presbyterianism, born in Hanover County, Va., December 20, 1733, ordained by Hanover Presbytery December, 1763, first taking charge of three congregations at the foot of the Blue Ridge, but finally confining his labors to the one at the Peaks of Otter, reached Kentucky in 1783.[2] For fifteen years Danville was his home. His later life was spent in Green County, where he fell asleep, June 18, 1816, in the eighty-third year of his age.[3]

As Makemie had drawn from the old country reënforcements to form the first Presbytery, and as Davies had assembled about him the little band that constituted "old Hanover," so did David Rice attract from Virginia a notable company of ministers. Adam Rankin came from Augusta County in 1784, and James Crawford arrived the same year. Terah Templin, ordained in 1785, though he had reached Kentucky three or four years earlier, had

[1] Davidson's "Kentucky," pp. 64-6.
[2] Bishop's "Memoir of Rice," pp. 13-64. This rare old book contains the only contemporary accounts of several other Kentucky pioneers.
[3] A suitable monument to Rice was erected, 1892, by Kentucky Presbyterians in McDowell Park, Danville.

been a member of Father Rice's congregation at the Peaks of Otter. Thomas Craighead and Andrew McClure reënforced the struggling missionaries in 1786.

On the 17th of October of that year, according to the direction of Synod, the Presbytery of Transylvania was organized.[1]

Tuesday, October 17, 1786. The Rev. David Rice, Adam Rankin, Andrew McClure, and James Crawford met in the Court House at Danville, on the day and year above written, by an appointment of the Synod of New York and Philadelphia; which appointment Mr. Rice read from the extract of the proceedings of the Synod, dated May 17th, 1786, the substance of which is as follows: The Synod divided Abingdon Presbytery into two Presbyteries, the one by the name of the Presbytery of Abingdon, the other by the name of the Presbytery of Transylvania, comprehending the district of Kentucky from the settlements upon Cumberland River, consisting of the Rev. David Rice, Thomas Craighead, Adam Rankin, Andrew McClure, James Crawford, and appointed the Presbytery of Transylvania to meet at Danville, in the district of Kentucke (*sic*), on the third Tuesday of October, 1786, the Rev. David Rice to be moderator or in his absence the senior minister present. Ubi post preces sederunt qui supra, except Rev. Thomas Craighead.[2]

Craighead's distant settlement was the occasion of his frequent absence. It will be observed that all the original members of the new Presbytery were from Virginia.

Thus, from Scotland's sufferings under Charles, and from Scotland's scattered sons, through Makemie, a pioneer of the American Presbyterian Church, through Samuel Davies of Hanover and Princeton, and through David Rice, Davies's son in the gospel and the founder of the Kentucky Church, is to be traced the establishment of Transylvania Presbytery, which Indiana Presbyterians venerate as the mother of us all.

[1] This "backwoods" Presbytery had very indefinite boundaries. Besides Kentucky, Indiana, and the settlements on the Cumberland River in what is now the state of Tennessee, it also subsequently included the churches along the Miami in Ohio. "It had no definite limits in a southern direction."

[2] "Minutes Transylvania Presbytery," Vol. I., p. 1.

CHAPTER II.

THE SETTLEMENT OF INDIANA.

NOT until nearly two hundred years after the discovery of America by Columbus, and fully half a century later than the landing of the Pilgrims from the *Mayflower*, is it probable that the first white man touched the present boundary of Indiana. As early as June, 1541, De Soto had reached the Mississippi with his Spanish explorers, but no other Europeans appear to have looked upon the Father of Waters until 1673,[1] when Marquette descended the river nearly to the Gulf. During the years 1665-73 another French Jesuit was engaged in exploring the Lake Superior region and the territory near the southern extremity of Lake Michigan,[2] in which labors he was most of the time assisted by Marquette and Claude Dablon. They must have found the portage from the St. Joseph to the Kankakee.[3] There is an Indian tradition that Catholic missionaries were at Kekionga (Fort Wayne) about this

[1] Cf. Parkman's "Discovery of the Great West," introduction, p. xx.

[2] "In the year 1665 the resolute ardor of Father Allouez, a Jesuit missionary, prompted him to undertake the hazardous experiment of executing his mission in these remote and unknown countries. Arrived at the Falls of St. Mary he threw himself boldly among the savages, relying on his powers of persuasion to win their confidence, and the purity of his motives to secure success. His hopes were not disappointed. He visited the tribes on the southern borders of Lake Superior and was everywhere received with kindness. Three years afterward he was joined by Marquette and Dablon, and during the five succeeding years these courageous missionaries explored the territory between Lake Superior and the southern extremity of Lake Michigan, fulfilling their vocation as messengers of Christianity with a devotedness and self-sacrifice rarely surpassed, preaching to numerous tribes and subduing their wild hearts by gentleness of manners and by inculcating the mild precepts of the gospel. They likewise established the posts of Macinac, St. Mary's, and Green Bay, which soon became the first rallying points of civilization on the upper lakes."—Sparks's "La Salle," p. 2.

[3] They "probably visited that part of Indiana which lies north of the river Kankakee."—Dillon's "History," p. 2.

THE SETTLEMENT OF INDIANA. 21

time.[1] In December, 1679, La Salle went down the Kankakee from its mouth,[2] and his own report to the governor-general of Canada leaves no doubt that on his perilous return in the following year he passed through Fort Wayne. It was in 1682 that La Salle, passing down the Illinois into the Mississippi, discovered the mouth of that river on the 9th of April, and in the name of Louis XIV. took possession of the country.[3] The survivors of La Salle's second and fatal expedition, on the 19th of August, 1687, a few months after their leader's assassination, "came to the Mouth of the River call'd *Houabache*, said to come from the country of the *Iroquois*, toward New England." "That is a very fine River," proceeds the description, "its Water extraordinary clear, and the Current of it gentle. Our *Indians* offer'd up to it, by way of Sacrifice, some Tobacco and Beef Steaks, which they fixed on Forks, and left them on the Bank, to be disposed of as the River thought fit."[4] The *Houabache* was no doubt the Ohio,

[1] "England permitted the French to establish their influence along the banks of the Allegany to the Ohio. They had already quietly possessed themselves of the three other great avenues from the St. Lawrence to the Mississippi: for the route by way of the Fox and Wisconsin they had no opponents but in the Sacs and Foxes; that by way of Chicago had been safely pursued since the days of Marquette; and a report on Indian affairs, written by Logan in 1718, proves that they very early made use of the Miami of the lakes, and after crossing the carrying-place of about three leagues, floated down the shallow branch into the Wabash and the Ohio."—Bancroft's "History," Centenary Edition, Vol. II., p. 481.

[2] Sparks's "La Salle," pp. 45, 46. "On the 3d of December the party reëmbarked, thirty-three in all, in eight canoes, and ascended the chill current of the St. Joseph, bordered with dreary meadows and bare gray forests. When they approached the site of the present village of South Bend they looked anxiously along the shore on their right to find the portage or path leading to the headwaters of the Illinois."—Parkman's "Discovery of the Great West," p. 151.

[3] Father Hennepin, in his "Description de la Louisiane," gives an account of this tour; but according to Joutel (p. 185) "the Truth of his Relations is much controverted," and according to Bancroft (Vol. II., p. 366) he is "a boastful liar." See Charlevoix's "New France," Sparks's "La Salle," and Parkman's "Discovery of the Great West," for authentic details.

[4] "A Journal of the Last Voyage Performed by Monsr. de la Sale, to the Gulph of Mexico, to find out the Mouth of the Mississippi River." Written in French by Monsieur Joutel, a commander in that expedition, and translated from the edition just published at Paris. London, 1714, p. 163. (The original French edition appeared in Paris the previous year.)

but Monsieur Joutel's narrative is accompanied by a map which with tolerable accuracy suggests the course of a tributary of that stream, the present river Wabash, which now at last was known to French explorers.[1]

The possession of the vast territory thus acquired by France was for many years only nominal. Early in the eighteenth century, however, the ambitious scheme was accomplished of connecting the French settlements in Canada with the northern lakes, the valley of the Mississippi, and the Gulf, by a line of military and trading-posts and Jesuit mission stations. It was this design that led to the first actual occupancy of Indiana by Europeans, a fort having been located on the Wabash in 1710[2] by Captain Morgan de Vincennes at the point which has since borne his name. Subsequently settlements were made by the French at Fort Ouiatenon (La Fayette) and at the Twightwee village (Fort Wayne), near the junction of the St. Joseph and St. Mary Rivers.[3]

The war which deprived the French of their possessions in Canada also secured to Great Britain the "country of the Illinois,"[4] and the posts on the Wabash were occupied by the latter power. The English dominion was soon dis-

---

[1] Joutel's description of the region near the mouth of the *Houabache* might certainly have been written for the Wabash country. "The country about was full of Hillocks," he says, "cover'd with Oaks and Wallnut-Trees, Abundance of Plum Trees, almost all the Plums red and pretty good, besides great Store of other Sorts of Fruits, whose Names we know not, and among them one shap'd like a middling Pear, with Stones in it as big as large Beans. When ripe it peels like a Peach, the Taste is indifferent good, but rather of the Sweetest."—"Journal of La Sale's Last Voyage," p. 164.

[2] This is the date fixed by Judge Law ("Colonial History of Vincennes," p. 12), who finds a reference to "the Post," as already established, in a letter written by Father Marest, from Kaskaskias, November 9, 1712. (See "Lettres edifiant et curieuse," p. 333.) Volney, who was at the Post in 1796 and fixed upon 1735 as the year of its establishment, seems to have given the date of a subsequent arrival of French emigrants there. (Cf. Volney's "View of the Climate and Soil of the United States," London, 1804, p. 373.)

[3] Not more than three or four hundred whites were settled within the present limits of Indiana when the French domination ceased. Cf. Dillon, p. 84.

[4] Treaty of Paris, February 10, 1763.

THE SETTLEMENT OF INDIANA. 23

turbed, however, by the colonial struggle for independence, and in the expedition of 1779 under the gallant Virginian, General George Rogers Clark, it was finally terminated. Post Vincennes was surrendered by Hamilton on the 24th of February. Upon the conclusion of the revolutionary contest the country northwest of the Ohio,[1] which since Clark's conquest of it had been nominally under the jurisdiction of Virginia, was, by a formal deed of cession, transferred[2] to the United States. By the Ordinance of 1787 the Northwestern Territory was organized, including what now comprises the states of Indiana, Illinois, Michigan, Wisconsin, and much of Ohio.[3] From this vast tract Ohio was set off as a distinct territory May 7, 1800, when the residue of the original Northwestern Territory became the territory of Indiana, with William Henry Harrison as its first governor. In 1805 Michigan was erected into a separate territory, and in 1809 Illinois was placed under its own government, leaving Indiana with its present limits. The state was constituted December 11, 1816.

Though the authority of the United States had been extended over the region northwest of the Ohio by the Ordinance of 1787, the Indians for years afterward remained substantially in possession of the country. St. Clair's expedition against the savages reached its disastrous termination in 1791. The frontier was in a state of

[1] It is startling to observe how narrowly the United States escaped the loss of the whole Northwestern Territory, when negotiating the treaty of 1782. "Great Britain insisted on making the Ohio River a boundary of the United States. . . . The pertinacity with which the claim was insisted on induced Dr. Franklin to suggest to his colleagues, Mr. Adams and Mr. Jay, whether it would not be better to yield that point than to fail in the main object, it being understood that the French government was favorable to the claim. Mr. Adams very promptly answered, No. . . Mr. Jay was equally determined and Dr. Franklin concurred." See Burnet's "Notes on the Northwestern Territory," p. 315, foot-note. Cf. Law's "Vincennes," p. 131.

[2] March 1, 1784.

[3] Major-General Arthur St. Clair, first governor of the Northwestern Territory, was appointed by Congress October 5. 1787.

constant alarm until "Mad Anthony" Wayne's decisive victory of August 15, 1794, and his treaty with the Indians at Greenville, August 3, 1795. Thereafter, as confidence increased, settlers began to venture toward the rich bottom lands along the Wabash. But it must be remembered that as late as October 3, 1818, when by the treaty at St. Mary's the territory was yielded to the United States by the Delawares, Miamis, and Pottawottamies, the red men had still claimed the greater part of Indiana as their own. Even then they expressly reserved the right of occupying their former hunting grounds for three years longer.[1] It was not until a much more recent period that they entirely withdrew from the forests whose abundant game fed their hunger and whose thick shadows concealed their crimes.[2]

Transient fur-traders knew the region well and had been drawing immense profit from it for nearly a century before the quiet pursuit of agriculture was possible.[3] It was not to be expected that the most enticing reports of the fertility of Indiana's soil would be able to attract any large number

[1] "The Indians settled on White River, about twelve miles above Indianapolis, between the years 1790 and 1795, and built several towns a short distance above that. There now lives twelve miles above here a white woman who was with them when they first settled there, having been taken prisoner when Morgan's Station was overpowered, and all those who were in it either slaughtered or captured. She was nine years old when taken, and has lived among the Indians ever since, until the late purchase made by the United States brought the white people into the neighborhood."—*Indianapolis Gazette*, June 11, 1823.

[2] "One cold cloudy day in January, 1831, setting out to ride ten miles in the wilderness to acquaint a family with the appointment to form a church, I mistook the trail of an Indian hunting party, which led me to their encampment. Retracing my way by night I became bewildered in the woods and snow, and sat down by a burning log till morning, and at noon, twenty-four hours after leaving, emerged at Logansport."— "Retrospect after Thirty Years' Ministry at Logansport," by the Rev. Martin M. Post, D. D., p. 11.

[3] "The Miami villages, which stood at the head of the river Maumee, the Wea villages, which were situated about Ouiatneon on the Wabash River, and the Piankeshaw villages, which stood on and about the site of Vincennes, were, it seems, regarded by the early French fur-traders as suitable places for the establishing of trading-posts. It is probable that before the close of the year 1719, temporary trading-posts were erected at the sites of Fort Wayne, Ouiatneon, and Vincennes. These points had, it is believed, been often visited by traders before the year 1700."—Dillon, p. 54.

of immigrants with their families to the haunts of savages.[1] In 1800 the white population of the territory, which still included Illinois and Michigan, was only four thousand eight hundred and seventy-five. Eight years afterward, within the present boundaries of Indiana, there were only about seventeen thousand inhabitants, a number which had increased to about sixty-four thousand when in 1816 the territory became a state.

Of the character of the original population of Indiana Volney gives a striking and evidently correct representation. He reached Vincennes on the 2d of August, 1796. He says :

> The day after my arrival there, was a sitting of the judges of the district, to which I repaired to make my observations on the natural and moral state of the inhabitants collectively. As soon as I entered I was struck at seeing the audience divided into two races of men, totally different in feature and in person. One had a fair or light brown hair, ruddy complexions, full faces, and a plumpness of body that announced health and ease ; the other, very meager countenances, a sallow tawny skin, and the whole body as if emaciated with fasting, not to speak of their clothes, which sufficiently denoted their poverty. I presently discovered that the latter were the French settlers, who had been about sixty years in the place ; while the former were Americans, who cultivated the land they had bought only five or six years before. The French, three or four excepted, knew nothing of English, and almost all the Americans were nearly as ignorant of French, but as I had learned English enough in the course of a year to converse with them I had the advantage during my stay of hearing the stories of both parties.[2]

Still further to diversify this scene there were no doubt occasional representatives of Spain and Germany, and sometimes the Indians, taking possession of the little town,

[1] For a trustworthy and minute account of the perils of pioneer life see "Reminiscences of Col. John Ketcham," by the Rev. T. M. Hopkins, Bloomington, 1866. For abstract of treaties by which Indian rights to lands lying within the present limits of Indiana have been extinguished see Dillon, p. 578.

[2] "Climate and Soil of the United States," pp. 369, 370.

made it as bizarre and miscellaneous as Cairo or Jerusalem. Volney adds:

> My stay at Fort Vincents gave me an opportunity of observing the savages, whom I found assembled to sell the produce of their red hunt. There were reckoned to be four or five hundred men, women, and children, of various nations or tribes, as the Weeaws, Payouries, Saukies, Pyankishaws, Miamis, etc., all living toward the head of the Wabash. It was the first time of my observing at leisure these people, already become rare on the east of the Alleghanies. Their appearance was to me a new and whimsical sight. Conceive bodies almost naked, embrowned by exposure to the sun and air, shining with grease and soot; a head uncovered, hair coarse, black, sleek, straight, and smooth; a face disguised with black, blue, and red paint, in round, square, and rhomboidal patches; one nostril bored to admit a large ring of silver or copper; earrings with three rows of drops reaching down to the shoulders and passing through holes that would admit a finger; a little square apron before and another behind, both fastened by one string or ribband; the legs and thighs sometimes naked, at others covered with long cloth spatterdashers; socks of leather dried in the smoke; on some occasions a shirt with short, wide sleeves, variegated or striped with blue and white, and flowing loose down the thighs, and over this a blanket or square piece of cloth, thrown over one shoulder and tied under the opposite arm or under the chin. On particular occasions, when they dress for war or for a feast, the hair is braided and interwoven with feathers, plants, flowers, and even bones; the warriors wear round their waists broad rings of copper or silver, resembling our dog collars, and round the head a diadem formed of silver buckles and trinkets of glass; in their hand they have their pipe or their knife or their tomahawk, and the little looking-glass, which every savage uses with more coquetry, to admire so many charms, than the most coquettish belle of Paris.[1]

No doubt this singular miscellany might also have been found, though upon a smaller pattern, at Fort Ouiatenon and at Kekionga, the aboriginal La Fayette and Fort Wayne.

From this mixed population the savage element was

[1] "Climate and Soil of the United States," pp. 392-5.

rapidly removed. The French, who had been masters of the soil, gradually yielded to the more hardy and energetic Americans, although Congress in 1792 had given

four hundred acres of land to every one who paid the capitation, and a hundred more to every man who served in the militia. These would have been a fortune to an American family [continues the impartial Frenchman whom we have quoted before], but to the French, hunters rather than farmers, they were only a transitory gift, which these ignorant and imprudent men sold to Americans for less than eight guineas the hundred acres, and even this small sum they were paid in clothes and other goods on which a profit of twenty or five and twenty per cent was laid. These lands, which were of excellent quality, sold as early as 1796 at two dollars an acre and I will venture to say that they are now worth ten. Thus reduced for the most part to their gardens, or the land with which they could not dispense, the French settlers had nothing to live on but their fruit, vegetables, potatoes, Indian corn, and once now and then a little game. No wonder therefore they became lean as Arabs.[1]

As the French degenerated and receded the native immigration perceptibly increased. Each of the various military expeditions, especially that of Wayne, had left behind the natural deposit of stragglers from the army. Older communities in the East began to think of such investments of capital in the Indiana wilderness as at an earlier day had drawn George Washington, the young diplomatist of the "Ohio Land Company," far into the western woods.[2] The vast "Illinois grants" made by the Virginia legislature in 1784 to General Clark and his victorious troops included most of Clark County, Ind., and now were alluring immigrants from beyond the Alleghanies. In 1796 Dufour explored the country along the Ohio, and finally secured from Congress three thousand acres of land for a Swiss colony, in what is now Switzerland

---

[1] "Climate and Soil of the United States," pp. 371, 372.

[2] See Irving's "Life of Washington," Vol. I.

County. It was, however, the hardy woodsmen just beyond the southern border who most readily yielded to the attractions of the wild region, where the French had been supplanted and from which the savages were now being inevitably forced. At the opening of the present century the settlements were therefore strongly Kentuckian, and for a considerable period afterward it was chiefly by families from Kentucky, with a smaller number from Virginia, Tennessee, and the Carolinas, that the clearings were made and the primitive cabins builded.

It will thus be seen that local chroniclers are not without justification for the pride they take in the early Indiana history. Judge Law writes as follows with especial reference to Vincennes:

> I know of no portion of our country richer in historical incident. For surely a town which is one of the oldest on the continent; one for the possession of which the greatest nations of the earth have contended—France, England, and the United States; one located upon the beautiful stream which flows before it, the Ouabache, a river known and noted on the maps of the West long before the Ohio was known in the geography of the Mississippi valley, a river which for nearly a century bore upon its waters the bateaux of the three great powers above mentioned, bringing their armed warriors to occupy, and if possible to preserve it; one which has seen within its garrison the mousquitaire of Louis XV., the grenadier of George III., the riflemen of Clark, and the regular troops of Harmar, St. Clair, and Harrison; one above which has floated the "Fleur de Lis," the "Cross of St. George," and the glorious stars and stripes of our beloved country, is surely worthy of at least a passing notice by those who are now reaping the rich fruits of a conquest made under the most adverse and trying circumstances and with a skill and bravery not unsurpassed in the most glorious triumphs of the Revolution.[1]

Of the Kekionga of the Miamis, the present Fort Wayne, almost a rival of Vincennes in antiquity, and furnishing, though for a somewhat humbler page, abundant

---

[1] "Colonial History of Vincennes," pp. v. and vi.

THE SETTLEMENT OF INDIANA. 29

materials for story and song, the records are less complete. The junction of the St. Mary and St. Joseph may claim, however, a place

in the annals of that momentous contest between French and English civilization, between Romanism and Protestantism, which was waged with alternating success, and with short intervals of repose, for more than a hundred years, terminating soon after the fall of Quebec in the establishment of Anglo-Saxon supremacy by the treaty of 1763. The massacre of the little English garrison three fourths of a mile north from [Fort Wayne] on the 27th of May, 1763, during Pontiac's war, was accomplished through the treacherous influence of French traders over the Indians. This was among the last exertions of French power on this continent, east of the Mississippi. It was a subsiding wave on the outer circle of the long agitated waters.[1]

The population thus sifted and disciplined by providence, and at last receiving its characteristic tendencies from the region immediately beyond the Ohio, was one that naturally appealed to the Presbyterian Church for sympathy and help. The response came heartily and promptly from Kentucky.

[1] " Historical Sketch of the First Presbyterian Church, Fort Wayne," by Judge Jesse L. Williams, pp. 3, 4.

CHAPTER III.

THE FIRST MISSIONARIES.
1800–1806.

THE first decided drift of population toward Indiana set in at a period especially favorable to the work of evangelization and to the establishment of Presbyterian institutions. It was soon after the opening of the present century. Kentucky, upon the southern border, with a large Calvinistic element among her people and a considerable number of ardent and able Presbyterian ministers, had been aroused to the highest pitch of religious enthusiasm by what is still described as "the Great Revival." They could not be indifferent to the spiritual condition of the settlers across the Ohio, among whom were their former neighbors and friends. The General Assembly was under a like impulse from on high, and was appointing itinerants for the regions beyond.[1] At the same time the great missionary awakening began to move New England, and resulted in the formation of those home and foreign missionary societies which have since exercised so vast a power. A little later, too, there was a movement westward from Ohio, which contributed valuable aid, particularly to settlements near the eastern line of Indiana. From a variety of sources, therefore, and from widely separated regions, the gospel came, at this auspicious epoch, to what was now the farthest West.

Naturally the first laborers were from Kentucky, the nearest neighbor, still under the stress of the revival. They were volunteers. As early as 1804, 5, and 6 they

[1] In 1805 the Assembly commissioned Thomas Williamson, and in 1806 Samuel Holt, to Indiana.

made "short missionary excursions" to the neighborhood of Vincennes.[1] They were members of Transylvania Presbytery—Rannels, Robertson, McGready, and Cleland.

SAMUEL RANNELS was born December 10, 1765, in Hampshire County, Va., where he remained with his father until he was nearly twenty years of age. He graduated, March, 1792, at Dickinson College, then under its able president, the Rev. Dr. Charles Nisbet. He received licensure from the Presbytery of Lexington, Va., in 1794. In the following spring he came to Kentucky, having a call to the united congregations of Paris and Stonermouth, which he accepted. Ordained in 1796 he returned to Virginia and was united in marriage, May 10th of the same year, with Margaret Gilkison. Coming to Kentucky he labored in the field to which he had been called for more than twenty years, the relation being terminated by his death, March 24, 1817.

Mr. Rannels was about six feet in height and well proportioned. He was of an amiable disposition and agreeable manners. Solemn and affectionate in the discharge of his office, he was orderly and punctual in all his transactions. His pulpit exercises were of various degrees of excellence, sometimes far above mediocrity, but on other occasions noticeably deficient in power. In the great religious excitement prevailing in Kentucky in 1802–3, and which was attended with much irregularity, finally producing heresy and schism, Mr. Rannels was among the first and foremost to raise a note of warning. It was then that he gave some of the happiest illustrations of his impressive pulpit abilities. To him and a few others in those perilous times, the church in Kentucky, particularly the Presbyterian body, owed its defense and support so far as human agency was concerned.[2] He was one of the first of

[1] Dickey's "Brief History," pp. 11, 12.
[2] Bishop's "Memoir of Rice," pp. 166–8. Davidson's "Kentucky," p. 115.

the Kentucky ministers to cross the Ohio into Indiana.

SAMUEL B. ROBERTSON received ordination in 1801 and became pastor of the congregations of Cane Run and New Providence, where he continued until 1811, when he removed to Columbia, Adair County. Subsequently he was pastor of Lebanon church for four years. "He lived to a good old age and, having fallen upon sleep, he chose to be buried in the graveyard of this church by the side of the wife of his youth."[1] Admired as a preacher,[2] though not a man of commanding abilities, his name is prominent in the Indiana history, as by him was effected the organization of the first church.

JAMES MCGREADY not infrequently repeated his early excursions to Indiana. Nature had commissioned him as an exhorter, and with the populace he was a great favorite. On special occasions, during the ten years previous to 1817, the pastor at Vincennes often summoned him to his aid. His tremendous oratory at "the Presbyterian Stand" in the woods, addressed to thousands of people attracted from an incredible distance, was as stern and faithful as the "crying in the wilderness" of Judæa. A large man, inclined to corpulency, with a voice of thunder, the "hideousness"[3] of his face seemed only to render his habitual denunciations of sin more terrible. He was born of Scotch-Irish parents, on the Monongahela, in western Pennsylvania, in 1763, but while he was still a child the family removed to North Carolina, near the present Greensboro. In 1783 he was converted, was soon persuaded of his call to preach the gospel, and after a course of study in Dr. McMillan's school, subsequently known as Cannonsburg College, he

---

[1] Hogue's "Historical Discourse preached in the Presbyterian Church, Lebanon, Ky.," 1857, p. 13.

[2] See "Life of Cleland," p. 127.

[3] Davidson's "Kentucky," p. 132.

THE FIRST MISSIONARIES. 33

received licensure from Redstone Presbytery. Returning to North Carolina, at a funeral, in compliment to the young minister he was invited to ask a blessing preparatory to the usual unstinted dispensation of whisky on such occasions. His prompt refusal to "insult God by asking a blessing on what was wrong"[1] produced great excitement, and the pungency of his subsequent preaching resulted in a remarkable revival which extended through Guilford and Orange Counties—the second general revival in North Carolina after the War of the Revolution.

This revival was attended with no unusual appearances or exercises. The opposition to the close and practical preaching and renewed discipline never broke out into violence but in one case. At Stony Creek there were some families of wealth and influence that had become loose in their religious views and morals during the disturbance of the war and the presence of the armies; these opposed Mr. McGready's course and preaching, and proceeded from one step of opposition to another, till their dislike exceeded all bounds. Some of these, during one of their nights of revelry, made a bonfire of the pulpit, near the church, and left in the clerk's seat a letter written with blood, warning him that unless he desisted from his way of preaching, their vengeance would not be satisfied with the destruction of the pulpit, and his person would not be inviolate. McGready, as might have been expected, not in the least intimidated by the burning of the pulpit or the letter, continued to preach as usual,[2] and the opposition, confined to a few, died away. In a few years the dissipation of these families became the ruin of their character and property, and after the lapse of a short period not a descendant of theirs could be found in the congregation.[3]

In 1796 McGready removed to the southwestern part of

---

[1] Foote's "Sketches of North Carolina," pp. 371, 372. Later in life, when suffering from exposure, he unfortunately indulged too freely in a needed stimulant, and was so ashamed and penitent that he ever afterward observed that day of the month as a day of fasting and prayer. See Davidson, pp. 260, 261.

[2] The following Sunday he gave out the psalm beginning "How are the seats of worship broke."

[3] Foote's "Sketches of North Carolina," p. 375.

Kentucky, and assumed charge of the Gasper, Muddy, and Red River congregations. His fearless proclamation of the law produced here the same results that had been witnessed in North Carolina, the revival of 1800 having its commencement under his ministry. Its earliest manifestations are described by McGready himself.

In July the sacrament was administered in Gasper River congregation. Here multitudes crowded from all parts of the country to see a strange work, from the distance of forty, fifty, and even a hundred miles; whole families came in their wagons; between twenty and thirty wagons were brought to the place, loaded with people and their provisions, in order to encamp at the meeting-house. On Friday nothing more appeared during the day than a decent solemnity. On Saturday matters continued in the same way until in the evening. Two pious women were sitting together conversing about their exercises; which conversation seemed to affect some of the bystanders; instantly the divine flame spread through the whole multitude. Presently you might have seen sinners lying powerless in every part of the house, praying and crying for mercy. Ministers and private Christians were kept busy during the night conversing with the distressed. This night a goodly number of awakened souls were delivered by sweet believing views of the glory, fulness, and sufficiency of Christ to save to the uttermost. Amongst these were some little children, a striking proof of the religion of Jesus.[1]

The subsequent extravagances of this period found in McGready a sincere and powerful apologist, and he was finally involved in the controversies out of which grew the Cumberland church. He was, however, too clear in his theological views, too thoroughly in sympathy with Presbyterian forms, and too strongly attached to the old church, to be contented in the work of schism. He went far enough to receive censure, but made suitable acknowledgments and was restored to his former ecclesiastical standing. The Cumberland church, however, still revere

[1] McGready's " Posthumous Works," pp. ix., x.

him as their founder,[1] and after his decease, which occurred in Henderson County in 1817, most of his adherents united with that body.

Too eccentric and excitable to be safe in his leadership, no doubt the evangelical preaching of McGready was most useful to the feeble Indiana church. It is likely that many of the discourses which constitute the volume of his "Posthumous Works" were heard by the immense audiences attracted by his fame to the sacramental meetings along the Wabash and the Ohio. Their titles sufficiently suggest their vividness and force—"The Blinding Policies of Satan," "The Sinner's Guide to Hell," "The Hope of the Hypocrite," "The Deceitfulness of the Human Heart," "The Doom of the Impenitent." In a letter addressed to Samuel J. Mills, during his tour of observation in the West, McGready writes, April 27, 1815, from Red Banks, Henderson County, Ky.:

If some religious tracts were in my possession showing the vanity and soul-destroying nature of giddy balls and vain amusements, some treating of the importance of secret prayer, some of the danger of quenching conviction, some giving an account of extraordinary conversions—such, I think, I could distribute to advantage.[2]

Everything this mighty backwoodsman said and did showed the singleness, the intensity, and the sagacity of his aim.

To those who at this period came from Kentucky upon an occasional preaching tour must be added the name of James Kemper. He had been from 1791 to 1796 the first settled minister[3] of the First Church, Cincinnati, constitu-

[1] Smith's "History of the Cumberland Presbyterian Church" contains full notices of his character and career.
[2] "Report of Smith and Mills's Tour," p. 52.
[3] Kemper came from Virginia to Tennessee as early as 1783, and thence to Kentucky in 1785. He was licensed to preach, after four years' study under David Rice, being already the father of ten children. He was the first minister ordained north of the Ohio, and preached the first sermon at the first meeting of the first Presbytery that convened in Ohio, it being his own ordination sermon. Born in Fauquier County, Va., November 23, 1753, married July 16, 1772, to Judith Hathaway, he died August 20,

ted by "Father Rice," but he afterward returned to Kentucky. As early as 1804, and for several years subsequently, he visited Rising Sun, Samuel Fulton, a worthy pioneer, opening his cabin for the religious services which Mr. Kemper conducted.[1]

Such irregular and infrequent efforts as have been described could effect but little however. There was need of systematic ecclesiastical supervision, and Transylvania Presbytery may claim the honor of making the earliest recorded appointment of missionaries to Indiana. At Danville, April 14, 1803, it was resolved that Archibald Cameron supply "in the Illinois grant and at Post Vincennes settlements,"[2] James Vance being associated with him; and although neither performed the duty assigned, their reasons for failure being presented and sustained at Hardin's Creek, October 5, 1803,[3] as Archibald Cameron is a name well known in Indiana, whither subsequently he came more than once to preach, we may pause a moment to look at this Kentucky John the Baptist, the forerunner of the whole vast army of missionaries since commissioned to the same field. A native of Scotland, brought by his parents to America when a child, he became a thorough mathematician and classical scholar, studied theology under Father Rice, after seven years' service at Simpson's Creek took charge in 1803 of the Shelbyville and Mulberry churches, and remained with them until his death, which occurred in 1836. He was an old bachelor, blunt in his manners, independent as a Highland chief, shrewd, satirical, and orthodox to a fault.[4] "He often preached

1834, his widow following him March 1, 1846. Fifteen children were born to them. Cf. "Presbyterianism North of the Ohio," a semi-centennial discourse delivered before the Presbytery of Cincinnati, April 9, 1872, by the Rev. Joseph G. Monfort, D.D.

[1] Goodrich and Tuttle's "History of Indiana," p. 491.
[2] "Minutes Transylvania Presbytery," Vol. II., p. 72.
[3] "Minutes Transylvania Presbytery," Vol. II., p. 75.
[4] His orthodoxy, at least on one occasion, was the cause of some embarrassment to him. Dr. Beatty was fond of relating that in the Assembly of 1835, when the irregulari-

three full hours, and when he got waked up on baptism could preach six hours." In his later years, helpless from paralysis, surrounded but often neglected by his blacks, contented with corn and bacon, on a small plantation near Shelbyville he maintained a gruff baronial hospitality. He published a number of able pamphlets[1] and in the Cumberland controversy was a prominent and useful conservative.

"Supplications for supplies" were now frequently submitted to Transylvania Presbytery. At Danville, October 17, 1804, "a petition was received from Post Vincennes praying for supplies."[2] April 9, 1805, "a petition from a number of inhabitants of Knox County, Indiana territory, praying for supplies was presented and read." Two days later "Mr. Cleland was appointed to supply in Indiana territory as much of his time as he can with conveniency."[3] He discharged the duty, and thus became the first official delegate who labored upon this field. If his own qualities had been less captivating, and his service of the church in Indiana less important, the lending of a son for so many years to that service would still require us to review his career and character.

THOMAS CLELAND was for many years the most popu-

ties in the Western Reserve were under review, and when he himself had to make his maiden speech in the Assembly, Cameron, jumping upon a seat, delivered a violent philippic against the disorders in the region referred to. Upon the Assembly's adjournment, Cameron, returning home, was overtaken by the Sabbath at Cleveland, and called upon young Mr. Aiken, the pastor there, expecting to be invited to preach. But Aiken, who had been at the Assembly and had heard Cameron's speech, slyly suggested that upon the " Reserve " they had had so much trouble with impostors that they were compelled to refuse admission into their pulpits to ministers without written credentials. So the doughty Kentuckian had to listen patiently next day to two good " New-school " sermons. See also Sprague's " Annals," Vol. IV., pp. 168-72.

[1] Among these are: "The Faithful Steward, being an impartial investigation of the subject: is the church justifiable in baptizing adults without evidence of their faith and repentance, and in baptizing the children of any parents who do not likewise give evidence of being the subjects of faith and repentance," Louisville, 1806 ; and " A reply to some questions on Divine Predestination, with some remarks on a pamphlet entitled, ' The Trial of Cain,' " Shelbyville, 1822.

[2] " Minutes Transylvania Presbytery," Vol. II., p. 103.

[3] " Minutes Transylvania Presbytery," Vol. II., p. 111.

lar Presbyterian preacher in Kentucky. Born in Fairfax County, Va., May 22, 1778, removed in childhood to Maryland, and afterward in 1789 to Kentucky, educated at the Kentucky Academy and at Transylvania University, though he had chosen the law for a profession he was seized upon by the Presbytery and licensed April 14, 1803. He had previously made effective addresses at religious meetings, crowds being easily drawn together when "it was noised abroad that little Tommy Cleland had commenced preaching." His success made such an impression that the Presbytery soon interpreted it as a manifest call to the ministry. The night of his marriage to a daughter of Captain John Armstrong Presbytery convened in Mr. Armstrong's house. Then and there he was examined, as he supposed with a view of giving him license to exhort, but notwithstanding his protestations they enrolled his name as a candidate for the ministry. He urged his new domestic responsibilities, his limited education, his want of theological books and teachers. It was quite impossible, he argued, that he should now think of the ministry as a profession. The hour of midnight drew on. Alexander Cameron, bachelor though he was, said, "Let the young man alone. His wedding day is not the time to consider such a call." But, as the captive declares in his autobiography, he was "completely taken in by the Presbytery," which "assigned me as a part of trial for its next spring meeting a sermon from the text, 'Woe is me if I preach not the gospel.'"[1] Thus entrapped Cleland soon made good proof of his ministry, becoming an acknowledged leader in the work so well begun by the older generation under Father Rice. He was settled first in Washington, and afterward at New Providence in Mercer County, where he remained until his life was gently closed, January 31, 1858.

[1] "Life of Cleland," p. 70.

The Presbytery could have sent no better man to the wilderness. Of small stature, but lithe and hardy ; plain in dress and manners ; prudent and sensible ; not without wit ; a sturdy controversialist though loving peace ; a diligent writer for the press ; in the pulpit full of pathos and of Scripture ; a tireless itinerant and revivalist, his selection was an admirable one, and the service required just at the beginning of his public career must have proven a valuable experience to himself. Of his tour to Vincennes we have an account from his own pen :

Transylvania Presbytery had no definite limits in a southern direction. It also included Indiana, etc., on the north. In the spring of 1805 I was directed to visit Vincennes and the adjoining regions. It was an uninhabited route I had to go. A small wilderness trace, with only one residence on the way, in the most destitute part of the way, to entertain me during the night. Here was my poor animal tied to a tree, fed with the grain packed in a wallet from Louisville, and myself stretched on the puncheon floor of a small cabin, for the night's rest. All passed off, however, without any detriment or discomfort. The next evening made up for all previous privations. I was welcomed and agreeably entertained at the governor's palace during my stay at Vincennes. The late William H. Harrison, then a young man, with a Presbyterian wife, was governor of the Indiana territory, as it then was. He had recently held a treaty with a certain tribe of Indians, who assembled at Vincennes.

The first sermon I preached, and it was the first ever preached in the place, at least by a Presbyterian minister, was in the council-house, but a short time before occupied by the sons of the forest. I preached also in a settlement twenty miles up the Wabash, where were a few Presbyterian families, chiefly from Shelby County, Ky. They were so anxious to have me settle among them that they proffered to send all the way to Kentucky to remove my family, without any trouble or expense to myself, besides offering me a generous support. I somehow or other, from the beginning of domestic life, had my mind determined on residing in a free state, and here was an inviting prospect. I was indeed anxious to comply with their wishes. But besides the heavy contest for my land with old Colonel Shelby, now in process of litigation, the

Lord was showing me special favor with my people at home by an unusual blessing upon my labors. But still they were not willing to give the matter up, and that we might have a little more time to reflect and inquire of the Lord what was his will and pleasure concerning the wished-for change in my field of labor, I engaged to make them a returned visit the next year. I did return at the time appointed. The prospect seemed brighter than before. I was welcomed on all sides, by men of the world as well as by men of the church. And what was more I was welcomed by some poor sinners too, whom the Lord gave me as souls for my hire. And though I was prevented from settling among them, for the reason already specified, yet for a number of years afterward I received messages from those who claimed me as their spiritual father; and for aught that I know some remain there till the present day.[1]

The following year (1806)[2] this mission of Cleland bore fruit in the establishment of the first Presbyterian church in Indiana. Dickey supposes it to have been the earliest Protestant organization in the territory, but this is perhaps an error. The Baptists seem rightly to claim precedence. A competent authority says:

It was not until the year 1798 that the first Protestant congregation was organized in Indiana territory. This was a Regular Baptist church, composed of four members and established on the Philadelphia confession of faith. The organization was effected a

[1] "Life of Cleland," pp. 87-9.

[2] This has been questioned, an effort having been made to substitute 1802 as the correct date. But the following facts are conclusive in the matter: (1) The later date rests on the authority of Dickey, who wrote in 1828 and was familiar with the whole history; (2) Cleland distinctly says that in 1805 he preached the first Presbyterian sermon in Vincennes ("Life of Cleland," p. 88); (3) A few aged persons still survive who came to Vincennes several years subsequent to 1802, but remember being present at the organization of the "Indiana" church; (4) Accounts agree that Scott came to Vincennes to preach the year after the organization; but he did not receive licensure until December, 1803, and was installed pastor of the Mt. Pleasant church in Kentucky in 1805. The records of West Lexington Presbytery report him absent, October, 1807, on a mission, the Assembly having appointed him ("Minutes," 1806) to "be a missionary for three months in the Indiana territory and especially at Vincennes"; (5) Samuel J. Mills, in a letter dated January 20, 1815, speaks of Scott's "valiantly maintaining his post for *six* years past." After his tour in 1807 he had gone back to Kentucky for a time.

few miles northeast of the Littell settlement,[1] but the first house of worship was subsequently erected on the east bank of Silver Creek, near Mr. Littell's farm, where it became widely known as the Regular Baptist church at Silver Creek. There it still stands, the oldest Protestant church in the state.[2]

The Methodists came only a little later. The Rev. George K. Hester says:

It is believed that the first society formed in the state was organized at Father Robertson's.[3] This must have been in the spring of 1803. Then came McGuice and Sullivan. In 1805 Peter Cartwright[4] preached in "the Grant," and in the fall of 1805 Asa Shinn and Moses Ashworth preached there. In 1807 the work on this side of the river was organized into Silver Creek circuit with Moses Ashworth for their preacher.[5]

The "Church of Indiana,"[6] the oldest Presbyterian society in the state, was organized by the Rev. Samuel B. Robertson, in 1806, the service being held in the barn of Colonel Small, about two miles east of Vincennes. Though not large, the congregation was composed of excellent material. William Henry Harrison, the young governor, had married a Presbyterian wife, and was himself a steadfast friend of the society. Its members were, however, chiefly from Kentucky. Well instructed at home, by the occasional visits of Rannels, McGready, Robertson, and Cleland their duty to the faith of their

[1] Near Charlestown, Clark County.

[2] "Pioneer Preachers of Indiana," by Madison Evans, p. 43.

[3] Five miles north of Charlestown. "The first Methodist was Nathan Robertson, who moved from Kentucky to Charlestown in 1799."—Stevens's "History of Methodism," Vol. IV., pp. 152, 153.

[4] Cartwright seems to have considered the society he organized in 1808, in the Busroe settlement, the first among the Methodists. See his "Autobiography," p. 55.

[5] See Holliday's "Methodism in Indiana," pp. 37, 38.

[6] This society was divided into "Upper" and "Lower" Indiana churches by Vincennes Presbytery, April 6, 1842. The former retains its original designation. The latter became the "Indiana" church by act of Presbytery, April 15, 1847. The two fragments have equal claims to antiquity. A third division of the membership of the original society became the nucleus of the church which was organized in the town of Vincennes in 1832.

fathers had been kept in mind, and they were now to be greatly favored in securing a pastor whom they could love and trust, and for many years retain in a most successful service.

SAMUEL THORNTON SCOTT, to whom belongs the distinction of having first settled as a pastor within the territory, came to the "Indiana" church in 1807. His early years were spent in Woodford County, Ky., near Lexington, where he married Miss Margaret Dunlap. He pursued a literary course at Transylvania Academy and studied divinity with Dr. James Blythe. Before the completion of his education he came to Vincennes as a teacher. To this work he was probably summoned by former acquaintances, now removed to the neighborhood from Kentucky—the Dennisons from near Lexington and the Buckanans from Gallatin County.[1] He thus became, if we except the French priests, one of the first of the great army of Indiana schoolmasters. December 31, 1803, he received licensure from West Lexington Presbytery, and having preached at various places within its bounds by Presbyterial appointment, he was ordained and installed pastor of Mount Pleasant church December 28, 1805. At a meeting of his Presbytery in October, 1807, he is reported absent upon a missionary tour to Knox County, Ind., whither the Assembly of 1806 had commissioned him for three months. This was probably the occasion upon which, while fording the west fork of White River, he lost his hat and his shoe, and was restored to a clerical and presentable condition by General Harrison, to whom he had letters of introduction. Returning home Mr. Scott at once arranged his affairs for a permanent removal to Indiana. He was dismissed from the pastorate of the Mount Pleasant church October 10, 1808, and soon after

[1] "Life and Times of Stephen Bliss," by S. C. Baldridge, p. 71.

began the twenty years of continuous service in Knox County, which only his death, December 30, 1827, terminated.

Mr. Scott long held his post in the wilderness alone, unsupported except by brethren whom on special occasions he called from Kentucky. He "had erected a rude platform in the woods, and supplied a plentiful amount of rustic benches, and thither his fervent spirit had gathered the people for religious worship. Here in this sequestered sylvan sanctuary God had been pleased to show his faithful servant his glory in times of spiritual blessings, and the whole romantic scene was sacred."[1] This outdoor pulpit was known as "the Presbyterian Stand." Here it was that McGready sometimes addressed and overpowered great congregations.[2] Subsequently, under the pastor's diligent labors, there were three preaching stations in his parish, and no doubt the toil imposed by his isolation in so wide a field shortened his days.

This patriarch of Indiana pastors was of a very social temperament, a fine talker, and a good preacher. With old and young he was always a favorite. He diligently catechized the children, meeting them on Saturdays at private houses.[3] So scrupulous was he in observing the Sabbath that he once declined a carefully-dressed haunch of venison, prepared for him by a parishioner who had had a Sunday hunt, and thereby secured the man's life-long enmity. He was fond of "log-rollings" and "corn-huskings," where, if occasion permitted, he was sure to perpetrate some innocent practical joke. By one[4] whom

[1] "Life and Times of Stephen Bliss," p. 75.
[2] The records indicate that meetings of the session previous to 1815 were held at "the Stand."
[3] At one of these appointments he was late. On his arrival he explained that he had sent his only hat to Vincennes to be pressed, and forgetting it until the hour of starting, had been compelled to despatch a messenger to a colored man, his nearest neighbor, to borrow a hat.
[4] The Rev. John Crozier.

in 1825 he baptized at Paris, Ill., he is remembered as a man of medium height, of rather full habit, about fifty years of age, and wearing goggles.

Mr. Scott's family consisted of two sons and two daughters, Sallie Anne, Alexander Dunlap, Nancy Anne, and Samuel Thornton. The younger daughter became the wife of her father's successor, the Rev. Samuel R. Alexander. She died at the homestead, two and one half miles northeast of Vincennes, the estate having passed into the possession of her husband.[1]

[1] The burning of the old parsonage destroyed many valuable MSS., with which have perished authentic details of Mr. Scott's career and of the local history. Mr. Alexander coming to the parish in 1828, the year after the death of Scott, continued to cultivate either the whole or a portion of the field for more than thirty years and until age compelled his retirement. His death occurred February 17, 1884.

CHAPTER IV.

HINDRANCES AND DISORDERS INCIDENT TO WAR.
1807–1814.

NATURALLY the first foundations were laid by the Presbyterians in the midst of the oldest community in the territory, comprising as it did among its prominent citizens representatives of families beyond the southern border which had been conspicuous for their attachment to the church. It will, however, be remembered that while the French occupancy of Vincennes long preceded any other settlement by the whites on the northern bank of the Ohio, there was at a very early day a considerable population upon the "Clark grants," comprising nearly all of Clark County. There, not far from Charlestown, a second little band of Presbyterians was gathered in 1807.[1] It was called the "Palmyra" church, in accordance with what seems to have been a decided taste for antiquities in that region, where Bethlehem, Memphis, and Utica still hold their place amidst such modern and homely names as Muddy Fork and Bennetsville. This organization, which soon became extinct and was merged in the later society at Charlestown, was effected by the Rev. James Vance, who had been associated with Cameron in the previous unfulfilled commission to Indiana from Transylvania Presbytery. Early in 1807 Samuel B. Robertson was again appointed by the Presbytery "to attend in Knox County, Indiana territory, in order to answer the prayer of a petition from that place."[2] In 1809 James H. Dickey, bearing a name

[1] Dickey's " Brief History," p. 4.
[2] " Minutes Transylvania Presbytery," Vol. III., p. 184.

which his kinsman was by and by to render famous in the annals of the Indiana church, made a hasty missionary tour to the territory, crossing the border from Kentucky, the Egypt whose granaries then and for years afterward generously supplied the famine of the Word.

From a more distant region, however, a stalwart young minister came in 1810, and contrary to his design was detained at Lawrenceburgh. He was the second Presbyterian clergyman who settled within the state, and on that account, as well as for his ability and zeal, deserves a recognition which he has hitherto failed to receive.[1]

SAMUEL BALDRIDGE, the third of twelve children of Scotch-Irish parents, John and Margaret (Ferrel) Baldridge, was born near Guilford Court House, N. C., March 21, 1780. When he was about fourteen years of age the family removed to Cook County, Tenn., and settled on the French Broad River. As he approached manhood his brother James, the eldest of the children, in company with him built a saw and grist-mill on Clear Creek, an affluent of the French Broad. At this period occurred his conversion. Thereupon making known a desire to connect himself with the Presbyterian Church, his father, a determined adherent of the Covenanters, interposed, and assured his son that such a step should disinherit him. As Samuel persisted in following his convictions of duty the threat was executed.

In 1778 Samuel Doak, a man of strong faith and ardent zeal, having graduated at Princeton three years before, settled on the Holston, in the midst of a few families of Scotch-Irish emigrants from Virginia, organized a church, and in a log building on his farm opened a school. Thither, about thirty miles from home, the young convert went, and in due time graduated from Dr. Doak's

[1] There is no mention even of his name by Dickey, Johnston, or the other local historians. See, however, Monfort's " Presbyterianism North of the Ohio," pp. 8, 10.

academy, already chartered and known as "Washington College."[1] On the first Tuesday in September, 1805, being a candidate under the care of Abingdon Presbytery, he and two others, Reuben White and Alexander M. Nelson, were "directed to turn their attention to the study of divinity under the inspection of some member or members of Presbytery and they were allowed to prepare and deliver exhortations."[2] January 23, 1806, he married Lucinda Doak, daughter of the Rev. Dr. Doak, a lady of attractive person and of unusual intelligence and piety. He was licensed at Salem church, Washington County, the pastoral charge of his father-in-law, on the 5th of October, 1807, and on the eleventh of the subsequent October was ordained and installed pastor of the Rock Spring and Glade Spring congregations.

Meanwhile his father had removed, in 1808, to Ohio, and Mr. Baldridge, appointed commissioner to the General Assembly in 1809, visited him at Hamilton. The beauty and fertility of the region, together with his growing aversion to slavery, induced the young man to resign his pastorate in Tennessee and request a dismission to the Presbytery of Washington, Synod of Kentucky. With his wife and two children he came across the great wilderness of Tennessee and Kentucky, transporting all the household effects in wagons. They reached Lawrenceburgh, Ind., in safety in the summer of 1810, and were welcomed there by old friends from east Tennessee.[3] Mr.

[1] The Rev. Arthur T. Rankin, long a Presbyterian "bishop" in Decatur County, whose father's "little red house" at Ripley, Ohio, was a famous station on the "underground railroad," and whose mother was a Doak, well remembers the coming of his uncle Baldridge, on his bob-tail bay horse, to visit at the Ripley parsonage. He says that at the Doak Academy ambition was stimulated to the utmost by personal rivalry. The man who could first hasten through the curriculum was the first to receive his degree. At one time there was an eager strife for precedence between John Rankin and Samuel G. Lowry, whose name appears later in the Indiana history. By the hardest work the former got through first and became for a time the latter's tutor.

[2] "Minutes Abingdon Presbytery."

[3] Mr. Chambers had been a ruling elder there.

Baldridge was induced to remain in the settlement. It was missionary ground. The fertile valleys of the Ohio and Whitewater were attracting a large and enterprising population, but there were neither church organizations nor houses of worship. In order to secure a maintenance the missionary procured a large dwelling and opened an English classical school, like his former preceptor accustoming his pupils, during the recitations and at the table, to converse in Latin. Before he had connected himself with Washington Presbytery that Presbytery was divided, October 11, 1810, and Joshua L. Wilson, Matthew G. Wallace, William Robinson, James Welch, and himself were constituted into the Presbytery of Miami. He was appointed to supply statedly the vacancies at Lawrenceburgh and Whitewater. In this work he continued for two years, maintaining his school and preaching in private houses and under the forest's roof as he found opportunity. He also studied medicine at Lawrenceburgh, and became a successful physician, with a considerable practice.

Presbytery directed him, September 12, 1812, to spend two weeks in the vacancies above Dayton, "the barrens of Ohio," at his discretion. October 5, 1813, he was dismissed to the Presbytery of Washington, which received him at the spring meeting of the following year, when, April, 1814, he became stated supply of Washington and London. At the latter place he had several students in medicine. In 1815 he supplied London and Treacle's Creek. He was dismissed April 8, 1818, to the Presbytery of Lancaster, and the following spring took charge of the churches of Salt Creek (now Chandlersville), Buffalo (now New Cumberland), and Pleasant Hill (now New Concord), and was the next June installed as pastor. This relation continued until April, 1823, when he was released from Buffalo and Salt Creek congregations, remaining pastor of the Pleasant Hill church for another year. In 1824 he removed to Jeromeville, whose pulpit he supplied. Here he built a residence, apparently designing to make the place a permanent home. He continued a lucrative practice of medicine. He also supplied the Perrysville and Rehoboth congregations, and preached occasionally at many other points, a service in which he delighted. But here two misfortunes came. August 18, 1825, he lost his wife, and soon after was compelled to relinquish his property, held as security for another's debts.

In the summer of 1828, having previously, May 25, 1826, been united in marriage with Mary, daughter of Jonathan Coulter, Esq., of Perrysville, he returned to Indiana and settled at Eugene, Vermilion County. April 4, 1832, he was dismissed to the Presbytery of Vincennes, having removed to "Honey Creek parsonage" and taken charge of Honey Creek and New Hope churches. Says his son:[1]

My first recollections are connected with that old parsonage. It was a hewed-log building, and stood at the edge of a grove of wild cherry and mulberry trees. Fronting a wide low prairie, it looked out toward Sullivan, then known as Prairieton. The whole region was at times overflowed by the Wabash and looked like a sea. A June freshet once came within a few yards of the door. In this romantic and secluded spot it was that the great calamity of Dr. Baldridge's life occurred—an attack of palsy. He had just left a patient and was mounting his horse at the gate when the blow fell. He was taken home in an unconscious state and so remained for several weeks. Subsequently he woke as from a sleep. When he was able to sit up he one day noticed the books in his library, and after surveying them in silence at last asked what they were. My mother tried in vain, by reading their titles, to recall them to his mind. He subsequently asked that a book might be laid upon his lap, but even the letters were a mystery. My mother has said that she then had a full sense of the bitterness of her grief, and that she could never, yielding to his importunity, sit down with a book to teach him his alphabet

[1] The Rev. Samuel C. Baldridge, D.D., Hanover, Ind., who has furnished MSS. for the narrative of his father's life.

without uncontrollable weeping. One day, however, as she was going through the weary task her husband suddenly turned to her with dilated eyes and exclaimed, "I see it all." From this time the past gradually yielded up its lost treasures. But his power was gone.

He now removed to Paris, Ill., where he bought a farm and lived for some years. He afterward exchanged it for land within the bounds of New Providence church, between Paris and Terre Haute. "Here the family lived for some years, learning how God can supply all our need. 'He gave us bread to eat and raiment to put on.'" About 1840 Dr. Baldridge was invited to the church in Kalida, Putnam County, Ohio. He had preached occasionally before—"could not live without preaching"—but had no regular work since 1830. For a time he also preached at Dillsborough, Ind. Thence, about 1843, he removed to Oxford, Ohio, to give a son the advantages of the university, but thinking that the president was too little emphatic in his attitude toward slavery, he left Oxford for Hanover, Ind., in 1844. Two years later his home was finally broken up by the death of his wife, who had exhibited great prudence and cheerfulness in the midst of trial, and he found a resting-place at the house of his son, the Rev. Samuel C. Baldridge, where he died February 29, 1860. His remains were taken to Hanover, where they lie buried with his second wife.

Dr. Baldridge was adapted to his era. It was easy for him to move. Attachment to localities never hindered him. He rejoiced to preach in new and destitute regions, in private houses, and the summer woods. There are abundant testimonies to the power and ability of his preaching. At Jeromeville his overflowing congregations were gathered from the whole district around, many walking ten miles to hear him. After the lapse of sixty-six years a sermon preached in a private house near Lawrenceburgh was remembered vividly by one who was present, perhaps the sole survivor. He was recognized by his fellow-laborers as a "born missionary," and his zeal and energy were honored by frequent appointments to the most arduous itinerant labors. He accepted joyfully the heat and burden of the day. He was of the same spirit, had the same vigor of constitution and the same delight in preaching that characterized the Gallaghers and Nelsons and Hendersons—that whole generation of evangelists that sprang up in east Tennessee under the training of Dr. Doak. "I have heard him say," writes his son, "that in his prime after a hard day's ride as a physician it would rest him to preach in the evening."

Dr. Baldridge was an accomplished conversationalist. His Irish spirits were exuberant. His life began with brilliant promise, but the sun went down at noon. With the single exception of Mr. Scott, at Vincennes, he was the first Presbyterian minister to become a resident of Indiana. He preceded William Robinson nearly four years.

In 1811 (as also in 1819) the name of STEPHEN BOVELLE appears as a missionary to the state from the General Assembly. He had received licensure October 10, 1794, from Transylvania Presbytery, but his career was a checkered one.[1]

The following year the Charlestown church in Clark County was constituted by the Rev. Joseph B. Lapsley, a nephew of Cleland, an amiable young man, and a recent graduate of Lexington, Va.[2] But society was already in commotion on account of the opening war with Great Britain, a strife which sterner motives than those of patriotism brought home to the scattered settlements in the Ohio valley. The forests were still the haunts of savages, willing

[1] "Minutes Transylvania Presbytery," Vol. II., pp. 139, 178, 186, 187.
[2] "Life of Cleland," p. 76.

now, as often before, to sell themselves for British promises to Britain's emissaries. It was not a period for successful evangelistic labor. The war, however, summoned from Cincinnati to Fort Wayne a young man whose name has just been mentioned among the original members of Miami Presbytery. "When General Harrison, in September, 1812, marched to the relief of the garrison here, then besieged by the Indians, the expedition was accompanied," says Judge Jesse L. Williams, "by Rev. Matthew G. Wallace, as chaplain of the army. If, as may be presumed, he preached to the soldiers while here, his was the first proclamation of the gospel, in Protestant form, on this ground."[1] More than a century earlier the voice of the Romish priest had doubtless been heard at "Kekionga," and the rites of religion had been celebrated there, but not until the French had long been expelled and the English were once more struggling for their lost dominion was the Bible brought by a Protestant minister to this ancient home of the red man.

MATTHEW G. WALLACE afterward returned to Indiana to hold for years an important pastorate. A licenciate of New Castle Presbytery, the successor of Peter Wilson at Cincinnati, where he preached from April, 1800, to April, 1804, previous to 1809 he had supplied the churches at Springfield and Hambleton, and in 1814 he had charge of the congregations at Hamilton, Seven Mile, and Dick's Creek, Ohio.[2]

About the year 1831 two brothers named Wallace were successfully operating a saw-mill near where now stands Hulman's mammoth distillery [Terre Haute], and it having come to the knowledge of the people that their father was a Presbyterian minister, a subscription was circulated and a year's salary made up whereupon the Rev. Matthew G. Wallace was invited to

---

[1] "Historical Sketch of the First Presbyterian Church, Fort Wayne," p. 12.
[2] Gillett's "History," Vol. II., pp. 126, 151.

preach for one year. This was all done before the people had ever seen Mr. Wallace. He was a man of positive, severe character and kept charge of the church under many embarrassments, and notwithstanding various divisions, for nearly twenty years.[1]

In the winter of 1850-1, overtaken by the infirmities of age, Mr. Wallace resigned his pastorate, his death occurring July 15, 1854.

Though McGready, Robertson, Kemper, Vance, James H. Dickey, Bovelle, Lapsley, and Wallace occasionally preached the gospel in the territory during the seven years subsequent to Scott's settlement at Vincennes, and though for two years Baldridge was residing at Lawrenceburgh, it is evident that little was accomplished or attempted in behalf of the people north of the Ohio until peace was reëstablished. Under its pastor's care the "Indiana" church prospered in a quiet way, but the Palmyra society died and the Charlestown flock remained shepherdless. No doubt the accounts preserved by Bishop and Davidson[2] of the irreligion and disorder which characterized this period in Kentucky might be repeated with increased emphasis concerning the newer Indiana settlements. A Kentucky town containing two or three thousand inhabitants, and which ten years after sustained three large churches, could not now collect a congregation for a missionary who visited it.

The negroes were standing in the streets laughing and swearing; the boys playing and hallooing; the men in the outskirts of the town shooting at pigeons, of which immense flocks were flying over the place; the more respectable class of gentlemen riding out for amusement. In short, the only peculiar mark of attention by which the Sabbath day was distinguished was that there was more noise, more profanity, and more wickedness than on any other day of the seven.

[1] Sterrett's MS. "History of the Presbyterian Church in Terre Haute."
[2] "Memoir of Rice," p. 109. Cf. Davidson's "Kentucky," Chap XI. See also "The Western Sketch-Book," by Rev. James Gallagher, pp. 21, 22.

This was the experience of Samuel J. Mills, the leader of the praying band at Williams College, from which sprang our modern missions to the heathen world, and who, in 1814-5, with Daniel Smith, accomplished, under the direction of the Massachusetts Missionary Society, a tour of exploration through "that part of the United States which lies west of the Allegheny Mountains."[1] He says in his report :

Indiana, notwithstanding the war, is peopling very fast. Its settlements are bursting forth on the right hand and on the left. In 1810 there were in the territory 24,500 inhabitants; now they are computed by the governor at 35,000, by others at 30,000, and by some at 50,000. Its principal settlements are on the Miami and Whitewater, on the Ohio (extending in some places twenty miles back), and on the Wabash and White Rivers. Many small neighborhoods have received an addition of from twenty to forty families during the last summer. When we entered this territory there was but one Presbyterian clergyman in it, Mr. Scott of Vincennes. He was valiantly maintaining his post there for six years past. He has three places of preaching, and although he has not been favored with an extensive revival, yet his labors have been blessed to the edification of his congregations. His church consists of about seventy members. Between the forks of White River there is also a Presbyterian congregation in which there are about thirty communicants, and we have lately heard that a clergyman has settled among them.[2] In the state of Ohio we saw the Rev. William Robinson. He informed us that he expected soon to remove to the territory and establish himself at Madison on the Ohio. It is probable, then, that there are now three Pres-

---

[1] Associated with John F. Schermerhorn, Mills had attempted a similar service two years earlier. See "A Correct View of that part of the United States which lies west of the Allegheny Mountains, with regard to Religion and Morals," Hartford, 1814. In this rare pamphlet, prepared almost entirely from Schermerhorn's manuscripts, there is but slight reference to Indiana. "The best lands in this territory are still claimed by the Indians. . . Between the falls of Ohio and Vincennes there are a few houses. . . There is only one Presbyterian minister in this rapidly-settling territory."—Pp. 30, 31.

[2] This was the Washington church, Davies County, established by Samuel T. Scott in August of the previous year (1814), the fourth organization in the territory. The Rev. John M. Dickey had spent a few Sabbaths with the society in December, 1814, but he was not yet settled there.

byterian clergymen in the territory. But what are they for the supply of so many thousands? They are obliged to provide principally for their own support, by keeping school through the week or by manual labor. They have therefore very little time to itinerate. The settlements on the Miami and Whitewater we did not visit, but were informed by missionaries who have occasionally labored there that they afford promising fields of usefulness. Probably congregations might be formed there. Places of preaching where considerable numbers of people would assemble might be established with short intervals from Lawrenceburgh, near the mouth of the Miami, to Jeffersonville on the Falls of the Ohio. In the vicinity of the Falls are two other flourishing little villages, Charlestown and New Albany. It is of high importance that the standard of the truth should be immediately planted there, for these places or some of them must soon become rich and populous towns. At Charlestown there is a small Presbyterian church. But it languishes for want of the bread and of the water of life. Leaving the river and proceeding a little further west we came to other flourishing settlements. Corydon is the present seat of government for the territory. Salem, a county seat, has near it three other places where churches might be formed. These settlements are yet in their infancy. It is said, however, that they are able to support a minister. And yet there are people here who for five years past have not seen the face of a Presbyterian clergyman. Their hearts have been grieved at the neglect of their brethren to send them any aid. . . . When they saw us they shed tears of joy. In that part of the territory that lies on the Wabash there are settlements both above and below Vincennes that deserve the attention of missionary bodies, particularly those above, on Bussaron. An immense number of settlers have been crowding out on that frontier during the last season.

We have now given a brief view of the principal settlements in the Indiana territory. If one or two faithful missionaries could be sent into it to travel through it and search it out, to collect congregations and organize churches, who can tell how much good might be done? They might become the fathers of the churches there. Thousands would rise up hereafter and call them blessed.[1]

The date of this report of Mills is January 20, 1815.

[1] "Report of a Missionary Tour through that part of the United States which lies west of the Allegheny Mountains, performed under the direction of the Massachusetts Missionary Society by Samuel J. Mills and Daniel Smith," Andover, 1815, pp. 15, 16.

What was the religious condition of Indiana just as the second war with Great Britain was closing he presents with evident accuracy.

In December, 1814, WILLIAM ROBINSON, whom Mills "saw in Ohio," reached Indiana. Though directly from Miami Presbytery no doubt it was his former association with Kentucky ministers who had forded the Indiana streams and heard the bark of the Indiana wolves that turned him westward. He was a native of Ireland, but, coming to America with his father when a child, he found a home in Pennsylvania.[1] There he learned the wheelwright's trade, which enabled him afterward to defray the expenses of a literary course at Washington, Pa. About the year 1792 he emigrated to Kentucky, where he studied theology under the tutorship of the Rev. Samuel Finley. He was taken under the care of Transylvania Presbytery, October 3, 1793, and was ordained over the Mount Pleasant and Indian Creek churches, August 11, 1796.[2] These churches he had himself organized soon after his licensure and he continued to preach to them through the memorable revival of 1800. On the 13th of August, 1799, he married Miss Esther Grey, a member of the Mount Pleasant congregation.

In the autumn of 1803 he removed to Montgomery County, Ohio, and immediately organized the churches of Dayton and Sugar Creek. The following year he organized the Honey Creek society and labored as its minister until 1810,[3] when he settled at Lebanon, Warren County. Between the congregation there and at Monger's settlement his time was equally divided. At Lebanon he was

---

[1] He was a member of the "Buffalo congregation" (Davidson's "Kentucky," p. 121).

[2] "Minutes Transylvania Presbytery," Vol. II., p. 107, and filed papers. "Minutes West Lexington Presbytery," Vol. I., pp. 76, 95. Cited by Davidson.

[3] Gillett's "History," Vol. II., p. 126.

also engaged successfully as a teacher, some of his pupils afterward attaining high positions.

It was in the winter of 1814 that Mr. Robinson "came to the village of Madison to teach, and was soon engaged by the handful of Presbyterians here to preach to them."[1] The following year he organized a church and gathered a congregation. There was at the time no house of worship[2] and he was accustomed to preach in what some of the older generation still remember as the "buckeye" courthouse. He also continued to maintain his school.[3] Here and in the immediate vicinity, especially at South Hanover, his work proceeded until 1819. He then settled in Bethlehem, Clark County. In that village and in the surrounding district he preached regularly for two or three years, but in 1822 a dropsical malady proved so severe that he was almost entirely disabled for ministerial work. Sometimes, however, when unable to stand, he would deliver the gospel message from his pulpit chair. The disease making constant progress, he was at last rendered completely helpless, and in this condition he lingered for two or three years, until March 28, 1827, when, at a good old age, he died. He was laid to rest in the cemetery near Bethlehem. It was with difficulty that the unmarked grave was recently identified.[4]

Mr. Robinson was one of the original members of Salem Presbytery. He was also one of the four ministers set off

[1] Simpson's "History of the First Church, Madison," p. 1.

[2] There were but two Presbyterian meeting-houses in the territory, both of logs and both near Vincennes in the "Indiana" parish. The first residence in Madison was built in 1809, but in 1709 Vincennes was a town.

[3] Mrs. James H. Johnston was one of his pupils.

[4] The minister upon the field wrote April, 1876: "I can find no one who is able to point me to his grave. I found an ancient-looking grave, at the head of which there is a rough native limestone with the inscription, ' J. J. R., 1835,' supposed to be for one of his sons. By the side of it is a grave very much sunken, at the head of which is a small stone in its rough native state and uninscribed. This is supposed to be the grave of the Rev. William Robinson." According to the later testimony of a member of the family this surmise is correct.

to form Madison Presbytery, and at its first meeting, April 7, 1826, he preached the opening sermon from Jeremiah xlviii.: 10.

Like other pioneers, he suffered many privations, but happily he had been accustomed in early life to manual toil. Thus he was able to supplement the meager ministerial support while it continued, and afterward, when even that failed him with his failing health, his mechanical skill was almost his sole reliance. A wheelwright in his youth, in the "Buffalo congregation," Pennsylvania, in his old age, at Bethlehem, he turned to wool-carding. At various times he availed himself also of the scanty fees of a schoolmaster. But with thirteen children to maintain it is not surprising that "the family sometimes felt the pinching hand of poverty." The ministers of that day, doing their utmost to earn the opportunity of preaching the gospel, were content if they succeeded in saving those dependent on them from actual want.

During all his residence in Indiana Mr. Robinson seems to have also been hindered by feeble health. A pupil at Madison remembers his distressing cough in the school-room, his tall spare frame and pale face; and when, a few years later, he transferred his residence to Bethlehem, he was soon attacked by the disease which terminated his life. It will therefore be easy to account for the statement of one who knew him at Madison,[1] that "although living there several years he preached but little in the town"; and for the impression of another that he was "less engaged than some of the ministers of his time in missionary tours."[2]

The qualities of the man were those which a Scotch-Irish parentage so commonly implies. He was sturdy and pos-

[1] Dr. McClure.

[2] He is said to have made two journeys, however, through destitute regions of the state. The only society constituted by him, according to Dickey's "Brief History," was the church at Madison.

sibly in some instances stubborn and abrupt. Something of the old-country ideas as to the rights of a parish minister may have been born in him, and he did not care to have his labors supplemented by intruders, however respectable their commissions. A young man who ventured into the place in the winter of 1818–9, under the auspices of the General Assembly's Committee of Missions, was not warmly welcomed by the "incumbent." The minister in possession could not discern the necessity of the missionary's visit nor the value of his labors.

There was something of the same independent judgment in Mr. Robinson's attitude toward the new movement to promote total abstinence. The reform had few supporters, and among clergymen in the woods it was not unusual to indulge in a moderate daily dram.[1] Mr. Robinson's indulgence, according to abundant testimony, was not at all beyond what the habits of the day fully approved, but his liberty, such as it was, he was disposed to defend. In a neighboring pulpit it happened that the cause of temperance had a very zealous and able advocate.[2] From that quarter the whisky barrel got many a rap. When the echoes reached "Father Robinson" he declared that his brother "might preach against whisky if he pleased, but as for himself he would drink it."

There was also a trace of Scotch-Irish thriftiness in his character. It seems that at one time he had a little "store" in Madison.[3] "By secular employments he made much of his small salary," says one. Some of his neighbors, perhaps less prudent themselves, thought he carried his thrifty methods too far. But such devices were a necessity in those days, and all the pioneers were obliged to work their way

[1] Cf. Prime's "Memoirs of Goodell," pp. 18–21.

[2] We are fortunate in having a brief notice of Mr. Robinson from the MSS. of Father Dickey, who relates this incident and who was probably himself the preacher referred to

[3] This is the impression of Dr. McClure.

to a Sunday pulpit, or a "sacramental four-days' meeting," or a protracted preaching tour, through much intermediate "weariness and painfulness" on the farm or in the shop or school.[1] If there was any mistake in Mr. Robinson's case it was in his looking less than some are inclined to do for the falling of manna from heaven for his hungry children. His habits no doubt prevented those frequent and protracted missionary journeys which extended so widely the usefulness of many ministers of that day.

As a preacher Mr. Robinson, while not brilliant, had acknowledged elements of power. He must have retained something of the unction of the Kentucky revival through which he labored. Impenitent men were accustomed to say : " He cuts to the heart. No sermons I hear trouble me like his. There is no getting away from them."[2]

[1] Cf. "Report of Smith and Mills's Tour," p. 16.
[2] MS. of the Rev. John M. Dickey.

CHAPTER V.

THE WAR OVER AND THE WORK ADVANCED.

1815.

THE war was now over. The movement of immigrants to Indiana, already in progress according to Mills's report, notwithstanding the disorders and perils of the frontier, with the coming of peace received a fresh impulse. There was increased necessity for missionary effort and the call was promptly answered. In 1815 the General Assembly sent to the territory, for brief periods of service, Daniel Gray, from the Carolinas, Joseph Anderson, a Pennsylvanian, and James Welch, of Transylvania Presbytery. The Pittsburg Missionary Society was also instructed to engage others for the field. But these were all mere horseback riders. However faithful, their labors were too transient for large results.

The year is signalized by the appearance of a different company. The man rides a horse, indeed; but he has his wife and baby behind him, and his bed and kitchen stuff close by. He comes to spend his life for the people of the wilderness and to make his grave among them. It is John McElroy Dickey—plain, modest, resolute, tireless, true, sweet-voiced "Father Dickey." "His name," says Gillett, "will stand deservedly conspicuous as the father of the Presbyterian Church in Indiana."[1]

JOHN MCELROY DICKEY was born in York district, S. C., December 16, 1789. His grandfather, of Scotch-

[1] Gillett's "History," Vol. II., p. 397.

Irish descent, came from Ireland to America about the year 1737. His father, David Dickey, was twice married, first on March 28, 1775, to Margaret Robeson, who died four months after her marriage; and subsequently, September 4, 1788, to Margaret Stephenson. John was the first-born and only son of this latter marriage. He had four sisters, of whom one died in infancy.

His parents were in humble circumstances, but of excellent Christian character. David Dickey was a man of unusual intelligence, and, according to the testimony of his son, had remarkable self-control. "I never saw him angry but once," the latter declared; "nor did I ever see him manifest peevishness or fretfulness, even in old age." No pressure of business could ever induce him to omit the customary household worship or other religious duties. For years he taught the neighborhood school, and when John was but three years of age carried him to it daily. Of such a man the wife was a true helpmeet. Like Hannah, she had given her son to God and formally devoted him to his service. It was her habit, while at the wheel spinning flax or cotton, to gather her children about her for instruction in the Shorter Catechism. "To my mother," said Mr. Dickey, "more than to any other human being, am I indebted for what I am. In the midst of doubts, fears, discouragements, and toils, it has often been a source of consolation to know that I had a mother who, in covenant with God, gave me up to him and to the work of the ministry. If all mothers were like her, the Lord's vineyard could not long lack laborers."

Under such a home influence, the children all grew insensibly into the habits of piety, and were unable to fix the time when their early religious experience began. The son became familiar with the Scriptures, the Confession of Faith, and Form of Government of the Presbyterian Church—the reading books of that day—and the foundations were permanently laid for the clear theological views of his subsequent ministry. At four years of age it is said that he had read the Bible through. Not much later he was acquiring a considerable knowledge of mathematics, under his father's instruction, and aided by a coal and pine board. He eagerly improved his humble opportunities for study, until new advantages were providentially opened to him by the removal of the family northward in 1803. David Dickey, though reared in a slave state, looked upon slavery as a curse, and sought to deliver his family from its influence ; but upon leaving South Carolina he found himself obliged by circumstances to remain in Livingston County, Ky. After assisting for two or three years in the labor of clearing and cultivating his father's land, John went to study under the direction of his cousin, the Rev. William Dickey,[1] about a mile from his own home. The manse, however, had but one room, and the proprietor had several children of his own. Young Dickey, therefore, built a shelter near the house where he might keep his books and study. Thus he read Virgil and the Greek Testament, remaining with his cousin for about eighteen months. A school was then opened by the Rev. Dr. Nathan H. Hall, at Hardin's Creek church, two hundred and fifty miles distant, whither he determined to make his way. His father was quite unable to assist him, but John had secured a colt on the farm and raised it, so that he was now in possession of a fine young horse. Thus mounted, with perhaps two dollars in money, he set out upon the long journey. For board and lodging he

[1] The valuable notice of Mr. Dickey, in Sprague's "Annals," is marred by several inaccuracies. The Rev. William Dickey appears as *Wilson*; Mr. Dickey's great-grandfather is said to have emigrated from Ireland about 1740, whereas it was his grandfather, who came several years earlier than that date; Muhlenburg Presbytery is changed to *Mecklenburg*; the date of the organization of Salem Presbytery is set forward seven years; Columbus, *Ohio*, is substituted for Columbus, Ind. The appended communications from Mr. Dickey's ministerial brethren are singularly pictorial and just.

sold his horse to a Mr. McElroy, and entered with zeal upon his studies. The horse ran away and was never recovered, but the student was already a favorite, and continued a member of the McElroy household until his course at Dr. Hall's school was completed. He gave such assistance as he could in the labors of the farm, and all further compensation was refused by the hospitable host. It was thus that afterward, to avoid confusion often arising from the commonness of his own name, Mr. Dickey added McElroy to John. Soon becoming an assistant teacher in the school, he was enabled to support himself, at the same time working hard at his own course of study.

Here he remained nearly two years, when he entered upon the study of theology with the cousin who had previously been his instructor, and with the Rev. John Howe, at Glasgow, Ky. He was licensed to preach by Muhlenburg Presbytery, August 29, 1814, in the twenty-fifth year of his age, having already, November 18 of the previous year, been united in marriage with Miss Nancy W., daughter of William and Isabel (Miller) McClesky, of Abbeville district, S. C.

In December, after his licensure, he made a visit to Indiana, and spent a few Sabbaths at what is now Washington, Davies County, with a church that had been constituted, in August of the same year, by the Rev. Samuel Thornton Scott, Indiana's first resident Presbyterian minister. There were now but two other organized Presbyterian societies within the limits of Indiana territory— the "Indiana" church, near Vincennes, constituted in 1806, and the Charlestown church, established in 1812. A church formed in 1807, and known as the "Palmyra" church, had become extinct. There were but two Presbyterian meeting-houses, both of logs, and both in the "Indiana" parish. But two Presbyterian ministers were already settled in Indiana,[1] Mr. Scott and the Rev. William Robinson.

Mr. Dickey engaged to return to the Washington congregation, and accordingly, in May, 1815,[2] still a licentiate under the care of Muhlenburg Presbytery, he set out for his home in the wilderness, with his wife and their infant daughter. The family and all their earthly goods were carried on the backs of two horses. His library consisted of a Bible, Buck's "Theological Dictionary," Bunyan's "Pilgrim's Progress," and Fisher's "Catechism." When the ferriage across the Ohio was paid, they had a single shilling left.

Now began the self-denials and struggles of pioneer life. It was impossible to expect a comfortable support from the feeble congregation. There was little money in the neighborhood. Taxes were partly paid in raccoon skins, fox skins, and "wolf-scalps." People lived on what they could raise from the small clearings, by barter, and by hunting. Indians still occasioned annoyance and anxiety. Corn was pounded in mortars or rubbed on tin graters. Wheat flour was seldom seen. Fruit was rare, except the wild plums, grapes, gooseberries, and pawpaws. Mr. Dickey, therefore, aided the support of his family by farming on a small scale,[3] teaching a singing-class, and writing deeds, wills, and advertisements. He also surveyed land, and sometimes taught school. Much of this work was done gratuitously, but it secured the friendship of the people. His average salary, including money and gifts, of which he kept a record, even to the minutest detail, for the first sixteen years was eighty dollars. In some way he secured forty acres of land, to which he sub-

[1] The Rev. Samuel Baldridge, M. D., had, in 1810, settled at Lawrenceburgh, but before Mr. Dickey's arrival had removed to Ohio.

[2] Dickey's "Brief History," pp. 12, 13.

[3] The character of the man came out, however, in the style of his farming. It was so thorough and intelligent that the productiveness of his fields was proverbial.

sequently added eighty acres. Twenty or thirty acres he cleared, chiefly by his own labor. With his neighbors' help he built his first house in the woods. It was a small log-cabin—the floor of slabs split and hewed from oak and poplar trees; the windows small, greased paper serving instead of glass; the chimney partly of stone and partly of sticks, and daubed with clay. In later years he erected a schoolhouse on his farm, and made sash with his own hands for the small glass then in use. He was "handy" with tools, and fashioned the woodwork of his plows and other farming implements. Often would less skilful neighbors work for him in the field, while he "stalked" their plows, or made them a harrow or rake. He also had a set of shoemaker's tools, mending the shoes of his family and often those of his neighbors. He could himself cut out and make a neat shoe, but "never liked the work, and avoided it if possible." Music he read with great facility, supplying the lack of books with his pen, several of these manuscript volumes being carefully kept by his children. He was not unaccustomed, on special occasions, to compose both music and hymns for the use of the congregation. Under his management the winter singing-school became a prominent and happy feature of the life in the wilderness.

Preaching every Sabbath, and often during the week, he was compelled to do much of his studying while at work on the farm, or as he rode on horseback from place to place. The family were too poor to afford a lamp or candles, and often, after a day of manual labor, Mr. Dickey would gather pine knots, and having kindled a bright fire, would sit on the hearth and write the plan of a sermon. His best opportunities for meditation, however, came while riding to his preaching stations, through the forests, and along the quiet roads. With his Bible, hymn-book, and Confession of Faith in the saddle-bags, and a Testament and small concordance in his pocket ready for use, he pursued careful investigations of important themes. His son says :

On a pony that had learned to avoid the mud by going close to the rail fence, I have seen him riding for miles, and at every corner lifting his leg and drawing it up on the saddle to avoid the rails, too much absorbed in thought to observe what the pony or himself was doing. Occasionally returning to consciousness of things about him, he would rein the horse out into the road ; but the beast, preferring the harder ground, would soon go back to the fence, and creep so close to the sharp corners that the process of leg-lifting would begin again and go steadily on for another hour.[1]

At one time, returning from a preaching-tour to find the family entirely out of meal and flour, he remounted his horse, went to the mill several miles distant, procured a supply, and with the sack on the horse's back started homeward. But becoming engaged in meditation, the sack fell off without his notice. The hungry children, who had made several meals of potatoes, saw with dismay that he was returning without the supplies, and, calling their mother, met him as he rode up to the gate. A single question was enough to reveal the state of the case, and wheeling about, half-amused and half-ashamed, he hurried back to find the sack at the roadside. He often said that to think closely he must be on his horse. There was no subject engaging the attention of the world which he did not ponder as thoroughly as his opportunities allowed. He was well informed on questions of public policy, and sometimes addressed communications to those in power, always urging that " righteousness exalteth a nation." These communications were kindly received and often elicited respectful replies.

Mr. Dickey's cheerful labors were overshadowed, how-

[1] The Rev. Ninian Steele Dickey, to whom the writer is under many obligations for the use of MSS.

ever, and sometimes wholly interrupted, by the alarming diseases common in such new settlements. At first his own family escaped, but before a year had passed all were prostrated, and on October 23, 1816, Mrs. Dickey died. Added to these personal sorrows was the discouragement arising from frequent removals of his people to other neighborhoods. There was, moreover, no suitable place of worship. This latter want was soon supplied, however. Though it was difficult to select a site against which no one would object, scattered as his congregation were along White River, upon a track sixteen miles long by ten wide, they finally united upon a piece of "Congress land" whose sterile soil would not be likely soon to tempt a purchaser to dispossess them. The members of the little society met on a day appointed, and cut logs twenty feet in length, which, with their native covering of bark and moss, were laid together. The minister was present to encourage his people, and some of the logs were notched by his own hands. The roof was of clap-boards. The earth formed both floor and carpet. The seats were hewed puncheons. On this log meeting-house, the third, it would seem, which the Indiana Presbyterians possessed, the people looked with pride. Rude as was the humble sanctuary, it equaled, if it did not surpass, the houses in which several of the congregation lived. It continued to be the place of worship until shortly after Davies County was organized, when the county-seat was located at Washington, a temporary court-house was erected, and this then became the meeting-house.[1]

After four years' service[2] in this field, Mr. Dickey removed to Lexington, Scott County, and became pastor of the New Lexington and Pisgah churches, while he also had charge of the Graham church, situated on a creek of that name between Paris and Vernon, in Jennings County. His installation, August, 1819, over the two former congrega-

---

[1] MSS. of the Rev. Thomas S. Milligan, long a friend of Mr. Dickey's family, a man of studious tastes and noble character. His death (October 7, 1876) occasioned great and sorrowful surprise.

[2] Dickey's "Brief History," p. 4.

tions, was the first formal Presbyterian settlement in the territory.[1] Previously, however, April 2, 1818, Mr. Dickey had married Miss Margaret Osborn Steele. This wife shared his trials and successes for nearly thirty years[2] and became the mother of eleven children. The picture of the pioneer parsonage and its busy life would be sadly imperfect without the portrait of this Christian woman.

She was worthy of her husband. Much of his usefulness must be attributed to her. For the maintenance of the family she gave her full share of toil and self-denial, often living alone with her children for months together, disciplining them to industry and usefulness, while their father was absent upon long and laborious missionary journeys. She cultivated a garden which supplied many household wants. Reared as she had been on the frontier, her education was at first limited, but under her husband's tuition she became a respectable scholar, able to instruct her own and her neighbors' children. She was an adept at the spinning-wheel and loom, and for many years made with her own hands all the linen and woolen cloth and garments for the family. There were also frequent additions to the exchequer from the sale of jeans of her manufacture. Such was her trust in God that fear never seemed to disturb her peace. She had lived for a time where the dread of prowling savages forbade the lighting of a lamp, or of a fire at night, and ordinary trouble produced no visible disturbance of her mind. In every good work she was foremost, whether it were making husk mattresses for the students at Hanover College, gathering supplies for destitute missionaries, or caring for the sick and unfortunate at home. The meagerness of her own household stores did not prevent her from doing much for others. In the absence of her husband the family altar was regularly maintained, and the

[1] Reed's "Christian Traveller," pp. 91, 213.
[2] Her death occurred October 24, 1847.

Sabbath afternoon recitations from the Shorter Catechism were by no means omitted. Though her residence was on a farm and most of Mr. Dickey's public life was spent as pastor of a country church, she sustained a woman's weekly prayer-meeting. In the Sabbath-school and at public worship her place was seldom vacant, notwithstanding the claims of so large a family. It was the custom to begin the communion services on Friday, which was often a fast-day, and to continue them through the following Monday. Neighboring ministers and congregations attended these services in great numbers. Often was the hospitality of the parish taxed to the utmost. A member of Mr. Dickey's family says:

> Though I relished heartily the enthusiasm of these gatherings, especially the singing and the social enjoyment, I recollect that in my early days I dreaded these occasions, because I had to sleep on the floor, often without even a carpet or pillow, that room might be made for strangers. One of my father's neighbors, they used to say, had accommodation for sixty guests, while many young men and boys slept on the hay in the barns. Notwithstanding the claims of guests and the necessity of unusual work at these seasons, everything was ordered so that the women of the household might be present at all the public meetings. I do not recollect ever to have known my mother to be absent except on account of the severe illness of herself or some member of the family, and never did I hear her complain of the burden of entertaining so many strangers. I have known her to be much concerned as to suitable provision for their comfort, but what she had was cheerfully given.

Is it not natural to ask whether the dignity and gracefulness of these hospitable rites are often surpassed or equaled now? The preparations are more elaborate and the ceremonies more pretentious, but is the welcome as warm or as wise?

It is not surprising that a mother, so prudent and diligent, so religious in her denial of self and her generosity to others, aided, too, by such a husband, should be blessed with dutiful and noble children. Her sons and daughters grew up in piety, and most of them survive in prominent and useful stations.[1]

In the midst of the scenes now described, Mr. Dickey's indefatigable labors continued. He served the New Lexington and Pisgah churches until April, 1835, a period of sixteen years, when the care of the former congregation was committed to other hands, though he held the pulpit of the Pisgah society for twelve years longer, and until the infirmities of age admonished him that the end was near.

It is not as pastor of the small country flock that his usefulness is to be measured, however. He was a traveling bishop. From far and near he was called to assist in special services, in revivals, at communions, and in vacant churches. The whole southern half of the territory he often traversed in difficult horseback journeys, and frequently his mission work extended to the "regions beyond." In January and February, 1823, having received an appointment from the Assembly's Committee of Missions, he made an exploring tour to Vincennes and Crawfordsville, and returning fulfilled appointments for preaching which he had scattered as he advanced.

Before he had reached the end of his outward journey violent rains had fallen, and the Wabash, with its tributaries, became very high, and was for the most part without bridges. Yet he preached thirty-one sermons in thirty days, and kept all his appointments save two. In a number of cases if the engagements had been a

[1] It would seem that our pioneer history furnishes a notable illustration of the power of parental influence. Especially do the humble parsonages of the early days in the woods prove what worthy children God gives to faithful fathers and mothers. Of Mr. Dickey's children are: Margaret, wife of Dr. James F. Knowlton, Geneva, Kan.; Jane, wife of Dr. W. W. Britain, on the homestead, near New Washington, Clark County, Ind.; the Rev. Ninian S., for eighteen years pastor of our church in Columbus, Ind.; John P., a Presbyterian ruling elder, and James H., in Allen County, Kan.; Nancy E., wife of Mr. Mattoon, Geneva, Kan.; Martha E., wife of Thomas Bare, Esq., Carrolton, Ill.; Mary E., wife of James M. Haines, Esq., New Albany, Ind.; and William Matthews, a graduate of Wabash College, a student of medicine, a prisoner at Andersonville, and a resident of California. The oldest son died at the age of seventeen, while a student for the ministry.

single day earlier or later, the impassable streams must have detained him. And so he was accustomed to say, "The Lord delivered me out of the deep waters." In the summer of 1824 he spent two months in the counties of Bartholomew, Rush, Shelby, and Decatur, under the direction of the Indiana Missionary Society, which a short time before he had assisted in forming. During this journey he organized the churches of Columbus and Franklin and the church of New Providence, near Shelbyville. His custom was to make a tour of two weeks, preaching daily, and then for an equal length of time remain at home laboring in his own parish.[1]

We are aided in recalling the methods and sacrifices of those days by the vivid pen of one of Mr. Dickey's fellow-laborers.

At Madison, in 1829, I first met with Father Dickey, who came to assist Mr. Johnston[2] during a protracted meeting. He had been delayed a little by stress of weather and bad roads; the congregation were assembled when he entered the church, fresh from his horse and journey. I seem to see his figure, of full medium height, spare and bent, marching up the aisle in a well-worn and soldier-like overcoat, and drab leggings, with saddle-bags on his arm, and presenting a face, thoughtful, gentle, and earnest, expressive of an equable spirit, firm and mild. When he spoke from the pulpit he had an unnatural tone; he showed little rhetoric, little of the learning or art of the schools, but much good sense, faith, and fruit of study in prayer and love. The people listened with a kind and appreciative attention. His character evidently helped him. He was well known in Madison, and everybody felt that his words were those of a wise and disinterested friend. There I learned to revere him as one communing much with God and ever penetrated with everlasting things; whose mind and heart were habitually conversant with the greatest interests; who sought not his own, but was revolving plans of large usefulness; a man, sober and trusty of judgment, and of organizing ability; laborious and modest; stable in the truth; candid and liberal, but not lax; fraternal and broad in his sympathies, loving and, like Christ, loving the world.

[1] MSS. of the Rev. Thomas S. Milligan.

[2] The Rev. James H. Johnston, who died at Crawfordsville March 8, 1876, having completed the longest term of continuous service ever attained by a minister of our church in Indiana—more than fifty-one years.

A few days later I found Father Dickey at Indianapolis, attending the anniversaries of the State Benevolent Societies, in establishing which he had been among the prime movers and in which he continued to show an efficient interest. The legislature was in session, and on the Sabbath he preached to a large audience, from Jeremiah vi.: 16—"Thus saith the Lord, stand ye in the ways, and see, and ask for the old paths, where is the good way, and walk therein, and ye shall find rest for your souls." He spoke with unction and to general acceptance, notwithstanding his peculiar mode of delivery.

Two months afterward he surprised me with a visit at my bachelor's room at an inn in Logansport. He had come on an exploring mission from his home in the southern part of the state, in February, 1830, encountering such difficulties from the roads and high waters and rude beginnings of the settlers, remote from each other, as belonged to that period, and all from a desire, preaching as he went, better to know the spiritual destitutions of the state, and more intelligently to labor in removing them.

During a few more years I was wont to see him at Synods, where his presence was always valued, and notably I remember him in the General Assembly at Philadelphia, 1832. In the strifes of the times he was not a warm partisan ; he knew nothing of intrigue ; and beyond most men seemed to act above prejudice and in the light of conscience and the spirit of Christ.[1]

Though never of a rugged constitution, the contrast with his wife's vigor and endurance being the occasion of frequent remark on her part, indulging the hope, as she did, that she might be permitted to cheer him in life's decline, Mr. Dickey sustained such various labors as have been described for a long period. Not until April, 1847, was he compelled by failing health to surrender the pastorate

---

[1] MS. letter of the Rev. Dr. Martin M. Post, dated January 7, 1876. Born in Cornwall, Vt., December 3, 1805, Middlebury's valedictorian in 1826, a graduate of Andover, reaching his mission field at Logansport, Ind., December, 1829, he there continued to reside until his death, October 11, 1876. For the fathers of the Indiana Synod the semi-centennial year was a fatal one. Johnston fell asleep March 8, but three days before John Ross (æt. 92), these two having been the sole remaining representatives of the former times in the Synod, North. Dr. Post's demise occurred but four days later than that of Thomas S. Milligan. The five sons of the former all received a collegiate and theological training, the youngest, Roswell O., having become pastor of the flock so long cared for by his father.

he had held for twenty-eight years. After an interval of a few months his health was so far restored that he was able to labor in the service of the American Tract Society for nearly a year. On the termination of this work he sought no further fixed employment, but ministered in the pulpit and as a counselor, most usefully, as opportunity came.

In 1828 Mr. Dickey had published, under the direction of the Synod, "A Brief History of the Presbyterian Church in the State of Indiana," now the source of our best information with regard to the early days.[1] This small pamphlet it was his earnest desire to enlarge and complete. His son writes :

> The last work of my father's life, on which his heart was set, was the completion of the history. He was very feeble in body at the last, but vigorous in mind, and sat at his table and wrote as long as he was able. Industry was his characteristic. I never saw him idle an hour. When forced to lay down his pen it cost him a struggle. At his request I acted as his amanuensis and prepared several sketches of churches, of which he said no other living man knew so much as he.

All was, however, left quite unfinished. He lived but a day or two after laying aside his pen.[2]

---

[1] "In regard to the early history of Presbyterianism in Indiana, he was a sort of gazetteer or book of reference, from which we had rarely, if ever, occasion to appeal." —Dr. Henry Little, in Sprague's "Annals," Vol. IV., pp. 518–9.

[2] As to the origin of the " Brief History," and the various efforts to supplement and complete it, see " Minutes of Salem Presbytery," Vol. I., p. 20 ; " Minutes of Madison Presbytery," Vol. I., p. 26 ; " Minutes of Indiana Synod," Vol. I., pp. 13, 15, 31, 53, 59, 60, 549, 586, 612, 624 ; Vol. II., pp. 207, 225, 347, 384, 401, 419, 423, 436, 437, 446. Mr. Dickey's pamphlet, though accurate, is not infallible. I have before me the author's copy, with his manuscript corrections. The more important of these are the following: Page 5, as to Madison church read, "it was supplied by Mr. Robinson for two years. In the summer of 1819 the Rev. Thomas S. Searle located at Madison, and was installed the following year pastor of Madison and Hanover churches "; page 6, as to the date of the organization of Pisgah church read, " February 27, 1816 "; the name of Daniel C. Banks is substituted for that of James McGready, as having constituted the New Albany church, the latter having formed the church at Jeffersonville ; page 7, as to the date of the Rev. Isaac Reed's settlement in Owen County read, " October, 1822 "; page 8, read, " Mr. Proctor labored three fourths of his time (at Indianapolis) for a year, beginning October, 1822. Mr. George Bush commenced his labors there in June, 1824 "; page 10, read, " June, 1821," as the date of the organization of Evansville

The only meetings of the Presbytery and Synod he had failed to attend were those held at New Albany a few weeks previous to his death. He wrote to his brethren apprising them of his feebleness, and assuring them that his work was nearly done. Synod appointed a committee to suggest a suitable reply, on the reception of which Mr. Dickey was deeply moved, at the family altar with choked utterance giving thanks to God that the lines had fallen to him in such goodly places, among such loving and faithful brethren, and praying that God would greatly prosper them. Suffering intensely in the closing hours, his peace was great. Although for twenty-five years afflicted with a pulmonary disease, his endurance was remarkable. He finally fell asleep November 21, 1849. The Rev. Philip Bevan, a licentiate of Cincinnati Presbytery, at this time supplying the New Washington church, officiated at the funeral. On the following Sabbath the Rev. Dr. Harvey Curtis, then pastor of the Second Church, Madison, preached in the New Washington Meeting-house a commemorative discourse from the text descriptive of Barnabas: "He was a good man, and full of the Holy Ghost, and of faith."—Acts xi.: 24.

Mr. Dickey's remains lie buried beside his second wife and three of his children, in the cemetery of the Pisgah (now New Washington) church. His tombstone is a plain marble slab, inscribed with his name, age, the date of his death, and the text of the commemorative discourse.[1]

church; page 11, for James Balch substitute Nathan B. Derrow, the name of the "New Hope" church having been originally and until 1825, "Hopewell."

There are such typographical errors as Samuel B. Robinson for *Robertson*, and *Martin B.* for Nathan B. Derrow.

It is also to be observed that Dickey makes no allusion to the organization of Rising Sun church, September, 1816 (by Nathan B. Derrow), and of Concord church, Orange County, September 27, 1818 (by Orin Fowler), nor to the labors of Samuel Baldridge (1810-2), Samuel J. Mills (1814-5), William Goodell (1822), Lucius Alden (1825), and John Ross (1822-76).

[1] On the announcement of his death in Synod a movement was made to erect a monument to his memory at the expense of his brethren. The motion was opposed by

Of the man who so wisely and laboriously laid the foundations of Christian society in Indiana, the best estimate is presented in the simple record of his career. It is, however, to be observed how sagacious and determined he was in the advocacy of views which then were new, but now are generally accepted among good men.

In his personal appearance most unostentatious, his dress was usually homespun. Though in his later years he wore broadcloth in the pulpit, his every-day garb was of the jeans provided by the hands of his wife and daughters. Doubtless the necessity of economy determined this habit, but there was also still remaining among the plain people of the frontier that prejudice against imported stuffs which during the Revolution had been so violent.[1] Beneath such an unassuming exterior, however, dwelt a singularly broad and self-reliant mind.

The character of the man was indicated in his early and bold advocacy of the temperance reform. It has been asserted that he preached the first sermon in Indiana against intemperance.[2] A lady relates, as illustrating the propriety of such preaching at the time, that on one occasion, when a child, she was put out of a back window by her mother, and sent with great haste to one of the neighbors for whisky, "because they saw Mr. Dickey, the preacher, coming." One of his son's earliest recollections

Samuel Merrill, Esq., who said that he knew Mr. Dickey well enough to be sure that such display would have offended his modesty. Mr. Merrill suggested instead that funds be raised for a hall in Wabash College, to be known as "Dickey Hall." The suggestion met with cordial approbation, but was never carried out.

[1] The Rev. James Dickey, of South Salem, Ohio, a cousin of "Father Dickey," went to the General Assembly in Philadelphia dressed in homespun, and on a Sabbath was invited to fill one of the city pulpits. After ascending the pulpit the sexton first came to him, and subsequently the elders, to offer him a pew, as he was now occupying the clergyman's place. But they were soon surprised with a good sermon from the intruder. The next day the ladies of the congregation presented him with a clerical suit, but he gently declined it, saying that where he lived the people would not hear him preach in such clothes.

[2] The honor seems to belong either to him or to "Father Cravens," of the Methodist Church.

is of a stormy onset upon him by four of his parishioners, all distillers, as they were gathered under a spreading beech, after one of his discourses against the prevailing vice.

I expected that he would give them a severe castigation, and was indignant when afterward, with reference to the affair, he merely said, "Why, I didn't suppose they would like the sermon." And yet, so great was the influence of his teaching that two of these men never distilled whisky afterward. One of them would not even sell his distilling apparatus, but let it stand and rot. In a few years public sentiment, aided by a fire which destroyed one of the establishments, closed the other stills, so that intoxicating drinks were not manufactured within the bounds of his congregation.

He met the neighboring ministers in argument upon this subject, and so ably and with such good humor did he maintain his cause that, largely owing to his influence, the region where he lived and labored banished intoxicating liquors from use as a beverage. His reputation as a debater in behalf of total abstinence was so assured, and the unpopularity of opposing him so well known, that a young man who had represented the district in Congress, and was an aspirant again for the position, declined to debate the question with him, though he had issued a challenge to any one who would meet him.

"Father Dickey" was always an earnest anti-slavery man.[1] For several years he cast the only ballot in his township for Free-soil principles. By and by his convictions became so strong that, though he never introduced politics into the pulpit, privately and in debating societies he discussed the question, and ultimately won over nearly all his people to anti-slavery sentiments.[2] Living on the

[1] See Mrs. Stowe's "Men of Our Times," p. 548. Cf. Reed's "Christian Traveller," p. 152; Johnston's "Forty Years in Indiana," pp. 12, 13, 15, and 17; and Crowe's "Abolition Intelligencer."

[2] I have before me a thick, yellow manuscript, in the careful handwriting of Father Dickey, and entitled, "An Address to Christians on the Duty of Giving Suitable Instruction to Slaves." The argument is tender and convincing. It is dated December 20, 1822—a very early period for such an argument upon the Kentucky border.

border where runaway negroes were numerous, he fearlessly preached from such texts as, "Thou shalt not deliver unto his master the servant which is escaped from his master unto thee" (Deut. xxiii.: 15); and under his instructions the better men of the community ceased the lucrative business of hunting fugitives, although the practice had been thought innocent and necessary. The name of "the old abolitionist," which those "of the baser sort" gave him, rather pleased him. He said it would one day be popular.

I remember Father Dickey [writes Mrs. Harriet Beecher Stowe[1]] chiefly through the warm praises of my brother and my husband, who used to meet him at Synods and Presbyteries. They used to speak of him as an apostle after the primitive order —"poor, yet making many rich; having nothing, and yet possessing all things." He advocated the cause of the slave in the day when such advocacy exposed one to persecution and bodily danger. My husband, to whom I have appealed, says he remembers him well and loves his memory, but that he was a man that "didn't make anecdotes"; always constant, steady, faithful, he inspired younger ministers by his constancy and faith, and the simplicity of his devotion to Christ.[2] In my novel of "Dred," now changed in title to "Nina Gordon," the character of Father Dickson was drawn from my recollection of this good man, as described to me.[3]

The services which Mr. Dickey rendered to the cause of education were also important. His own early opportunities for study had been secured amidst manifold difficulties, and he sought the more earnestly to provide for his children and his neighbors' children an easier and better

[1] From Mandarin, Fla., February 5, 1876.

[2] A clergyman, who was at one time a pastor in southern Indiana, and went back to New England after a few years' trial of the frontier, relates that on a certain occasion he saddled his horse and rode fourteen miles to lay his discouragements before Mr. Dickey and obtain advice and sympathy. But when he observed how the latter was supporting a large family, without a thought of faltering, though in the midst of difficulties compared with which his own were trifling, he returned home without even mentioning the object of his visit.

[3] See Stowe's "Nina Gordon," Vol. I., pp. 300, 301 and *passim*.

way. In his first parish in Davies County he taught school.[1] Until the division of the Presbyterian Church in 1837 he was an active trustee of Hanover College.[2] Chiefly through his influence a wealthy Englishman, Mr. Thomas Stevens, was induced to establish and maintain a female seminary on the Ohio River near Bethlehem. In a suitable brick building, erected by Mr. Stevens for that purpose, Mr. Dickey resided several years, providing a home for the teachers and securing educational privileges for his children. The first principal of the school was Miss Longly, who, after two years in the seminary, became the wife of the Rev. Dr. Riggs, of the Sioux mission. Much was accomplished by the school for the whole surrounding region.

It is not surprising that a life so variously useful and a character so strikingly symmetrical have elicited affectionate eulogies. "He was always spoken of with great reverence by my mother," says one who in childhood was accustomed to see him at her own home. "I met him first in Presbytery," wrote another, "and I well remember that the impression of his goodness derived from others was heightened in me by the first day's observation . . . I was never with one whose flow of feeling savored so much of heaven."[3] "He has left a name," said Dr. Martin M. Post, "which suggests a wise counselor, a true worker, a thoroughly honest and godly man. May a double portion of his spirit rest on his successors in the Synods of Indiana."

It is with this era of restored tranquillity and growing missionary activity that the territorial history of Indiana

[1] The Presbyterian minister was almost inevitably the schoolmaster in the early days at the West. Scott, Baldridge, Robinson, Todd, Martin, Crowe—nearly all the earliest settled ministers taught schools.

[2] It is evident that in the first struggles of the school at Hanover, he, with Johnston, was Crowe's "brother beloved."

[3] Henry Ward Beecher, in Sprague's "Annals," Vol. IV., p. 519.

terminates. The population is about eighty thousand. William Henry Harrison, the first governor of the territory, had in 1813 been succeeded by Thomas Posey, a senator in Congress from Tennessee, an officer of the revolutionary army, and a Presbyterian ruling elder.[1] The last regular session of the territorial legislature is held at Corydon in December, 1815. On the 19th of April, 1816, the president of the United States approves the bill providing for a state government, and on the 10th of the following June a constitutional convention assembles. At the first state election, August, 1816, Jonathan Jennings is chosen governor. There are three settled Presbyterian ministers in Indiana at the opening of the year 1816, and four churches, with a membership of possibly one hundred. But good and wise men are laying the foundations for steady and substantial progress.

[1] October 9, 1817, " General Thomas Posey, an elder from the church of ' Indiana ' appeared in Synod and took his seat."—" Minutes Kentucky Synod," Vol. I., p. 115.

CHAPTER VI.

AID FROM NEW ENGLAND.

1816, 1817.

AGAIN appeared, early in 1816, tremendous McGready. Possibly he crossed the Ohio just before the year began. The next year his earthly career was to close, and it seems that these last labors[1] for the Indiana church were peculiarly energetic and useful. He established the Blue River congregation in Washington County, February 6, and the Pisgah church, Clark County, February 27. Thomas Cleland and Joseph B. Lapsley were also sent again by the General Assembly to the state, together with William Wylie and Samuel Brown. It is not certain that either of them performed the duty assigned.

But, apparently at his own charges, came, simultaneously with McGready and possibly in his company, another notable Kentuckian, who may claim especial attention since subsequently his hard service in Indiana was to cost him his life.

SAMUEL SHANNON was a graduate of Princeton College while under the presidency of Dr. Witherspoon. He was admitted a member of Transylvania Presbytery, as a transfer from the Presbytery of Lexington, Va., April 28, 1789, and was the third Presbyterian clergyman who settled north of the Kentucky River. He lived till the year 1806 in the lower part of Woodford County, and had the charge of a small church called Woodford church. . He then moved across the Kentucky River into Franklin County, where his family remained and where he had his home till his death.

[1] The Assembly of 1817 commissioned him to Indiana, but there was a higher call awaiting him.

The last years of his life were spent in missionary labors, chiefly in the destitute parts of the state of Indiana. In the summer of 1822, while engaged in one of these missionary excursions, he caught the fever of the season and of the place. Apprehensive of the consequences he made the best of his way home. His family met him a few miles from home, but were unable to move him any further. They had just an opportunity of expressing their affection toward him, and of receiving his departing blessing, when he expired.[1]

In the War of 1812 he volunteered to accompany the northwestern army as a chaplain. He was a man of great physical strength. His fist was like a sledge-hammer, and he was said to have lopped off a stout bough at a single stroke of his sword, when charging through the woods. Notwithstanding his strength he was one of the best-natured men in the world, and nothing could provoke or ruffle him. He had also a mechanical turn, and invented a piece of apparatus called "the Whirling Table."[2]

But in the pulpit he was awkward and his utterance was slow and stammering. His zeal, however, was untiring and his usefulness was unquestioned throughout the new settlements.[3]

It will be seen how exclusively thus far the foundations have been laid by Presbyterian agencies. We may have the pleasure now of observing the friendly alliance with other instrumentalities. In New England home missionary operations were carried on chiefly through the ordinary ecclesiastical organizations. Among these the missionary society of the Connecticut Association[4] was eminent for zeal and for the number and intelligence of its emissaries. Penetrating at last to Indiana they seem to have had no thought of establishing Congregational churches, but with all their strength aided the Presbyterian movement, now for more than twelve years under way. It is not difficult to explain their policy. Finding here a Kentucky and

---

[1] Bishop's "Memoir of Rice," p. 286.
[2] Davidson's "Kentucky," p. 83.
[3] He established the important churches of Livonia and Salem.
[4] See Appendix A. Cf. Dickey's "Brief History," p. 18.

Tennessee and Virginia population, descended from a Scotch-Irish ancestry and bound by prejudice, habits, convictions, and affection to the ancestral church, it would not require a Yankee's shrewdness to detect the hopelessness of an attempt to proselyte them. But these missionaries from New England had no desire to make proselytes. They came in the service of Christianity. They seem indeed in many cases to have been unconscious of any line whatever dividing them from Presbyterians. They adhered to the Westminster standards and raised no question about the Presbyterian form of government. In many instances they received ordination from Presbytery. The type of New England piety they brought to the West was that of Connecticut, among whose Puritan founders those of Presbyterian preferences balanced almost evenly the Independent element.[1] The period was one of beautiful harmony and signal success, and may be reviewed with unmingled satisfaction.

NATHAN B. DERROW appears to have been the earliest of all these devoted laborers from New England. Coming from Connecticut to western New York in 1802, on the 2d of February, 1803, he was ordained and installed over the Homer church,[2] which he happily served until 1807. He then moved westward again to "New Connecticut" (what is now known as the Ohio Reserve), and settled at Vienna, Trumbull County.[3] In 1815 he spent "eighteen weeks in various parts of New Connecticut," "publishing the gospel, reproving error, and strengthening the weak."[4] It was in 1816 that he came to Indiana, commissioned by the Connecticut society. "He traveled extensively through the state, and besides the church of Graham he consti-

[1] Hodge's "History," pp. 33, 34.
[2] Hotchkin's "History of Western New York," pp. 47, 421.
[3] Gillett's "History," Vol. II., p. 140.
[4] *Connecticut Evangelical Magazine*, Vol. V.

tuted a church at Brownstown"[1] which soon became extinct.

"In July 1817 CLEMENT HICKMAN, from the Presbytery of Geneva, N. Y., settled with his family at Princeton, where a small church had been previously formed by Mr. McGready."[2] A few months later, while visiting New Harmony, he was taken ill and died. He rests there in an obscure grave. A child of his lies buried in a field near Princeton. He had previously been a minister in the Methodist Church; but in the year 1810, coming to Painted Post, N. Y., and employed by the inhabitants to preach for them, he applied to the Presbytery of Geneva, and April 18, 1811, was duly licensed. The subsequent year, August 25, he was ordained and installed, but was dismissed, September 10, 1816, to journey westward, and to end his days soon after in Indiana.[3]

It was at this same period that WILLIAM DICKEY, another kinsman of "Father Dickey," for a month or two took his place among the frontiersmen; and DANIEL C. BANKS, settled at Henderson, Ky., near the border, rendered valuable service in organizing[4] and for a time preaching to the congregation at New Albany, who also, in 1821, under the Assembly's appointment, effectively aided the church at Evansville.[5]

Now occur two historic names, John Todd and James Balch, names that recall some of the most honorable national and ecclesiastical traditions. They arrived in the same year (1817), and both strikingly illustrate the fugitiveness of the most brilliant family distinctions.

[1] Dickey's "Brief History," p. 13.
[2] Dickey's "Brief History," p. 13.
[3] Hotchkin's "Western New York," p. 452. Cf. p. 107.
[4] In Dickey's "History" McGready is named as the founder of the New Albany society, but the error is corrected by the author in the margin of his own copy of the pamphlet.
[5] McCarer's "Memorial Sermon," p. 7. The Evansville church was organized by Mr. Banks, in June, 1821.

The name of JOHN TODD belongs to a classic region in American church history and introduces us at once to a courtly company. It was in old Hanover Presbytery, Virginia, and associated with James Waddel, David Rice, and Archibald Alexander[1] that John Todd of Indiana passed his early years.

His father, John Todd, was the companion of Samuel Davies, and before the latter's transfer in 1759 from Virginia to the presidency of Princeton College "was called to wear the mantle of Davies"[2] and "was for many years the leading man in the presbytery east of the Blue Ridge."[3]

The senior Todd immigrated to America about A. D. 1740[4] from the province of Ulster, Ireland, where his ancestors had taken refuge more than a century before from the persecution of Presbyterians in Scotland by Charles I. He is said to have been a weaver.[5] He graduated from Princeton College in 1749, a member of the second class admitted to a degree, and was taken on trial by the New Brunswick Presbytery May 7, 1750. About ten days after Mr. Davies "represented before the Synod of New York the great necessities of the people in the back parts of Virginia, where multitudes were remarkably awakened and reformed several years ago and ever since

[1] Cf. "Life of Alexander," p. 210.

[2] Gillett, 1st ed., Vol. I., p. 94. Cf. Briggs's "American Presbyterianism," pp. 296-7.

[3] Foote's "Sketches of Virginia," second series, p. 47.

[4] In "John Todd, the Story of his Life," Harper's, 1876, occurs (p. 526) the following: "There are in this country three distinct families of Yorkshire Todds. One of these sprung from an ancestor of unknown name who settled in Virginia, whence his descendants have spread into Kentucky. Thomas Todd, associate justice of the United States court, was one of them. He married the widow of Major George Washington (a nephew of General George Washington) and sister of Mrs. President Madison. James Madison Todd, of Frankfort, Ky., is a son of Justice Todd, as was also Col. C. S. Todd, aid to General Harrison and the first minister of our government to the United States of Colombia." The elder Todd of this narrative is the "ancestor of unknown name" above alluded to. Cf. Davidson's "Kentucky," p. 67, foot-note.

[5] Webster, p. 608.

have been thirsting after the ordinances of God."[1] Thereupon the Synod recommended "to the Presbytery of New Brunswick to endeavor to prevail with Mr. John Todd, upon his being licensed, to take a journey thither." He was licensed November 13, 1750, and from a report made to Synod in the autumn of that year it appears "that Mr. Todd is preparing speedily to go." It was at first designed that he should locate in Prince Edward or in Charlotte County, but the objections raised by the General Court, in sympathy with the Church of England, made it impossible to obtain houses of worship there. Mr. Todd was accordingly invited to occupy four of the places licensed for Mr. Davies.[2] A call was laid before New Brunswick Presbytery, May 22, 1751, and on his acceptance of it he was ordained. The civil license obtained as required by law in such cases curiously illustrates the difficulties in the way of "dissenting" preachers

---

[1] See letter of Jonathan Edwards, November 24, 1752, in which he also alludes to a recent interview in New Jersey with Mr. Davies, who told him then "of the probability of the settlement of Mr. Todd, a young man of good learning and of a pious disposition, in a part of Virginia near to him."

[2] Seven such places had with difficulty been secured. Foote's "Sketches of Virginia," second series, p. 45. In 1618 a law had been passed in Virginia which enacted that "every person should go to church on Sundays and holy days, or lie neck and heels that night, and be a slave to the Colony the following week." For the second offense he was to be a slave for a month, and for the third, a year and a day. Cf. Stith's "History," p. 148. In 1642 a law was passed providing that "no minister shall be permitted to officiate in the country but such as shall produce to the governor a testimonial that he hath received his ordination from some bishop in England; and shall then subscribe to be conformable to the orders and constitutions of the Church of England; and if any other person, pretending himself to be a minister, shall, contrary to this act, presume to teach or preach, publicly or privately, the governor and council are hereby desired and empowered to suspend and silence the person so offending; and, upon his obstinate persistence, to compel him to depart the country with the first convenience." Cf. Bishop's "Memoir of Rice," p. 38, foot-note. Mr. Samuel Morris and his friends who were accustomed to meet at his house, known as Morris' Reading-House, for the purpose of reading on the Sabbath "Luther on the Galatians," Boston's "Fourfold State," Whitefield's "Sermons," etc., were called upon by the court to assign reasons for their absence from the parish churches and to "declare to what denomination they belonged." Happily it occurred to them to suggest that they were Lutherans, and as no law or precedent was discovered to direct the court how to proceed against the Lutherans the suspected persons were released. Bishop's "Rice," pp. 43, 44.

in those days. The following is a copy of the record:

WEDNESDAY, APRIL 22, 1752.
Present, the Governor, William Fairfax, John Blair, William Nelson, Esqrs., William Dawson, D.D., John Lewis, Thomas Nelson, Philip Grymes, Peyton Randolph, Richard Corbin, Philip Ludwell, Esqrs.

John Todd, a dissenting minister, this day in Court took the oath appointed by the Act of Parliament to be taken instead of the oath of allegiance and supremacy and the abrogation oath, and subscribed the last-mentioned oath, and repeated and subscribed the test. And thereupon, on his motion, he is allowed to officiate as an assistant to Samuel Davies, a dissenting minister, in such places as are already licensed by this Court for meeting of dissenters.

This official paper looks more like a restraining order than a license, and doubtless was intended as such. But the compulsory arrangement, says Foote,

proved very agreeable to the seven congregations, as it left them all in connection with Mr. Davies; and equally pleasing to Mr. Davies, as it gave him more frequent opportunities for those missionary excursions in which he delighted, the influence of which is felt to this day; and no less acceptable to Mr. Todd, who enjoyed the experience and council of his friend, with the privilege of missionary excursions.

Mr. Todd was accordingly installed, November 12, 1752, by Hanover Presbytery, "into the pastoral charge of the Presbyterian congregation in and about the upper part of Hanover County, Va."[1] The discourse was by Samuel Davies, and was afterward published "at the desire of the hearers and humbly dedicated to the reverend clergy of the established church in Virginia, by S. Davies, V. D. M."[2]

[1] At Davies's suggestion Jonathan Edwards had previously, when dismissed from Northampton, been called to this field. See "Bellamy Papers," and Webster, p. 609.

[2] Extracts from the "Dedication" will be found in Foote. By a happy fortune the manuscript of this remarkable discourse has found a place of security in the region whither Todd's descendants migrated, and where many of them have been laid to rest.

Todd was now established in the work which he was permitted to prosecute in Virginia for nearly forty-two years. The field was soon visited, and a remarkable impulse given to religion, by Whitefield. To him Todd writes, June 26, 1755:

The impressions of the day you preached last here, at my meeting-house, can, I believe, never wear out of my mind; never did I feel anything of the kind more distressing than to part with you, and that not merely for my own sake, but that of the multitudes that stood longing to hear more of the news of salvation from you. I still have the lively image of the people of God drowned in tears, multitudes of hardy gentlemen that perhaps never wept for their poor souls before standing aghast, all with signs of eagerness to attend to what they heard, and their significant tears, expressive of the sorrow of their hearts that they had so long neglected their souls. I returned home like one that had sustained some amazing loss; and that I might contribute more than ever to the salvation of perishing multitudes amongst us, I resolved I would labor to obtain and exert more of that sound fire which the God of all grace had so abundantly bestowed upon you for the good of mankind. To the praise of rich grace be it spoken, I have had the comfort of many solemn Sabbaths since I saw you, when, I am persuaded, the power of God has attended his word, for sundry weeks together; and in my auditory, which was more crowded through your means than it had been before, I could scarce see an individual whose countenance did not indicate the concern of their souls about eternal things. And blessed be God those appearances are not yet wholly fled from our assembly.

I was by orders of Presbytery to attend the installation of Mr. Henry, the 4th of the month, at Lunenburg, about a hundred miles southwest of this place, and we administered the sacrament of the Lord's Supper the Sabbath following. We preached Thursday, Friday, Saturday, Sabbath, and Monday. There was comfortable evidence of the power of God with us every day; believers were

After a day in the library of Wabash College I was recalled by the president to examine a case of relics, where I discovered this very MS. of Davies, thick, firmly sewed, yellow, but perfectly preserved. The penmanship is precise, the wide margin crowded with scriptural references, the Greek mottoes from Clemens Alexandrinus and Chrysostom beautifully transcribed, points and all, and the psalm to be sung at the close written down entire.

more quickened and sinners were much alarmed. Many of them talked with Mr. Henry and me with great desire to know what they should do to be saved. One I remember came to me trembling and astonished, the nearest image I ever saw of the trembling jailor, crying, "What shall I do to get an interest in Christ?" In my return home I made an excursion to preach to a number of people who had never before heard a "New Light," as they call me. I hope the word of God was attended with divine power to many of their hearts.[1]

The negotiations which had already been opened to send Davies to England in behalf of Princeton College, and which resulted in his transfer to the presidency of that institution, alarmed the Virginia Presbyterians, who looked up to Davies as their father. No one was quicker to take the alarm than Todd, on whom the change would impose new and grave responsibilities. Of him Davies thinks when contemplating the Atlantic voyage. "I also am encouraged," he says, "from the reflection that my congregation will not probably suffer in my absence, as Mr. Wright, I expect, is well accomplished for the place ; and my cautious and prudent Rev. Mr. Todd will be so near at hand to assist in cases of difficulty."[2] Afterward, when the invitation to Princeton came, he was at first disposed to decline it,[3] but when he finally concluded to go Todd became the superintendent of affairs and bishop for our church "in the back parts of Virginia."

It is to be observed that throughout this period much labor was bestowed by the Presbyterians upon the slave population.

Last Sunday I had a sacrament [wrote Davies], assisted by my good brother and next neighbor, Mr. Todd. It was a time of unusual anxiety to me. I hope it was a refreshing time to some

[1] See Gillies's "Collections." The above letter is reprinted by Foote.

[2] Davies's "Journal," July 25, 1753.

[3] Davies's "Sermons," Barnes ed., Vol. III., p. 467, foot-note.

hungry souls. I had the pleasure of seeing the table of the Lord adorned with about forty-four black faces.[1]

As early as 1755 Todd had a hundred of these people "under his instruction."[2]

Public affairs also began to require the attention of our ministers. The discussions and conflicts which brought on the Revolution were warmly maintained in the valley of Virginia. Our ministers and people were loyal to liberty. Archibald Alexander says:

> That man will go on a desperate adventure who shall proceed to hunt out the Presbyterian Tories of the Revolution. Our ministers were Whigs, patriots, haters of tyranny, known abettors of the very earliest resistance, and often soldiers in the field.[3]

It is not surprising then that Todd was "a staunch Whig."[4] At the first meeting of the Presbytery of Hanover after the Declaration of Independence that body addressed a memorial to the Virginia House of Delegates, identifying themselves with the patriot cause. It was signed by John Todd as moderator.[5] In 1785, on the 13th of August, at Bethel, Augusta County, an important convention was held to oppose a scheme for general taxation in support of religion—a scheme which Patrick Henry and others advocated. Todd was chairman of the convention.[6]

To his other work the care of a classical school was now to be added. The chief motive seems to have been the preparation of young men for the ministry. David Rice, a member of Todd's congregation, who afterward became "Father Rice" of Kentucky, began the study of Latin at

[1] Foote's "Sketches of Virginia," second series, p. 47.
[2] Foote's "Sketches of Virginia," first series, p. 286.
[3] *Princeton Review*, Vol. XIX., p. 482. Cf. Miller's "Life of Rodgers," p. 146, and Bishop's "Memoir of Rice," Chap. XV.
[4] Foote's "Sketches of Virginia," second series, p. 47.
[5] Davidson's "History of the Presbyterian Church in Kentucky," p. 37, and Foote's "Sketches," first series, pp. 323-4.
[6] Davidson's "Kentucky," p. 37. Foote's "Sketches," first series, pp. 342-4.

this school.[1] James Waddel, Wirt's "blind preacher," who had emigrated from Ulster in Ireland, and whose family, it is possible, was there not unknown to Todd, became an assistant instructor, and under the principal's direction pursued the study of divinity.[2] The needed furniture of books was secured for the school from England, the London merchant, John Thornton, contributing fifty pounds sterling to promote the object, and the Rev. Dr. Gordon, with whom the correspondence was carried on and who interested others in the enterprise, himself giving liberally.[3] This donation of books was destined to serve most important ends beyond the original design. By and by, with Mr. Todd's increasing age, the classical school declined. No successor appeared to conduct it. Other academies, with more ambitious claims, had now been established. It was the venerable preceptor's happy suggestion, therefore, that the library be transferred to Kentucky, for the use of the students of Transylvania Seminary. In that region it was natural that he should be interested, where his old pupil Rice was making himself famous, and where James Moore,[4] who married Todd's daughter, was to have the new institution in charge. Accordingly, among the names of the founders of Transylvania University that of the Rev. John Todd of Hanover Presbytery in Virginia stands first,[5] with that of his nephew, Colonel John Todd, member of the Virginia legislature from the county of Fayette.

In the later years of his life Mr. Todd was unable to per-

[1] Bishop's "Memoir of Rice," pp. 28, 55.

[2] Foote's "Sketches," first series, p. 351. Sprague's "Annals," Vol. III., p. 236.

[3] Davidson's "Kentucky," pp. 292-3.

[4] The Rev. Dr. James Moore was originally a Presbyterian, but, upon his trials for licensure, meeting what he, perhaps rightly, esteemed too little charity, he took orders in the Episcopal Church. The Rev. Dr. Daniel McCalla, of South Carolina, also married a daughter of Mr. Todd.

[5] Davidson's "Kentucky," p. 289.

form all the duties of his pastoral charge. Severe labors in the Virginia wilderness, during the ardor of youth, had exhausted his vigor. Compelled to cease entirely from preaching tours in "the parts beyond," and often detained by ill-health from the church courts, both he and James Waddel were severely criticized by the younger men, who "knew not Joseph," though it was into Joseph's labors that they were so cheerfully entering. A foolish slander as to his laxity in the admission of candidates to the communion appeared to Todd's sensitiveness deserving of reply, and he made his way to Presbytery in the Cove congregation, Albemarle, July, 1793. Having fully vindicated himself he set out for home on Saturday, the 27th, but on the same day was found in the road lifeless. Either his spirited horse had thrown him, or he had suffered from an apoplectic attack.

John Todd of Virginia was evidently a man of solid and useful rather than brilliant qualities. With a vigorous and well-trained mind, in circumstances offering abundant scope for the highest abilities, he gave himself with entire devotion to the service of the church. He was an impressive preacher. "Heard Mr. Todd preach an honest sermon," is Davies's record in his diary. Colonel Gordon said, on hearing him at the communion, November 1, 1761 :

> I never heard a sermon, but one from Mr. Davies, that I heard with more attention and delight. Oh, if the Lord would be pleased to send us a minister of as much piety as Mr. Todd.[1]

It was of such a father that John Todd, the younger, was born, in Louisa County, Va., October, 1772. The region itself was in its variety and beauty of scenery well fitted to quicken the faculties of a boy, and the manse of Providence parish, which was at the same time the seminary, by its daily routine fostering a high intellectual life, also gave

[1] Webster's "History," p. 609.

frequent welcome to guests who would have shone in the most brilliant assembly. Here the pastor's son obtained his first knowledge of books, and here he was molded by the stately manners of the society around him. The preparatory course having been finished at the parsonage and at Washington Academy, he was sent to Dickinson College, Pennsylvania, where he graduated. His theological studies at Princeton were in the days of Dr. John Witherspoon, and when they were completed he returned to Virginia to begin his ministerial career in his native county. Licensed by Hanover Presbytery, September 13, 1800, he "preached his first sermon where his father preached his last."[1] For some time he served the churches left vacant by his father. Having previously, in 1795, married, he removed to the West in 1806,[2] and settled in Louisville, Ky., where he kept alive the family traditions in establishing a school. He first connected himself, October 10, 1809, with the Presbytery of West Lexington, but was received October 3, 1810, by Transylvania Presbytery. Though occupied with his school he was accustomed to preach at various points in Kentucky, and sometimes spent a Sabbath on the northern side of the Ohio in the territory of Indiana.

It was just at this time that Craighead's erratic theology was producing great excitement throughout Kentucky. Notwithstanding the previous admonition of Synod (October, 1806), he had in 1809 preached and printed the famous sermon on "Regeneration." He was understood to maintain, with other clearly Pelagian tenets, that faith and sanctification are effects of the written word, apart from any direct agency of the Holy Spirit. His views had attracted a considerable number of independent minds, and among them John Todd. It is not unlikely that the fasci-

[1] Foote's "Sketches," second series, p. 49.
[2] Not 1809, the date which Davidson, followed by Foote, gives.

nations of his oratory, acknowledged by jurists like John Breckinridge, had prejudiced Todd's judgment. The latter, however, maintained a correspondence with his father's former neighbor, Dr. Archibald Alexander, with reference to the points in dispute, seeking light and counsel. Such good-tempered discussion, with his own solitary reflection, would probably have led a candid man like Todd gradually back to the accepted theology. But these were times of war. Kentucky Presbyterians had suffered too much annoyance from heretics to be in a patient mood. They drew the scimitar at once. Todd, having been accused of teaching Craigheadism, was arraigned by Transylvania Presbytery August 14, 1812, and after trial was admonished. This Presbyterial onset not being calculated to calm one's judgment, it is perhaps not surprising that the accused continued to preach the views which admonition had failed to enlighten. Upon the advice of Synod he was therefore suspended, April 15, 1813, but October 13, 1817, the controversy was amicably adjusted.[1]

It will be remembered that Dr. James Moore, Todd's sister's husband, had experienced what he and his friends considered needless rigor when seeking licensure from Presbytery. Perhaps it will now be generally thought that a larger measure of kindness might have retained that valuable man[2] in the Presbyterian Church. At any rate

[1] "Minutes Transylvania Presbytery," Vol. IV., pp. 35, 52, 119. "Minutes Synod of Kentucky," Vol. II., pp. 31, 36, 61, 105. Cf. Davidson's "Kentucky," p. 276. The tone of Davidson's account of this affair is needlessly offensive. His book is valuable—the result of independent study of original documents and written not unattractively. It is, however, too warm for history. In his notice of the Cumberland difficulty, of Craighead, and of the separation of 1837, he put himself too near the fray. At the distance of forty years his expletives seem quite too fierce. The treatment of Todd is only a single instance illustrating the justice of Dr. Alexander's criticism: "We think that in some cases there is too much minuteness of detail, as in describing certain irregularities; and in others there is what may be called too rigid a fidelity in recording facts which might have been better left in perpetual oblivion." See *Princeton Review*, Vol. XIX., p. 308.

[2] Davidson's "Kentucky," pp. 295-6, foot-note.

this household tradition must have affected the mind of Todd and rendered a judicial process the more offensive. That indeed does not seem to be the successful means of curing, though doubtless it is sometimes the necessary instrument for cutting off heretics. But in this same region, where the ability and taste for theological debate yet survive, Todd had afterward the satisfaction of illustrating the advantage of milder methods A young Kentucky preacher, John A. McClung, who was creating a considerable sensation by his powers of argument and oratory, early in his career was distressed by serious doubts. His biographer says :

> He promptly stated his condition to Presbytery and asked to be relieved. In the discussion which ensued a motion was made to go to the extent of expulsion. The Rev. John Todd, a noble and venerable soldier of the cross, rose and said : " Brethren, I hope no such action will be taken. Brother McClung is honest ; he is a seeker after truth, but under a cloud. Give him time. Relieve him as he asks. Do nothing more. The light will again dawn upon him and he will surely return."[1]

The counsel of Todd was followed, and the light did dawn. A valuable reputation was spared and the usefulness of a minister's life defended.

During Mr. Todd's residence at Louisville he had occasionally preached, as early as 1808 apparently, at Charlestown, Ind., whither he sometimes took his family in the summer to avoid the heat of a southern city. These excursions were continued until the autumn of 1817, when, in October, the disagreement with Presbytery having been adjusted, he removed to Indiana and took the pastoral charge of Charlestown church.[2] Here he remained, a part of the time also maintaining a school, until September,

---

[1] McClung's " Western Adventure," p. vii.

[2] Dickey's " Brief History," p. 14.

1824,[1] when he returned to Kentucky and settled at Paris, there establishing a classical academy. Though his health was now somewhat impaired he also continued to preach as opportunity was presented, but in 1831 crossed the Ohio again, and took up his residence in the southern part of Marion County, whither two daughters, Mrs. Judge James Morrison and Mrs. Thomas J. Todd, had preceded him. The church of South Marion having been organized, he supplied it and the church of Eagle Creek, both now extinct, until his death, which occurred, unexpectedly, from apoplexy, December 13, 1839. His remains rest in the cemetery at Greenwood, Ind.

Mr. Todd had enjoyed better opportunities for literary culture in early life than most of his contemporaries in the western woods, and naturally the tradition of his scholarship survives him. He was especially strong in the Greek, employing constantly the Septuagint of the Old Testament and the original version of the New when prosecuting his biblical studies, and not uncommonly employing the latter at family worship. He habitually read the fathers in the original. A son of another of our Indiana pioneers retains vivid impressions of his "wonderful library."[2] "It was full of the old books," Mr. Kent recollects. Richard Baxter was a favorite, and in the peculiar views at one time entertained by Mr. Todd it was claimed that he was only Baxter's disciple. The style of his preaching was controlled by his studious habits, and was rather argumentative and biblical than rhetorical. It

[1] He was not dismissed to West Lexington Presbytery until April 5, 1827. See "Minutes Madison Presbytery," Vol. I., pp. 45, 46. The letter of dismission was presented to and received by Ebenezer Presbytery, April 15, 1829.

[2] It is probable that this library preserved a portion of the Gordon gift from England. Most of the books have been scattered and lost. By the courtesy of Dr. Henry G. Todd, of Danville, I have in my possession a volume of the *Monthly Review*, London, 1753, with the autograph of Samuel Davies on the title page, and on a fly leaf, in beautiful chirography, "John Todd's book, 1ober, 1760."

was usually extemporaneous, though the preparation was careful and often written.

By inheritance from both branches of his family Mr. Todd held a number of slaves, which he brought with him to Kentucky, but as he did not recognize the right of slavery he received these servants as a trust for which he was to be held responsible to God. He taught them to read the Scriptures and gave them careful religious instruction. As they arrived at the age of twenty-one they received their freedom, a condition which at that time was not prohibited by the state law.

The manners of Mr. Todd were of the old school, especially polite. The Rev. N. S. Dickey writes :

> I saw him at my father's. He came in with his hat under his arm, having taken it off before he reached the outer door, and with a very cordial but formal greeting met my father and mother. I noticed the old gentleman's politeness and dignity, and though but a child spoke to my mother upon the subject. She took occasion to commend him as a model of deportment. "Why, mother," said I, "a neighbor's boy declares that Mr. Todd takes off his hat to the niggers." "Well," she answered, "the negroes uncover their heads out of respect to Mr. Todd, and surely he would not allow them to excel him in courtesy. I wish all my sons might be as good and polite as he."

Mr. Todd seems to have been as hospitable as he was urbane. The manse at Charlestown was a well-known "missionary stopping-place."[1] The old logs listened to many an hour's noble conversation, while around the big fire the guests and the host recounted God's past mercies and laid plans for the highway in the wilderness. At that chimney corner Martin, Crowe, Dickey, Reed, Bush, Fowler, Day, Goodale, and indeed all the pioneers of that early day found a welcome.

In person Mr. Todd was rather stout, about five feet

[1] Cf. MS. diary of Orin Fowler.

eight inches in height, weighing usually one hundred and eighty pounds. His head was bald.

The following extracts from a letter written from Greenwood, February 7, 1835,[1] throw some light upon the occupations and spirit of his later years:

> My settlement after I came to this vicinity was in the midst of a people very generally possessing religion, but connected mostly with the Methodists and Baptists. Few as we are, however, and not generally in independent circumstances, there is a readiness expressed to build a house of worship. One of our members, in a situation the most central for the church, has offered to furnish the ground and to aid in the undertaking. And last season they expressed a particular desire that as I was unsettled I should make my residence among them, with the generous offer of aiding me in my support, furnishing ground necessary during my life, and erecting for me necessary buildings, with the consideration that I should give some aid to a few young persons, not confining myself from other duties. This was the offer of two families. . . . During the last year my preaching, with little exception, was confined to the people of this church[2] and New Providence,[3] to whom I preached on the Sabbath—once a month only at New Providence, except that occasionally I preached to them on other Sabbath afternoons, when in the forenoon I had preached to the people of South Marion.

The stately movement of these sentences and their dignified formality are as good as a portrait. It was evidently a Virginia gentleman of the olden time who held the pen.

Also in 1817 came to Indiana, the same year as Todd, JAMES BALCH, son of James and Anne (Goodwyn) Balch, who was born in Mecklenburg County, N. C., December 25, 1750. His three elder brothers were all distinguished

---

[1] The penmanship is remarkably precise and bears a striking similarity to that of his father.

[2] Eagle Creek church.

[3] This now extinct organization in the vicinity of Greenwood is not to be confounded with Shelbyville, which was first called New Providence. See Dickey's "Brief History," p. 9, and Sluter's "History of Shelbyville Church," p. 2.

Presbyterian clergymen. Hezekiah Balch, original, intrepid, imprudent, the first president of Greenville College, Tennessee, made himself conspicuous as a controversialist and was sooner or later summoned to the bar of almost every ecclesiastical court to which he was amenable. Hezekiah James Balch, five years younger, was a member of the Mecklenburg Convention (May 19, 1775), and had "an important agency"[1] in forming the "Declaration" which has been held to be the germ of the Declaration of Independence in Philadelphia the following year. His personal presence was impressive; he was an excellent scholar; and his early death in the summer of 1775 disappointed the hopes of many in the church.[2] Dr. Stephen Bloomer Balch, born April 5, 1747, lived until September 7, 1833, having been able after passing the age of fourscore to preach with power.[3] With such brothers James, the youngest of the four, passed his childhood. He seems to have been one of the first licentiates of Abingdon Presbytery, and took charge, October, 1786, the year after the Presbytery was formed, of Sinking Spring congregation. He was a member of the first board of trustees of Greenville College, and in the church courts was an earnest defender of sound doctrine and rigid order. Removing to Kentucky he was received from Abingdon by Transylvania Presbytery, October 1, 1799; settled in Logan County; and there had an opportunity to display the bold and independent qualities which characterized his family. An original member of Cumberland Presbytery, he put himself into prominent opposition toward the new

[1] He was a member of the committee of three which drafted the paper adopted by the convention May 20. Cf. Lossing's "Pictorial Field-book of the Revolution," Vol. II., p. 412.

[2] "There is nowhere a monument or tradition to direct to the grave of Hezekiah James Balch, or anywhere a living mortal to claim him as ancestor." — Foote's "Sketches of North Carolina," p. 441.

[3] The notices of the Balch family in Sprague's "Annals" contain but a single sentence, and that an inaccurate one, with reference to the youngest brother.

measures inaugurated by that body. He openly disapproved of the extravagant methods employed during the McGready revival. That he should have been censured by McGready[1] for his course need occasion no surprise, but his conservatism scarcely deserves the rebuke of a historian.[2]

In 1817 Mr. Balch removed to Sullivan County, Ind., already having completed his sixty-sixth year. Founding the Hopewell church, on Turman's Creek, he continued to labor there until his death, which occurred January 12, 1821. He was a resolute and sometimes no doubt appeared a stubborn man. His mental acquirements were what his favorable early opportunities would lead us to expect. He was a faithful and pungent preacher.

Until recently there had been no stone to mark in an open field the sunken grave of a pioneer who bore and honored one of the notable names of his generation. At the spring meeting of Vincennes Presbytery (1879) a committee was appointed to reinter the body. This was done on the 29th of the following October. At his own request Mr. Balch had been buried near the old Hopewell meeting-house—a comfortable log house near Turman's Creek, in Sullivan County, Ind. The church had long ago disappeared, and the land had fallen into the hands of one who knew nothing of the grave, which had been plowed over several years. The remains were removed to the Presbyterian burying-ground near Graysville, in the same township. Mr. James Johnson, who almost sixty years before attended the funeral, was present.

[1] "About this time the Rev. J. B. came here and found a Mr. R. to join him. In a little time he involved our infant churches in confusion, disputation, etc., opposed the doctrines preached here, ridiculed the whole work of the revival, formed a considerable party, etc., etc."—McGready's " Posthumous Works," p. viii.

[2] Cf. Gillett, Vol. II., p. 159.

CHAPTER VII.

A NOTABLE QUARTET.

1818.

THERE were now eleven congregations in the state. Except Mr. Balch's society on Turman's Creek all were within the oldest neighborhoods, and none ventured far from the Wabash and the Ohio. The roll of settled laborers is a short one, comprising but five names—Scott, Robinson, Dickey, Todd, and Balch. The year 1818 makes a most valuable addition to the force, bringing two remarkable itinerants, Orin Fowler from the Connecticut Missionary Society and Ravaud K. Rodgers from the General Assembly; besides William W. Martin, another Kentucky volunteer, and Isaac Reed from New England, both of whom became citizens of Indiana, laborious, influential, and useful in an eminent degree. In this quartet of 1818 there was a variety of gifts and graces as picturesque as can well be imagined. If they could have been seen together before the blazing logs of a frontier cabin the dullest observer would have hugged the chimney corner to watch their diversity of manner and mind. Mirthfulness and sobriety, loquacity and reticence, a polished urbanity and a homely eccentricity, would have been quickly apparent, with scholarship and piety quite evenly distributed. Of the four, Mr. Martin was the first to reach the state. He only left it for the better country. If providence had sent William Wirt to hear "Father Martin" preach, the famous description of James Waddel's eloquence might fitly have had a companion-piece. For many years he was the popular favorite throughout the southern half of Indiana, and his name was sufficient to draw to any rustic platform or pulpit an immense throng of admirers, accustomed to bow before the energy and pathos of his oratory.

WILLIAM W. MARTIN, of Scotch-Irish ancestry, was born in Bedford County, Pa., August 12, 1781. He was one of four children, all of whom became useful members of the Presbyterian Church. The piety of his parents made early and deep impressions on his character. He was accustomed to refer to the solemn reflections awakened by a sermon on "The Last Judgment" which he heard his father read one wintry day before he was eight years old. The regular observance of family worship, and especially the instructions and example of his mother, exercised a power over his childhood which he often gratefully acknowledged, and at the age of ten he had already begun to hope that he might become a Christian minister. Meanwhile, however, the family had removed to Westmoreland County, Pa., and in the spring of 1794 they sought a home in the wilds of Kentucky, the depreciation of continental money having reduced them from comfort to poverty. Notwithstanding the influence of reckless companions there was a renewal of former religious impressions when he was about sixteen years of age and he became a member of the Presbyterian Church at Paris, Ky., then under the care of the Rev. Samuel Rannels. During the summer he wrought upon a farm and in the winter at the cooper's trade. The desire to become a minister of the gospel was still cherished, and at the age of twenty-three he entered Bourbon Academy at Paris, under the preceptorship of the Rev. John Lyle. There he remained five years, and then for two years pursued a course of theology under the same instructor. Receiving licensure from the West Lexington Presbytery in October, 1812, he settled in

Winchester, Clark County, and was ordained in the fall of 1813. This first pastorate he held for six years, being also engaged a part of the time as teacher and editor.

But Mr. Martin was restless under the shadow of slavery. Neither his judgment nor conscience approved it, and he resolved to seek a settlement in a free state. He first crossed the Ohio upon a brief tour of observation in 1817,[1] and in May of the year following removed permanently to Indiana. Taking charge of the congregations of Livonia, Salem, and Blue River, he resided for a year at Salem in the family of Mr. Young, an elder, when he removed to the neighborhood of Livonia, securing there a little farm. It was in this immediate vicinity that most of his subsequent life was spent, for though he several times went to other fields, the old flock always called him back, and it never was in his heart to refuse them. Livonia was his home. Until his formal pastoral settlement over the Livonia church in April, 1821, the three congregations shared his labors equally, but from that date the Blue River society was entrusted to other hands. After thirteen years of continuous service at Livonia Mr. Martin finally asked Presbytery to release him from that charge, his service at Salem having ceased two or three years before.[2] He removed in 1831 to Paoli, preaching there for a year, and at the same time serving the Orleans church, which he had himself organized September 27, 1818. His subsequent removals were to Princeton, Gibson County, where he labored one year; to West Salem, where and in adjacent fields he preached until June, 1834; and to South Hanover, whose pulpit he supplied until the autumn of 1835. It must not be supposed, however, that Mr. Martin's influence was confined to his small rural parishes. Through-

[1] He then administered the communion in a grove near the village of Salem.

[2] The Rev. Benjamin C. Cressy, a polished preacher and a devoted man, came from New England and assumed the care of the Salem congregation in the autumn of 1829.

out this period, and through his whole career in Indiana, he was a tireless bishop, traveling far and near to serve the entire Presbyterian community.[1]

Since his departure from Livonia his former flock had been shepherdless, but their bleating was not in vain. In November, 1835, he resumed his pastorate, and on the twenty-fifth of November, 1837, occurred his second installation over this church. Eighty acres of land, one mile southwest of Livonia, were now presented to him by the congregation, and there he reëstablished his hospitable home. Six years later the pastoral relation was again dissolved (April 5, 1843) that he might remove to Bloomington and superintend the education of his sons. He occupied the pulpit in that place until April, 1845, when he once more came back to Livonia, continuing his ministry to the local society and to the contiguous neighborhoods until his death, which occurred September 10, 1850.[2] His body rests in the Livonia cemetery.

The position of Mr. Martin among the Indiana pioneers was unique. He was essentially an orator. Of slender form, quite six feet in height, and of fair complexion, he was in youth a very handsome man and was beautiful even in age. He was emotional in his nature, full of sentiment and of tears. His voice was both sweet and powerful. It is not strange that such gifts commanded the attention of the populace upon the frontier. Nor is it surprising that under the control of a piety uncommonly warm and true he was sometimes, in the pulpit, and especially during the sacramental seasons in the woods which captivated his heart and stirred him to the depths, in the highest degree eloquent. . Earlier academical advantages, and in later life

[1] In these self-denying labors he spent his entire private fortune, received mainly from his wife, and amounting to ten or twelve thousand dollars.

[2] During his ministry in Indiana Mr. Martin organized the churches of Franklin, Orleans, Paoli, Palestine, Bono, Princeton, West Salem, and Vincennes, assisting also in the organization of the First Church at Indianapolis.

larger opportunities for reflection, would no doubt have pruned his fancy, but there are abundant proofs that he was accustomed to sway the multitudes at his will by his impassioned addresses.

Father Martin's face was striking—large, serious, at times sad and stern, but usually genial in expression, often lighted up by a remarkably tender, wistful, and loving look, as though secretly yearning for your salvation. . . . In practical preaching or exhortations upon some of the great doctrines of the cross and in revival labors, he had few superiors in his day. His manner was grave, solemn, always earnest and often impassioned, having the "accent of conviction," so transparently sincere that every one who heard him knew that he himself had felt in his own heart the power of the truth. It was while attending the meeting of Salem Presbytery at Livonia in 1841 that one of the brethren described to me a scene during the sessions of the old Indiana Synod at Vincennes in early times, when Father Martin preached on Hebrews xiii.: 13 : "Let us go forth, therefore, unto him without the camp bearing his reproach." His heart was so full of the theme, so vivid was his conception of Jesus suffering without the gate, that he was transported, and transported and electrified the whole assembly. The Synod was melted to tears and there was audible sobbing in every part of the house.[1]

Perhaps the prayers, even more than the preaching, of Mr. Martin will be recalled by those who remember him, as characteristic of the man. His prayer before the sermon commonly consumed three quarters of an hour. " I have timed him," says one, " when his prayer lasted an hour and five minutes." On another occasion a son of Father Dickey measured a prayer that was an hour and thirty minutes long.

He seemed like Paul ; whether in the body or out of the body he could not tell. His prayers were full of the letter and the spirit of Scripture. Petition, confession, thanksgiving, and praise, expressed in the language of the Bible, poured forth like water from a living spring. The Bible was at his tongue's end. And oh, what

[1] MS. letter of the Rev. William M. Cheever, who was a student at Hanover while Mr. Martin supplied the pulpit there in 1834-5.

unction there was in his counsels and prayers by the side of the afflicted and the dying. Many a dear dying saint before dissolution has seen the gates of the City of God opening to the touch of Father Martin's prayer.

At the earliest opportunity, like other Presbyterian pioneers, he established a school, with his own means erecting a log house for its accommodation near his dwelling. His own classical attainments enabled him to prepare for the ministry and for the other learned professions a number of young men who became prominent in important stations. The school was long known as "the Log College." In this work Mr. Martin was greatly assisted by his wife, who carried it on uninterruptedly during his frequent and protracted missionary journeys.

Of the hospitality which marked the early times the minister's cabin near Livonia furnished a beautiful illustration. There was a tavern in the village, but it was said that the Presbyterian preacher had most of the custom. The Rev. John Crozier recalls an incident which pleasantly discloses the interior of the manse.

One Monday night, returning from Paoli, I stayed at Mr. Martin's. He had been in the harvest field but had come in early, and like Abraham had taken from the flock or the herd and prepared with his own hands what soon became a savory meal. During the evening the family and guests were gathered in the little parlor, busily engaged in conversation. In the middle of the room stood a small square table on which were a Bible, one or two books of reference, a big bundle of sermons, writing materials, and a tallow candle. By this table sat Father Martin, with a high leghorn hat, worn to shade his eyes, and amidst the hum of talk he began his studies. He was soon quite absorbed in thought. After an hour or more of silent meditation, he suddenly threw up his glasses and asked his clerical visitors whether they knew what was the color of the Apostle John's hair. One of the gentlemen had never heard the question suggested before. Another thought the New Testament was non-committal as to the color of anybody's hair. The younger people ventured to express no opinion and the inquiry was soon handed back to the questioner, who at once said that John's hair must have been black. He then began roguishly to read a passage he had just found in one of his youthful manuscripts referring to the "raven locks" of the apostle now "blanched by the frosts of fourscore winters."

Mr. Martin certainly belonged to the tribe of Levi. His three brothers-in-law were the Revs. Samuel R., Thomas, and William A. P. Alexander, the latter for many years a successful missionary in the Sandwich Islands. His only sons became ministers—Samuel N. D., Dr. William A. P., and Dr. Claudius B. H. Martin. The two former went to China, where one still remains, the accomplished president of the Imperial University. Not to be outdone, five out of the seven daughters entrapped Presbyterian ministers, and Drs. Newell, Venable, and Matthews, and Messrs. Camborn and Morton have added their Levitical luster to the family renown.[1]

ISAAC REED was born in Granville, Washington County, N. Y., August 27, 1787. There with his parents, Abraham and Thankful Reed, his early childhood was passed. He entered the junior class in Middlebury College, Vermont, and graduated from that institution in 1812.[2] After completing the college course his plans were seriously embarrassed, as they had previously been, by the delicacy of his health. He attempted to teach, securing a position in the academy at Jamaica, L. I., but in a few weeks was compelled to rest. December 28, 1812, he entered the law office of John C. Parker, Esq., at Granville. A second time making the attempt to endure the labor of the school-

[1] It will be seen that there were attractions for guests at the Livonia parsonage, and Father Martin was fond of making the young theologians who came to his cabin go up into the pulpit too. On one occasion three of them, hiding in separate corners of the meeting-house, were led to the desk, directed to "make their own arrangements," and then abandoned to their fate.

[2] Another member of the class, the Rev. Stephen Bliss, also became a missionary in the Synod of Indiana. Cf. "Life and Times of Stephen Bliss," p. 90.

room he was again compelled to desist, and resumed his legal studies in the office of Messrs. Bradish & Sedgwick, New York City.[1] With improving health, however, his original preference for the ministry as a profession was confirmed, and while again conducting a school on Long Island he began the study of divinity under the advice of the Rev. Dr. Woolworth, of Bridgehampton. He was taken under the care of Long Island Presbytery, but, removing to Connecticut, concluded his theological preparations at Norwalk under the tuition of the Rev. Roswell R. Swan,[2] and received licensure at North Stamford, May 29, 1816, from the Fairfield Congregational Association. At Norwich, near Utica, N. Y., as a missionary of the Oneida Female Missionary Society, and at Manlius, N. Y., his labors were especially useful for brief periods. But serious pulmonary symptoms reappeared and his thoughts were turned toward the Southwest. Mounting his horse he traveled from Manlius, over the Allegheny Mountains, and in four months made a journey of nine hundred miles. His first resting-place was in central Kentucky. The month after his arrival he was "severely attacked," December, 1817, "with a bilious fever,"[3] and quite naturally he thinks himself "greatly deceived respecting the climate." He was soon able, however, to establish a projected "preaching circuit" and early in the February following had gone over it once. He says:

> It includes two Sabbaths at Lancaster, one at Point Lick, two at Richmond, another at Point Lick, and the next at Lancaster again. In these two counties there are four Presbyterian churches but no minister able to preach. I have compassion on them and have concluded to cast my lot among them for the winter.[4]

The "lot" certainly did not prove to be lucrative, and

[1] Cf. Reed's "Christian Traveller," p. 15.
[2] Cf. "Christian Traveller," p. 14.
[3] "Christian Traveller," p. 42.
[4] "Christian Traveller," p. 57.

as the good man had been entirely at his own charges since leaving New York he was compelled after a few weeks to relinquish the field. Near Lancaster, March 19, 1818, in the pious but somewhat unsophisticated vein which apparently characterized him everywhere, he wrote:

After preaching the last Sabbath I dined in town and saw a large collection of blacks about a grocery, swearing and contending; and as I came out of town a large number of white boys and some young men were playing ball in the seminary yard. Oh, how is my heart pained with the immoral and impious ways of people here. To see such things take place immediately after I have been preaching, in the most solemn manner of which I am capable, how discouraging it is![1]

Mr. Reed now resumed his travels, preaching in Kentucky wherever opportunity was offered, until July 23, in company with the Rev. Dr. Thomas Cleland, he crossed for the first time into Indiana and found a welcome at the house of Dr. D. McClure, in Madison.[2] Explorations of the adjacent country immediately began. At New Albany he spent five weeks. "The town was rude in appearance, had few good houses, but was fast improving and contained seven hundred inhabitants."[3] Brought hither, as he thinks, by providence, the naïve and prayerful ejaculation recorded in his journal is, "O that I may be submissive!" Here overtures are made for his settlement, and having returned to Kentucky, to be ordained by Transylvania Presbytery, in Dr. Cleland's New Providence meetinghouse, Saturday, October 10, before the close of the month his stated ministry in New Albany begins.

[1] "Christian Traveller," p. 58.

[2] In a MS. memorandum Mr. Reed makes the following reference to the pioneers already on the ground: "Six Presbyterian ministers, viz.: Wm. Robinson, very infirm; John Todd, mild and but little known; W. W. Martin, active, eloquent, and popular; J. M. Dickey; Samuel T. Scott; James Balch, an old and blunt man."

[3] "Christian Traveller," p. 79. The types here make the figures *seventeen* hundred, but this seems to be an error, as nine years later (see p. 222) the population is estimated at *eight* hundred.

The engagement was for one year. The salary was five hundred dollars. Fifteen members composed the Presbyterian church. Over most of the town plat lay thickly the trunks of trees which had been felled but were not removed. There was a little frame covered in for a Methodist meeting-house; the Presbyterians had none. But during the year a house of worship was built. A considerable addition was made to the membership. And a Sabbath School of sixty members, the first ever formed in Indiana, was gathered.[1]

Thus far the missionary had no help from abroad, but at the close of his labors at New Albany,[2] he obtained a commission from the Connecticut Missionary Society. Again he became "the Christian traveler," preaching in Kentucky and for several weeks in Granville, Ohio. On Christmas Day, 1819, in Danville, Ky., his hand "and the hand of Elinor Young were joined in the marriage covenant, in the presence of the minister, the Rev. Samuel K. Nelson, the family of Mrs. (widow) Young, an attending young gentleman and two female friends."[3] He preached two years at Nicholasville during that period, in the autumn of 1821 crossing the Ohio once more upon a mission tour of about four weeks to Owen County and the frontier of Indiana. Having completed a journey to Philadelphia, as commissioner to the General Assembly, chiefly upon horseback and in a "dearborn" wagon, he started again, September 25, 1822, for the region which seemed to attract him from all his wanderings, though here poverty and hardship and suffering united to cool his ardor and try his faith in God. During the four weeks' excursion the year before he had wisely made his way with his

[1] "Christian Traveller," pp. 86-9.

[2] The considerable salary promised here was not paid. The little band had promised far beyond their ability.

[3] "Christian Traveller," pp. 98, 99. An older sister of Mrs. Reed became the wife of the Rev. Dr. Baynard R. Hall, another pioneer of our church in Indiana. See "Christian Traveller," p. 111. In Hall's "New Purchase" Reed figures as the "Rev. James Hillsbury" (see p. 86).

brother-in-law, president of the State Seminary at Bloomington, "through the woods by the forks of the Eel River, to the land office in Terre Haute, . . . and entered a half quarter-section of land."[1] Here he arrived in October, 1822,[2] and "settled," if a man who was half his time in the saddle could be said to "settle" anywhere.

In explaining the motives of his return to Indiana Mr. Reed unconsciously reveals his own indefatigable and unselfish mind :

> As none others had given themselves up to settle in those new parts of the state the writer resolved to venture forward and lead in this way. His scheme for improvement was this: to locate with a little infant church already formed, to instruct and encourage them, to appropriate one half of his ministerial labors to their benefit, and to receive from them in return as much salary as they should be able to raise, paid in their personal labor or in the produce of their farms. The balance of his time he held to be devoted to missionary service, and his plan and his practice were to spend alternately one week at home and the next abroad. The preaching places were distant from each other and most of them distant from the writer's residence and charge. The consequence was that to be punctual in the attendance upon his appointments, and to keep up the hopes of the Presbyterian people, subjected him to a vast deal of riding. Respecting this plan and this field of action, before his removal from Kentucky, he wrote to a friend, a student of theology at Princeton, "that it opened to the view of his mind such a field for Christian enterprise and usefulness as almost raised him above himself."[3]

But on the "half quarter-section" there was no dwelling.

> I found much difficulty to obtain labor from the people, they being hurried with their own work. As far as my own personal labor could supply this deficiency it was supplied. But with all my efforts the building progressed slowly, and to increase my difficulty the winter closed in early. We entered our house

---

[1] "Christian Traveller," p. 121.

[2] "Christian Traveller," p. 139.

[3] "Christian Traveller," pp. 138, 139.

the week before Christmas and occupied it that winter, without a loft, with no plastering between the logs, above the joist plates, and with a large wooden chimney-place cut out of the end of the house and built up a little above the mantel-piece.[1] Wood was plenty and well did it need to be for a situation like that. Yet many were the comforts which were mingled with those difficulties, though the trial sat heavily on my Elinor. And indeed I have often wondered since that time how I could have ever had resolution enough to have voluntarily brought myself into that situation. But now necessity pushed us on and hope cheered us with the return of spring and a better prospect in the future. Nor do I remember that I ever felt a wish that I had not ventured upon this service. It always appeared to me to be worthy of my trials in it.[2]

Is not this a bit of real heroism? Possibly there may be too many clergymen. But there is no danger that there will ever be too many self-forgetting men, ready to imitate such an example.

The approach of summer must have had a peculiar welcome after such a winter in such a hut. The only creature at the "Cottage of Peace" that could have imagined "December as pleasant as May" was the missionary's horse. He had at least had a rest. But with spring came work again, the usual interminable preaching tours. Mr. Reed is now in correspondence with the "United Domestic Missionary Society." In August occurs his installation as pastor of the Bethany church.[3] To this society he gives half his time and during the alternate weeks traverses the whole wilderness around. The horse is not to be congratulated now. The mud, the forests, the swollen fords,[4] the widely scattered congregations, make the necessary labor severe. Thus three years go by. Mr.

[1] This is the "Cottage of Peace" of Mr. Reed's book.
[2] "Christian Traveller," pp. 139, 140.
[3] "Christian Traveller," p. 142.
[4] An amusing description of Mr. Reed—"Bishop Hillsbury"—is given by his brother-in-law in the first edition of "The New Purchase," Vol. I., pp. 278-83.

Reed organized more churches than any other man.[1] He is at Salem, at the first meeting of the Salem Presbytery, April, 1824. During the year he travels twenty-four hundred and eighty miles.[2] At "sacramental meetings," licensures, ordinations, installations, he is sure to be present, in every corner of the southern half of the state. The exposure and suffering implied we can now scarcely conceive.

Meanwhile the missionary's pen is busy. He sends communications to eastern newspapers. He prints his first little book. He contributes to the local press.[3] Other publications are issued under the sanction of Presbytery. A dedication sermon is published.[4] He diligently keeps the journal which now constitutes "The Christian Traveller." The log house in Owen County is the center of a most tireless activity. Every opened path of usefulness is pursued to the end.

Until the close of 1825 these labors continue. Mr. Reed is then released from his pastoral charge. For two years "he had not received a dollar in money from his congregation." The claims of his family required him to "depend on farming as a business" or seek another field. He still clings to the Indiana woods. Possibly he may move "further up White River." His journal describes his tour in the spring of 1826.[5] This proves to be his last missionary work before leaving Indiana. The conclusion he finally reaches is to return with his family to the East,[6]

[1] See "A Ministry of Forty Years in Indiana," by the Rev. James H. Johnston, p. 5; "Quarter-Century Discourse," by the Rev. P. S. Cleland, p. 14.

[2] "Christian Traveller," p. 145.

[3] See *Western Censor and Emigrants' Guide*, Indianapolis, June 7, 1824, and July 20, 1824.

[4] "Christian Traveller," pp. 144, 147, 148, 150.

[5] "Christian Traveller," pp. 177-84.

[6] It is probable that Mrs. Reed's judgment was not opposed to the removal Her mother, Mrs. Ann Young, the "Mrs. Glenville" of Hall's "New Purchase," Chapter XXXII., had recently died at the "Cottage of Peace." In the wilderness there was little opportunity for the education of her children. This latter consideration would have great weight with one whose ambition was as persevering as hers. It is said that at one time hopes were entertained of a brilliant dramatic career for one of her children.

a congregation at Moriah, N. Y., having desired him to visit them. His allusion to the early stages of this journey of a thousand miles strongly suggests the discouragements with which the missionary had been accustomed to contend.

It was Wednesday, the 31st of May, when we left Indianapolis and entered the woods in the road to Centreville. To a traveler with a wheel carriage, in so new a road as this, through a country where the settlements are so few and distant, some difficulties might be expected at any season of the year, but at present they were numerous and truly discouraging. The country is moist and the soil very rich, and the road but partially cut out. Over the small streams log causeways had been made, but the high waters of the spring season had raised them and floated the logs in every direction, so that at these places the cut-out way was utterly impassable. The resort was to turn into the woods and choose some other place to venture through the waters and wet grounds, till we were beyond the entire causeway, or at least the raised part of it. Often at these places, and at others, from the length of the stretches of deep mud, had Mrs. Reed to get out with the youngest child in her arms, and the oldest walking with her, and thus to make her way on foot, while I had to lead the horse by the check-rein, walking before him, and frequently with the mud and water deeper than my boots. In many places it appeared extremely doubtful when the horse went in whether he would ever be able to come out. Thus we traveled for three days, in one of which, starting at eight o'clock in the morning and traveling with the utmost diligence till sunset, we made only thirteen miles. And this was the second day of June.[1]

The travelers safely reached their destination, however, and Mr. Reed made an engagement for five years with the Moriah congregation. His letters in the *New York Observer* show his continued attachment to the scene of his former toil, whither he was soon to return. After a single year the Moriah engagement was terminated, and he looked westward once more, coming, in 1828, to Bloomington, where his brother-in-law, Professor Hall, still

[1] "Christian Traveller," pp. 233, 234.

resided. This place "the wanderer," as he styled himself, made the center of the usual missionary labor for a number of years. He left Bloomington in the fall of 1835 and transferred his family to South Hanover, having himself accepted an agency for the college. A little later he was conducting a school in Kentucky, near Shelbyville. He is then successively at various points in Indiana, Kentucky, Ohio, and Illinois, until in the spring of 1854 he removed to Waterloo, N. Y., and immediately after to Auburn. During all these latter years, aided by his wife, he had joined the work of teaching to that of a missionary. A severe winter now seriously threatened his health, and he came West again to Olney, Ill. Here his family remained while he moved on to Missouri. Connecting himself with the Presbytery there, he was assigned to a mission field at Versailles; but returning to his family at Olney he suffered a severe hemorrhage of the lungs, and imprudently attempting to fulfil an engagement to preach, was attacked with typhoid pneumonia, and after a brief struggle died Thursday night, January 14, 1858. A plain marble slab marks his resting-place in the Olney cemetery, and bears the inscription, "The wanderer here finds rest." His widow survived until May 9, 1869, when she fell asleep at the residence of her daughter, Mrs. Williams, near Putnamville, Ind.

In person Mr. Reed was tall and spare, with dark hair and blue eyes. He enjoyed society. "I am a great talker," said one who knew him well,[1] "and he talked

[1] Dr. Henry Little. It was in the winter of 1830, when Dr. Little was making his first journey through the state, that a characteristic incident occurred. Says Dr. Little: "Finding Mr. Reed at Bloomington, he told me that he was to go to Bedford, to marry a couple, the next day, and that I must go with him. At five o'clock on a December morning we breakfasted and were off. At an Indian wigwam we halted and talked a while. Father Reed, having long yarns to tell, lost his saddle-bags afterward, and had to go back two miles to find them. Just at sunset, having traveled twenty-eight miles in all, we reached Bedford and went to the double log cabin where the preacher was expected. It was full of company. The family was from New Jersey. At seven o'clock the wedding came off and we sat down to supper. Everything was nice and in

two thirds more than I." He was perhaps lacking in shrewdness. For practical affairs he had little aptitude. Sometimes human nature surprised and baffled him. In social meetings he would often speak wonderfully well, though his ordinary preaching was not especially attractive. He stooped and leaned in the pulpit, the thumb of his right hand hooked under his waistcoat at the suspender button. But "he had as little selfishness as any of the unselfish men about him—would do anything for the Master's sake." "He was laborious, persevering, patient, pure-minded, affectionate, and simple in his tastes and public ministrations."[1] "He performed prodigies of labor as an itinerant."[2] His life was one of "arduous and unrequited toil."[3] His monument he reared while laying the foundations of the church in the wilderness. It was in this early period, before his almost aimless "wandering" began, that his usefulness was most assured.

ORIN FOWLER was another of the quartet of missionaries reaching Indiana in 1818. The eldest son and sixth child of Captain Amos[4] and Rebecca (Dewey) Fowler, he was born at Lebanon, Conn., July 29, 1791. In boyhood he worked on his father's farm, though when sixteen and seventeen years of age he was for two winters engaged in teaching school, the inevitable resource of young New Englanders. He fitted for college under the instruction of his pastor, the Rev. Mr. Ripley, and entered Williams College in the autumn of 1811. At the end of the first term he took his dismission,

abundance. But after I had got one little biscuit, the embarrassed bride and groom shoved back their chairs; others, equally confused, followed their example; no suggestion of our emptiness came from unworldly Father Reed, and I was too much a stranger to protest; so the groaning table was almost untouched, and I had to go to bed hungry as a bear. Next morning, however, I made up for lost time."

[1] MS. of the Rev. Ransom Hawley.
[2] "Life and Times of Stephen Bliss," p. 90.
[3] "Quarter-Century Discourse," by the Rev. P. S. Cleland, p. 14.
[4] A soldier of the Revolution.

and after studying again for a while under Mr. Ripley's direction, and also for one term at the academy at Colchester, he entered the sophomore class at Yale College in October, 1812. Here he maintained an excellent standing, being distinguished in the more solid and practical courses of study.[1] A few months previous to his graduation he accepted the preceptorship of the academy at Fairfield, Conn., and held the place, discharging its duties with great fidelity and acceptance, until the autumn of 1816. He then presented his resignation in order to devote himself more exclusively to theological studies, Dr. Humphrey, then minister of Fairfield, afterward president of Amherst College, becoming his instructor. He was licensed to preach on the 14th of October, 1817, by the Association of the Western District of Fairfield County.

Having preached occasionally in different places, chiefly in Fairfield County, but without any reference to settlement, he decided March, 1818, to attempt a missionary tour in the West. With this in view he was ordained at Farmington, at a meeting of the North Association of Hartford County, on the 3d of June following, and on the same day rode twenty-one miles toward his field.[2]

For the proposed service Mr. Fowler was admirably fitted. A sound judgment, a tenacious will, system, industry, and uncommon bodily vigor would all be requisite, and it will be seen that these were among the striking features of his character. "He had rather a large frame," says his college classmate, Dr. Sprague, "indicating what he really possessed, a vigorous constitution."[3] Dr. Shepherd, his friend and neighbor, declares that he seldom if ever knew a pastor "who could perform unremittingly such an

[1] Among his classmates at Yale were the Rev. Drs. Sprague and Nevins, and Judge Jessup of Pennsylvania.

[2] Thus far I have followed the statements in Sprague, originally furnished by Mrs. Fowler, and after her husband's death reprinted in his "History of Fall River."

[3] "Annals," Vol. II., p. 650.

amount of labor."[1] Young Fowler was just the man to ride into the woods alone and lay the foundations of Christian society there. Throughout his journey he carefully kept a diary, precise and practical in every page. The faded manuscript has been recovered. A few extracts will best reproduce the early days, at the same time that they fittingly unfold Mr. Fowler's character.

Wednesday, June 3d, 1818. Left Farmington and rode twenty-one miles to Barkhamsted.

Sabbath. Preached twice at Canajoharie to an attentive audience in the Baptist house.

Sabbath, June 14th. Spent the day at Seneca Falls with Mr. Stark and preached twice from Isaiah 55th, 6th, and Isaiah 5th, 4th.[2] Received from individuals two dollars for the missionary society.

Tuesday. Rode to Murray, thirty-nine miles, an unpleasant country. Passed the growing village of Rochester, and had an opportunity to converse with one young person.

Wednesday. Rode forty-four miles to Cambria. Saw several deer.

Thursday. Rode forty miles to Black Rock in Buffalo. Passed Queenstown and Chippewa battle-ground and saw the soldiers' bones.

Friday. Rode on the border of Lake Erie to Hamburg, twenty-two miles. Passed village of Buffalo, a lonely way.

Saturday. Rode to Portland, thirty-eight miles. Passed the awful four-miles woods.

Tuesday, June 30th. Rode to Plain, thirty-five miles. Passed Wooster, a pleasant county-seat. Very poor country. Providentially lodged with a Presbyterian family who gave me my fare, and with them I attended family duties.

Thursday. Rode thirty-four miles to Harrison, through an awfully muddy country, and woods the most of the way. Was met near the middle of an eight-miles wood in a terrible thunder storm. But the Lord preserved me.

Sabbath, July 12th. Preached in Oxford.

[1] "Annals," Vol. II., p. 651.

[2] The MS. of the latter discourse is before me, its first page covered with memoranda of dates and localities, indicating its frequent extemporaneous repetition upon this journey and especially in Indiana. It seems to have been his first written sermon.

Monday. Rode through Brookville in Indiana to a town on Whitewater, twenty-six miles.

Friday. Passed through Vevay, where wine is made by the Swiss, twenty-five miles to a place on the mountains near Madison. Was overtaken by hard rain and stopped at a very miserable hut. Oh, how many poor creatures have I seen. How many destitute of this world's goods and perishing for lack of vision. Was lost in the wood, but providentially found the way to a Connecticut family, where by lying on the floor I lodged comfortably.

Sabbath. Preached (in Madison) to a crowded and solemn audience.

Monday. Rode to the skirt of the town and preached. Received one dollar from Judge Dunn and Elder Simington.

Saturday, August 1st. Rode five miles to Paoli and had opportunity to hear preaching by Mr. Martin.

Tuesday. Rode fourteen miles to Salem and preached. Lodged with brother Martin, an excellent man.[1]

Thursday. Rode fifteen miles to Brownstown. Visited the school under the care of Mr. Kenshaw. Held a long conversation with two drunkards. One confessed that he was miserable, that he had the horrors. The youth cried when he asked if he could yet be saved.

Monday, August 10th. Visited a school. Found the instructor sitting with an ox goad in his hand, so large that he could reach every scholar.

Tuesday. Rode thirty-four miles to Lexington, eighteen of them through the woods. Called at one house and saw a woman rocking her infant in a little log, shaped like a pig-trough.

Thursday. Rode ten miles to Judge Dunn's and found brother Reed of Connecticut, who preached toward evening.[2]

Friday. Visited the school under the care of Dr. Maxwell, which is large and interesting.

Saturday. Visited the school under the care of Mr. McKey. Found them accurate in the catechism as far as they had gone.

Sabbath. Preached in Judge Dunn's barn.

---

[1] It will be found that the journal is very sparing in epithets. This "excellent" is a rarity, as Father Martin was.

[2] "I felt happy to-day in meeting at W. Dunn's, Esq., the Rev. O. Fowler, missionary from Connecticut. We had been acquainted there when students of divinity and were licensed by the same association. . . . I preached and he prayed after sermon. In prayer he was able, devout, and solemn. . . . O that many like him may be sent into the harvest in these parts."—Reed's "Christian Traveller," p. 75. See also pp. 96, 97, 112.

Thursday, August 28th. Rode to Mr. McCartney's, where I preached. Baptized his children, eight in number. The names of James and Jane McCartney's children, this day baptized, are Polly, Margaret (Peggy), Sally, Martha, John, James, William, Jane, and Miriam Dunn.[1] From there I rode five miles to Captain Graham's. Passed the village of Mount Pleasant, which consists of one log house about fifteen feet square, and one other log building about half raised, with about half an acre of partially cleared ground. There is a sugar camp between the village and Captain Graham's.

Friday, September 18th. Rode thirty-four miles to Judge McGee's, Velona. Went till four o'clock without food or drink, and saw but one house for a distance of twenty-two miles. Had much trouble on account of high water. Lost my horse in the woods, but found him again after traveling about three miles through the mud. How great are my fatigues and trials, but the Lord delivers me at all times. One family visit.

Sabbath, September 20th. Administered the sacrament of the Lord's Supper to the Brownstown church, there being only four communicants. It was the first sacrament ever administered in Brownstown and the first Presbyterian sacrament ever held in Jackson County.

Tuesday. Rode twenty miles by Brother Martin's and Salem to Livonia, a village consisting of about twenty log cabins. There is not a shingled roof in the place.

Sabbath, September 27th. Assisted in organizing the Concord church,[2] which consists of eleven members: Mr. James Fulton and his wife Catharine, Mr. John Magner and his wife Sally, Mr. James Donnell and his wife Elizabeth, Mrs. Nancy Fisher and her son Telek and daughter Celia, Mr. Moses Mather and his wife Caty. Then administered the sacrament of the Supper in connection with brother Martin, and preached. Rode three miles to Mr. John Magner's. This is Orange County. The first Presbyterian communion in the county.

Friday, October 9th. Sat with Presbytery at Charlestown and preached in the evening.

Friday, October 16th. Rode five miles to Mr. Bergen's and preached to an interesting congregation. After preaching pro-

---

[1] The missionary's record is equally explicit on each similar occasion. The names, and frequently the nicknames, are religiously preserved.

[2] This church Dickey's "History" does not mention. It was afterward merged in the neighboring churches of Orleans and Paoli.

ceeded to form a church. Commenced with prayer ; then read the certificates of such as had them and heard the relation of others and questioned them on doctrines as well as on experience. Led the brethren to the choice of three elders, and it appeared that Christopher Bergen, Samuel Ryker, and Jeduthan Dodd were elected. Postponed further consideration till to-morrow morning at 10 o'clock.

Saturday. Met and held further consultation and appointed a clerk. At 12 preached to a large, solemn congregation. After preaching proceeded to read the Confession of Faith, and install the elders, they having been ordained. The members of the church[1] are fourteen in number and their names are as follows : Christopher Bergen and his wife Anna, Samuel Ryker and his wife Barbara, Jeduthan Dodd, John L. McCoskey, Peter Ryker and his wife Susannah, John Ryker and his wife Nancy, Theodorus Vanosdol, Peter Vancleve, Rachel Vanosdol, Rachel Weatherford. Afterward met with session and admitted Mary Benepiel and Hannah Hamilton by profession. . . . Twenty-five persons are now in this room around me, all to tarry through the night.

Sabbath. Administered the sacrament to the church yesterday constituted, there being nearly forty communicants present. While administering the ordinance one young man, G. B., was so struck with the expression, "My God, my God, why hast thou forsaken me," that he was pressed down, and kept his bed till night. Many were much affected and after the meeting was over two other young persons were so powerfully impressed that they could not refrain from crying out, "What shall I do?" While at supper an aged sinner of sixty-six, and directly after another of seventy-four cried out, "We are undone, we are lost."

Saturday, October 24th. Preached to a large congregation at New Lexington, and then proceeded to form a church. Received and read the letters of such as had them and heard the relation of others. Alexander McNutt, William Wilson, and Solomon Davis were elected elders. One young lady who had been a Baptist wished to join us, having given up her Baptist sentiments, and accordingly she was received.

Sabbath. Met with the brethren and sisters for further consultation, and at 11 o'clock proceeded to the place of preaching, delivered a sermon to a very large, solemn congregation and then

---

[1] Jefferson church. Cf. Dickey's " History," p. 7.

proceeded to constitute the church.[1] Read the Confession of Faith and covenant, declared them a church, and consecrated them to the Lord by prayer. Then proceeded to ordain the elders, and charge them and the congregation. Afterward baptized eight children. . . . The members of the church are twenty in number and their names are as follows : Alexander McNutt and his wife Margaret, William Wilson and his wife Margaret, Solomon Davis and his wife Mary, Jacob Hollenback and his wife Elenor, William Bowles and his wife Jane, David Walker and his wife Jane, Frederick Sipes, Robert Woodburn, Margaret Patterson, Mary Robinson, Susannah Arbuckle, Fanny Terril, Nancy Roe, and Mary Davis.

Sabbath, November 15th. Rode three miles to Mr. Magner's in the evening. Mr. and Mrs. Shields, with thirteen children, were at meeting last night.

Thursday. Rode nine miles through Vincennes to Judge McClure's, and preached to an attentive audience. V. is built upon the bank of the Wabash. Its local situation is beautiful, but its appearance is very mean. But few of the buildings are well made and many of them are erected with mud walls.

Monday, November 30th. Continued at Vincennes. Attended the funeral of Mr. Emanuel L. Dubois, and delivered an address. Spent the most of the day with brethren Derrow, Tenney, and Robinson, all of them being missionaries. Heard brother Robinson preach in the evening from John v.: 45.

Wednesday, December 9. Rode thirty-nine miles to Smith's Ferry on White River ; thirty miles of the way without a single house. Saw about twenty deer, and many buck and elk horns.

Thursday. Rode thirty miles alone to Judge Ketcham's on Clear Creek ; twenty miles without a house. Alas, how great my fatigues. For five nights I have lodged on the floor, and for two days have found but very little to eat. But the Lord has supported me.

Saturday. Preached at Bloomington,[2] from Psalms cxix.: 165. Received from George Anderson, a Methodist preacher, half a dollar for the missionary society.

Tuesday. Rode twenty-five miles to Mr. Steele's, on Steele's Prairie. Was very glad to get where there are some of the comforts of life again.

[1] Cf. Dickey's " History," p. 7.

[2] Probably the first Presbyterian sermon in the place. Cf. Moore's " History of Indianapolis Presbytery, " p. 3.

Sabbath, Dec. 27th. Preached a funeral sermon on the death of Sally Ann Scott.[1]

Sabbath, Jan. 10, 1819. Preached twice to very large and solemn audiences; first, to Father Balch's people, and baptized Amelia Witherspoon, daughter of John and Letitia White, members of Mr. Balch's church.

Sabbath, Jan. 17th. Preached at the court-house in Vincennes. Alas, how great is the wickedness of this place. Every species of wickedness is committed on the Lord's day, this day being devoted to it. May the good Lord have mercy and not destroy the city.

Friday, Jan. 29th. I have a new trouble. My horse is very lame and I fear I must leave him, but I will trust in the Lord.

Sabbath, Jan. 31st. Preached at Mr. Hall's to a very large and solemn congregation. After preaching proceeded to constitute a Presbyterian church, having previously made the necessary arrangements and examinations, when nine persons came forward and were constituted a church of Christ (the Carlisle church). Their names are as follows: William McCrary and his wife Mary; James Watson; Rachel Porter; Mary Gould; Lydia Silliman; Anna Brody; Mary Wasson; Martha Wasson. Mr. McCrary was chosen to the eldership and ordained.

Monday, Feb. 8th. The citizens of this place (Vincennes) have this day presented me with one hundred and one dollars for my personal benefit; and learning that my horse had failed generously purchased me another, for which they paid eighty dollars. May the Lord reward them for their kindness, and may I have grace and gratitude according to my day.

Sabbath, Feb. 14th. The season is very mild and I have this day had greens with dinner.

Wednesday, Feb. 24th. Rode four miles to Louisville, found brother Rodgers, a missionary from New York. Attended a prayer meeting with him, brother Reed, and brother Banks.

Thursday. Rode to Charlestown. Found brother Todd and family well.

---

[1] Here the journal is interrupted by a list of "missionary stopping places"—a sort of roll of honor. *Livonia:* Alex., James, and Elder McKinney; *Orange County:* David Findley and Mr. Fisher; *Camp Creek:* Elders Walker, Rodgers, and Henderson; *Bethlehem:* Mr. Armstrong; *Washington:* John Allen and Mr. Thompson; *Vincennes:* Drs. Hale and Wood; *Carlisle:* Capt. Wasson; *Princeton:* Mr. Brown, Innkeeper, and Esq. Goodlet; *Clear Creek:* Judge Ketcham; *Bloomington:* Wm. Harden, Esq., postmaster; *8 Miles West:* Judge Berry; and *N. W.*, Mr. Kirkum; *Steele's Prairie:* Mr. Steele; *Between Vincennes and Carlisle:* Judge McClure, Mr. Ockletree, and Mr. Watson.

Friday, March 18, 1819. Left Madison and crossed the river. It was indeed trying to part with my good friends in Indiana. They have manifested much affection for me. May the Lord crown their years with loving kindness, and if I may meet them no more here grant that I may meet them in his kingdom.

From these scattered extracts it is evident how painstaking and thorough and successful were Mr. Fowler's labors in Indiana.[1] Entering the state July 13, 1818, and leaving it March 18 of the following year, his fine health had been taxed to the utmost, his assiduity had entirely broken down a valuable saddle-horse, he had organized three churches, through the southern section of the state he had everywhere scattered seeds of truth, large tracts of country like that about Vincennes he had traversed again and again, and it is easy still to discover the lasting influence of his discreet zeal.

Turning homewards he passed through Kentucky, Virginia, Maryland, and Delaware, and reached New York May 13, in time for the spring anniversaries, which then formed a prominent feature of religious life in the Eastern States. He soon sought a settlement, and was installed pastor of the Congregational church at Plainfield, Conn., March 1, 1820, having previously for several months supplied its pulpit. After eleven years' labor there he removed to Fall River, Mass., where he was installed July 7, 1831.

In the year 1841 Mr. Fowler delivered three discourses containing an historical sketch of Fall River from 1620 to that time. In this sketch he referred to the boundary line between Massachusetts and Rhode Island, that had been in dispute for about a century. Not long after, at a meeting of the citizens of Fall River on the subject of the boundary, Mr. Fowler, without his consent or even knowledge, was placed upon a committee to defend the interests of the town before commissioners appointed by the two

---

[1] He was, however, unable to sing, and found himself on that account often embarrassed. Nor could he become accustomed to the rude frontier life. It will be seen from his diary how it cheered him to meet anybody " from Connecticut."

states. This service he promptly and ably performed; but the commissioners came to a decision in which the people of Fall River were little disposed to acquiesce; and they resolved upon an effort to prevent the establishment by the Massachusetts legislature of the line fixed upon by the commissioners. Mr. Fowler now published a series of papers in the *Boston Atlas* designed to present before the public mind the historical facts sustaining the claims of Massachusetts, but even his most intimate friends did not know that he was the author of them. When the authorship was ascertained there was a general voice in favor of his being chosen to the Senate of the commonwealth, at the next session of the legislature. He was accordingly elected in the autumn of 1847, and the Senate, chiefly, it is said, through his influence, rejected the report of the commissioners by a unanimous vote. Such was the estimation in which he was now held as a legislator that in the autumn of 1848, before his senatorial term had expired, the people of his district elected him to the Thirty-first Congress. Here his influence was extensively and benignly felt and his advocacy of the cheap postage bill particularly is said to have been highly effective.

Mr. Fowler, during the time that he was a member of the Massachusetts Senate, supplied his own pulpit, either in person or by proxy, and continued to perform his pastoral duties until the last of November, 1849, when he left Fall River to take his seat in Congress. Agreeably to a previous understanding, he was dismissed from his pastoral charge by the same council that installed his successor, in the spring of 1850. During his connection with Congress he often supplied the pulpits in Washington and the vicinity and preached for the last time in the autumn of 1851.

On the night of the 27th of August, 1852, he had a slight attack of illness, but the next day was able to be in his seat in Congress as usual. A day or two after the attack was repeated, but relief was again obtained after a few hours. It was soon found, however, that his disease, so far from being dislodged from his system, was taking on an alarming form, and that his system was rapidly sinking under it. After he became convinced that his recovery was hopeless he requested to be left alone with his wife, when he offered a comprehensive and affecting prayer, without wandering or repetition, and mentioning especially both the churches of which he had been pastor. After this he began to speak of his spiritual state, and said: "I have tried to live in peace with God and man"; but the difficulty of respiration did not allow him to proceed. He languished until the 3d of September, and then gently fell into his last slumber. His remains were taken for burial to Fall River, and were received by his former charge as well as his fellow-citizens generally with every testimony of consideration and respect. His funeral sermon was preached by his successor, the Rev. Mr. Relyea.[1]

The eulogy in the House of Representatives was delivered December 8, 1852, by his colleague, the Hon. Zeno Scudder.

Mr. Fowler was married October 16, 1821, to Amaryllis, fourth daughter of John How Payson, of Pomfret, Conn., and niece of the Rev. Dr. Payson, of Portland, Me. They adopted two children, Mrs. President S. C. Bartlett, of Dartmouth, and her brother, Mr. Learned, of Chicago.

Besides various speeches in Congress and contributions to periodicals and newspapers, Mr. Fowler published a sermon at the ordination of Israel G. Rose, at Canterbury, 1825; "Short Practical Essays on the Sabbath" (anonymously), 1826; a "Disquisition on the Evils Attending the Use of Tobacco," 1833; "Lectures on the Mode and Subjects of Baptism," 1835[2]; "History of Fall River," 1841; and "Papers on the Boundary," 1847.

From what Mr. Fowler did we may readily see what he was.

He had an air of great dignity, bordering perhaps a little upon stateliness; a mind of more than ordinary capacity, always delighting in hard labor; an eminently social and friendly spirit; and a disposition to turn all his talents and opportunities of doing good to the best account.[3]

His mind was not of that class which takes in things intuitively. He was a severe student. His books of Hebrew and Greek and historical reference were always near by and showed marks of being often used. The bent of his mind was rather for facts than

---
[1] Sprague's "Annals," Vol. II., pp. 649, 650.
[2] These lectures received warm encomiums. See Scudder's "Eulogy."
[3] Dr. Sprague, in "Annals," Vol. II., p. 650.

consecutive reasoning. He made thorough work with historical documents. His most elaborate performance, for a single discourse, was a lyceum "Lecture on Cotton," which was listened to by large audiences, in several manufacturing towns, with deep interest.[1]

Were we to review the traits of his character which were the source of his success and usefulness, none would appear more prominent than his industry, firmness, teachableness, honesty, and goodness. These were the elements which made him the learned divine, the influential statesman, and useful citizen.[2]

He was shortish and stoutish in physique; a short neck (according to pictures I frequently see); a broad white neck-cloth; with a broad squarish face, and (physically) thick head above it. He was of "ye olden style"—called in the children and catechized them not infrequently; was very systematic and precise in habits and manner; regularly went round the parish in his calls every quarter, and was a confidential adviser in every household. He made an appointment to meet a genial lawyer of his parish one afternoon at five o'clock. About five minutes before five the lawyer saw him coming near on the street and momently expected his rap. It did not come till the town clock was striking the hour. When the lawyer remonstrated because he had not sooner entered he replied that in the five minutes he had made another call. He had considerable ability. I suspect he had little or no humor. His principle was as exact for others as for himself. He had arranged an exchange with a minister some dozen miles away. On reaching that man's house, latish Saturday evening, he found the minister at home, expecting to drive over the next morning. He immediately went out, got into his carriage, drove home that night, and supplied his own pulpit the next day.[3]

The venerable Dr. Ravaud K. Rodgers, whose year of missionary service in Indiana was contemporaneous with that of Mr. Fowler, from Athens, Ga., writes warmly of his acquaintance with him, referring to him as "a very agreeable companion, and a very acceptable preacher, whose heart was in his work."

[1] Dr. Thomas Shepherd, in Sprague's "Annals," Vol. II., p. 651.

[2] "Eulogy" by the Hon. Zeno Scudder, delivered in the House of Representatives, December 8, 1852.

[3] MS. of the Rev. William W. Adams, D.D., Fall River, Mass.

RAVAUD K. RODGERS, last of the quartet referred to in the beginning of this chapter, is still remembered by a few of the oldest residents of southeastern Indiana, to which portion of the state his work, in the winter of 1818-9, was mainly confined. In Madison especially, which he revisited a short time before his death, there are very distinct traditions of the young eastern minister's force, wit, courtesy, and kid gloves. Though from Princeton, and bearing credentials from the General Assembly, his entrance into the Madison parish, which had a settled minister, was not without opposition. Writing from Athens, Ga., March 7, 1876, Dr. Rodgers says:

> It was ———— ————, as I learned, that called in question my right to preach the gospel in Indiana, and among other things charged that my views of Christian theology were very incorrect. Upon consultation with the elders of the church and some of the private members it was thought proper that I should on the then approaching Sabbath read from my commission from the board to satisfy the minds of all that I was not that impostor which Mr. ———— would make me out to be. He also gave it as his opinion that I had no religion about me! I could not but think on that point as our dear old Dr. Alexander thought when he was inquired of by an impudent ignoramus, "Do you think that you have any religion?" calmly replying, "None to brag of." The good people of Madison, notwithstanding all that was said, treated me with great kindness.

In another communication, February 17, 1876, referring to an invitation he had received to visit Indiana once more, he says:

> I dare not even think of such a visit. I had better be preparing for a visit elsewhere. I have the pleasant hope of meeting some beyond the dark river with whom I took sweet counsel in the days when, as an inexperienced youth, I endeavored to preach Christ in the young state of Indiana.

Dr. Rodgers was born in New York City, November, 1797. His father was John Richardson Bayard Rodgers,

M.D., surgeon of a Pennsylvania regiment in the revolutionary army. His grandfather was Dr. John Rodgers, so long pastor of the Wall Street Presbyterian Church, New York, and first moderator of the General Assembly. He graduated at Princeton College in 1815, in the class of Drs. Charles Hodge, Symmes C. Henry, and Bishop John Johns. After his graduation from Princeton Seminary in 1818, and the brief missionary tour in Indiana, he was settled at Sandy Hill, N. Y., for ten years, removing from there to take the pastorate at Bound Brook, N. J., which he retained for forty-four years. He was stated clerk of the Synod of New Jersey for thirty-six years, and in councils of the church occupied a place of prominence. When increasing infirmities admonished him to relinquish active labor he retired to Athens, Ga., the residence of his only child, the wife of R. L. Bloomfield, Esq., where he enjoyed the serenity of a beautiful old age. His death occurred January 12, 1879. He was buried in the Bound Brook cemetery, where his children rest, and many to whom for so long a period he ministered in the gospel.

It was late in 1818[1] that CHARLES STEBBINS ROBINSON, a representative of the Young Men's Missionary Society of New York City, on his way to Missouri crossed the state of Indiana, where he preached the gospel and made careful observation of the religious destitutions. A page from his experience on the frontier well exhibits the self-denials and sufferings from which the church and the nation have gathered so rich a harvest.

I have worn myself out in the missionary service and now I have not the means of taking a journey, the only way that remains

[1] Not in 1816, as Gillett says (Vol. II., p. 397), and Roy in his "Historical Sketch of Congregationalism and Presbyterianism in Indiana." Born at Granville, Mass., May 29, 1791, a graduate of Williams in 1814, and of Andover in 1818, reaching St. Charles, Mo., December 7, 1818, Robinson made that the center of missionary operations until his death, February 25, 1828. His widow survived until August 28, 1833.

of restoring my health; and indeed scarcely of procuring for myself the comforts of life as I sink into the grave, and leave my family none knows to whose care, except there is a God of the widow and the fatherless. Since I have been in St. Charles I once had, for a considerable time, nothing to eat but milk. I went to the store for necessary food, and was refused because I had not the money to pay for it. I returned to my destitute family, you may imagine with what feelings. None knew of our distress but those who felt it. It was November, the cold wind found ready entrance to our cabin, and we had no wood. I procured a spade with a view of remedying the evil as well as I could, throwing up a bank around the house. I had scarcely dug into the earth a foot when to my surprise I threw up a silver dollar which had long been bedded beneath the surface. The goodness of God filled my heart, and I must say I wept plentifully at the sight of it. I could not help it. This served to furnish us with a little wood and a few necessaries. But I could not have remained there at that time had it not been for the kindness of a friend.[1]

[1] See *Missouri Presbyterian Recorder*, Vol. I., No. 6, pp. 169-71. Cf. *The Home Missionary*, Vol. I., p. 115; also, *Indiana Religious Intelligencer*, Vol. I., pp. 245-6.

CHAPTER VIII.

BETTER ECCLESIASTICAL SUPERVISION.

1819–1821.

THE labor expended upon the frontier at this early period would have been much more effective had it been directed by an intelligent supervision. It was easier to detect than to remedy the difficulty, however, and many of the missionaries, choosing their own methods, were also compelled to select their own fields without trustworthy information as to the most needy vacancies or the most favorable openings. With a desire to introduce something like system into these affairs, the Synod of Kentucky had already submitted to the General Assembly the inquiry "whether it would not be proper for a stated missionary to be settled somewhere in the western country (say on the Wabash) and for him to be constantly employed in the missionary service."[1] This suggestion of a superintendent of missions, had it been at once adopted, might have saved many a year of toil at a period when it was peculiarly important to economize all the energies of the struggling church.

The small number of permanent pastors was a further disadvantage. At first nearly all the missionaries came upon horseback, rode over an immense circuit, and then returned to their parishes, or to other circuits, in other states. It required but a brief experience to teach the missionary societies the waste of such expenditures. The

[1] "Minutes Kentucky Synod," October 15, 1810, Vol. I., p. 193.

fourth annual report of the United Domestic Missionary Society says:

> Under a deep conviction of the prime importance of a stated ministry, and in conformity to the usage of this society from the beginning, we have expended the income of the year to aid feeble churches and congregations in the support of ministers who were already settled over them as pastors, or who had the prospect of being permanently employed to watch for souls as they that must give account. We have, accordingly, in general discountenanced the system of itineracy, which has been pursued in too many instances, in this and other countries, to comparatively little effect. It has been required of the missionaries of this society to confine their labors principally to a specified field, embracing one or at most two or three churches or congregations. Experience has convinced this committee, and we rejoice to perceive in the recent usage of other domestic missionary societies, that the Christian public are beginning to be convinced that the system of charitable aid, which furnishes weak congregations with the means of supporting a settled ministry, is far more effective in its permanent results than that which embraces a wider field, and plants but does not water. The latter too often disappoints and discourages those whom it excites and interests; the former pours upon its beneficiaries a perennial stream of those saving benefits which it has already taught them to value. To maintain a permanent ministry, therefore, on as wide a field as we have had ability to occupy, has been our settled purpose.[1]

But this purpose was continually thwarted by the lack of men. The great majority of missionaries to Indiana were still itinerants, concerning whom Dickey observed that "from the brevity of the commissions and the extensive field of operations which they embrace, the good effected has been by no means proportionate to the time and treasure expended."[2]

In 1819 and the two succeeding years the names of eleven new missionaries appear, but it seems that of these only a single one had at the time any intention of settling

[1] "Fourth Annual Report of the U. D. M. S." (May, 1826), pp. 18, 19.
[2] "Brief History," p. 18.

within the state, and he after a brief service was removed by death. In 1820-1 came, from Tennessee, Francis McFarland, who soon went westward to Missouri ; Adams W. Platt, who returned to New York ; William B. Barton,[1] who settled in Woodbridge, N. J.; Ahab Jenks, from Ohio, a sturdy representative of the Connecticut society ; and George S. Boardman and John Vancourt,[2] commissioned by the Assembly. Thompson S. Harris also received an appointment from the Assembly, but preferred to go directly to the Seneca Indian Mission, near Buffalo, N. Y.

To the year 1819 belongs an old record, recalling a pioneer who until a much later day was chiefly occupied beyond the eastern boundary of Indiana. The record, signed by Lowes, Lowry, Jacobs, McLean, Decker, Brooks, Kennedy, Laremor, Harper, Gardner, etc., is as follows :

We, the undersigned, promise to pay the Rev. David Monfort the sum of money annexed to our names—the one half to be paid in six months, the other half in one year from the date (April 1, 1819), in compensation for his labor in preaching one day in every four weeks at Centre School House, four Sabbaths, the remainder on week days, for one year. In witness whereof we have set our names.[3]

DAVID MONFORT, son of Lawrence and Elizabeth Cassat Monfort, was born in York, now Adams County, Pa., March 7, 1790. His ancestors were Huguenots,

[1] His work in Indiana, continued for about six months, was chiefly given to the Jefferson church, Jefferson County.

[2] Vancourt seems to have returned his commission without visiting the field, the vacancy being filled by Barton. Boardman was sent to Madison and the adjoining settlement, but finding the field preoccupied by Searle he itinerated chiefly on the White and Indian Kentucky Rivers. Cf. Gillett's "History," Vol. II., pp. 406, 407.

[3] Centre School House was in Franklin County, Ind. While preaching there one Sabbath each month Mr. Monfort preached on the remaining Sabbaths at Bethel church, on Indian Creek, Ohio. The salary for one fourth of his time was twenty-nine dollars per annum. John Brooks and Simeon Jacobs paid in sugar.

driven from France to Holland by the revocation of the Edict of Nantes, a race whose representatives in Johnson County, Ind., may still be recognized from such names as Aten, Bergen, Bonte, Brewer, Brinkerhoff, Conover, Demaree, Pieterson, Seburn, Voris, Vannuys, Van Dyne, Van Dyke, etc. Young Monfort lived with his parents on a farm in Warren County, Ohio, until he passed his minority. When seventeen years of age his religious life began, in the midst of the New Light Revival. He became a member of the Presbyterian Church, and in preparation for the ministry studied privately under the Rev. Richard McNemar, near his home, and with the Rev. John Thomson, at Springfield, now Springdale, near Cincinnati. He completed his literary course in Transylvania University and his course in theology at Princeton, graduating in 1817. Licensed by the Miami Presbytery, at Lebanon, April 4, 1817, he supplied Bethel church for a few months, received a call as pastor, and was ordained and installed October 20 of the same year. This pastorate continued ten years and was both happy and useful. Mr. Monfort was strong, active, of fine personal appearance, a good student, an attractive writer and speaker, and withal an excellent singer. His church became the largest in the state, with the exception of the First Church, Cincinnati. Besides the regular engagement at "Centre School House," already alluded to, he also occasionally preached during the Bethel pastorate at Lawrenceburgh, Brookville, Mt. Carmel, Dunlapsville, Connersville, and other points in Indiana.

In 1828 he took charge of the church at Terre Haute, where he remained but two years, in the midst of affliction and suffering. He lost his wife and daughter, and was himself visited with severe sickness, causing a lameness from which he never recovered. Returning to Ohio he spent one year in Wilmington and its neighborhood, when he again came to Indiana and began his long pastorate at Franklin. He was now in feeble health, but worked incessantly and with great success. Death once more visited his house, removing his second wife, Rhoda Halsey, of Lebanon, Ohio, immediately after his settlement at Franklin. Until 1838 he was also pastor of the Hopewell church, receiving a salary of three hundred dollars from both societies. After a service of nineteen years at Franklin he retired, in 1850, living for a time at Kingston, Ind., Decatur, Ill., and finally at Macomb, Ill., where he died, suddenly, of paralysis, October 18, 1860.[1]

Dr. Monfort[2] was a man of wide and varied learning. He was trimly built, though undersized in person, had dark hair and eyes, a narrow high forehead, and was remarkably neat in his dress. His manners were engaging. Whilst always serious he was never gloomy and forbidding. He held in scrupulous regard all the proprieties and conventionalities of life. No incident is preserved to indicate that he had the slightest tendency to wit or humor. He was possessed of a sound and discriminating judgment; knew how to gain the good will of men and how to hold their esteem. His views of religious truth were clear and decided, and what he believed he preached with all the might that was in him. As a speaker his most marked characteristic was his great clearness. He was a teacher of men, excelling in doctrinal discourse, but on occasions he preached with great feeling. His manner was deliberate, calm, solemn, and earnest.[3]

He was thoroughly versed in ecclesiastical jurisprudence and his opinions as to principles and precedents had in the church courts almost the force of law.[4]

[1] Cf. " History of the Half-century Celebration at Franklin " (address of Dr. J. G. Monfort), pp. 160-4.

[2] Hanover College conferred upon him the doctorate.

[3] " History of the Half-century Celebration at Franklin " (Judge Banta's address), pp. 149, 150.

[4] He was thrice married. Of his first wife, Phebe, daughter of Judge Isaac Spinning, of Dayton, Ohio, three children survived him: Elizabeth, wife of the Rev. John C. King, Isaac Pierson, and Lawrence. Of his third wife, Ann Ray, of Indianapolis, were the Rev. Cornelius V., Mary, wife of the Rev. Robert M. Roberts, John, Andrew, and Phebe.

To the one Presbyterian minister who in 1819 came to take up his residence in the state a tragic interest belongs. He traveled half-way across the continent to his field on the Ohio at Madison. At that time this perhaps seemed the most important Indiana parish. Established four years previously by William Robinson, and by him irregularly supplied, though the congregation had not grown rapidly its position gave it a sort of metropolitan influence. Until a much later period Madison was the market for Monfort's future parishioners at Franklin, and even for the stragglers still further north who were soon to build their cabins in the neighborhood of the coming capital of the state. The church on the Ohio needed and was now to secure a master-workman.

THOMAS C. SEARLE came to Indiana under the auspices of the Young Men's Missionary Society of New York City. A graduate of Dartmouth College and of Princeton Theological Seminary, he began his ministry at Montgomery Court House, Maryland.[1] Chosen in 1817 to the professorship of logic at Dartmouth he retired from that position to enter the missionary service. He was present, August 15, 1819, with Thomas Cleland and John M. Dickey, at the second communion season, of which a record is preserved in the Madison church. From that date he assumed the care of the parish. On March 4, 1820, he constituted the Hanover church, Clifty Creek forming the boundary between it and the Madison congregation. His New Hampshire attachments determined the name of the society, and thus also of the future college.[2] He was installed over the Madison and Hanover churches,

[1] Cf. MS. of the Rev. Isaac Reed, who in 1829 was appointed to prepare a history of Vincennes Presbytery, and has left the notes he had begun with some assiduity to collect. With regard to Searle see also Reed's "Christian Traveller," pp. 92, 213.

[2] The same circumstances likewise gave a name to the church which Mr. Searle constituted in Jennings and Ripley Counties, August 17, 1821, and called "Dartmouth." This organization soon disappeared in the Graham and Vernon churches.

August 13, 1820. With great zeal and with flattering success he prosecuted his work ; but the autumn of 1821 was in a marked degree unwholesome, and the young pastor was soon prostrated with a bilious fever. Descending too soon from his chamber to preside over the nuptials of a niece, he suffered a relapse, and October 15, at the age of thirty-three, he died. Over the entire community not only, but over the whole region, the shadow of this event long rested, Mr. Searle's capacities, devotedness, and popularity having justly excited the highest anticipations. Of slight and trim figure, attractive in appearance and manner, he had at once become a favorite. With affectionate laudation, seldom more fully deserved, the afflicted church inscribed upon his tombstone in the old cemetery their sense of his worth : "As a man he was universally loved and respected ; as a Christian he was a pattern for all ; as a scholar and promoter of learning he held the first rank ; as a preacher of the gospel he excelled.''

CHAPTER IX.

INDIANAPOLIS.

1821.

THE seat of government of the Indiana territory was originally at Vincennes, its oldest settlement and safest military post. By the legislature of 1813 the capital was transferred to Corydon, where, in December of that year, Governor Posey delivered his first message to the General Assembly. Having created a state government by the act approved April 19, 1816, the national Congress donated four sections of land, to be selected by the legislature, for a permanent capital. Ten commissioners were accordingly designated, January 11, 1820, to choose a suitable location near the center of the state, and three of the five who served upon the commission reported in favor of the present site.[1] The report was approved January 6, 1821, and at the suggestion of Judge Jeremiah Sullivan, of Madison, Indianapolis[2] was fixed upon as the future city's name.

When the legislative commission made their report the whole region comprising the new seat of government was still in possession of the Indians. Ceded by them to the white men, October 3, 1818, the treaty at St. Mary's, Ohio, then expressly stipulated that they should not be ejected until 1821. The reported fertility of "the new purchase" had, however, already begun to attract settlers.

[1] Naturally William Conner, "the Father of Central Indiana," at whose house the commissioners met, about sixteen miles north of the present capital, strongly favored the selection of that locality, now Noblesville.

[2] By General Marston G. Clark, brother of General George Rogers Clark, "Tecumseh" was suggested. Another commissioner advocated "Suwaroff."

George Pogue, a blacksmith, according to tradition came to the site of Indianapolis from the Whitewater,[1] March 2, 1819. About the same time came also John and James McCormick. These were the earliest arrivals. Late in 1820 and in the following spring, this patch of forest having now acquired celebrity from the commissioners' report to the legislature, other frontiersmen appeared. In April, 1821, the surveyors, under Alexander Ralston, commenced the labor of laying off the town, and on the tenth of October following the state agent, General John Carr, opened the public sale of alternate lots in Matthias Nowland's log tavern, on Washington, west of Missouri Street. The sale occupied several days, and three hundred and fourteen lots were disposed of. The Indianapolis history was thus fairly begun.

These beginnings were in the literal wilderness. The forests were most dense. What sort of trees stood compactly for a hundred miles in every direction from this classical clearing may be suspected from the fact that in the winter of 1820 under the river bank, near Washington Street, a hollow sycamore log furnished Wyandotte John a commodious dwelling. The undergrowth of hazel and pawpaw and spicewood was nearly impenetrable. To all ordinary effort the region was inaccessible on account of the mud, the level surface and the thick shade effecting a direful conspiracy of bogs. An Episcopal missionary sent from Philadelphia declared that, though an old traveler, he had never in any part of the world felt himself to be in greater peril than when attempting to ride a horse through the mire from Madison to the new capital. The agues were as colossal as the swamps and the timber. At times the whole population was prostrated. It would not seem that the attractions of the place were remarkable. A Pari-

[1] The first emigrants from the eastward and from Kentucky were nearly equal in numbers. The former were known as the "Whitewater" people.

sian transported over the poplars and walnuts in the summer of 1821, and set down at Carter's tavern on "Berry's Trace," would soon have begun to sigh for home.

But let it not be supposed that the isolated, sallow, log-cabined settlement was either puny or pitiable. The truth is that a singularly hardy and energetic population were already here, and such were their mental and social qualities that at least on its well days and intermittently the hamlet had an air not only of cheerfulness but of dignity. Calvin Fletcher, Harvey Gregg, and Obed Foote were the attorneys. Isaac Coe, Samuel G. Mitchell, and Livingston Dunlap dispensed the Peruvian bark and calomel, and were assisted by Jonathan Cool whenever old rye and old rhymes could spare him. Daniel Shaffer, the Pennsylvania Dutchman and the hero of the early "raisings," opened, on the south bank of Pogue's Creek, the first store. He soon had important rivals in John Givan and Nicholas McCarty. Colonel James Blake was the steam-engine of the place in those days when steam-engines were almost unknown. James M. Ray, the clerk at the sale of lots, became the first county clerk. Caleb Scudder was the cabinet-maker, Wilkes Reagan the butcher, and John Van Blaricum the horse-shoer. Amos Hanway made the wash-tubs and buckets, and Samuel S. Rooker, the first sign-painter, soon had orders from Carter's "Rosebush" and Hawkins's "Eagle" Tavern. Samuel Henderson was postmaster until 1829; Morris Morris and Daniel Yandes were projecting corn-fields and tan-yards; George Smith, of the coming *Gazette* newspaper, made himself queer with a long queue superstitiously tied with an eel-skin string; and John McCormick was the crack fisherman, who, it was said, could in two or three hours load a canoe with "gar" from his lucky gig.

Of the primitive population it will be seen that a large

and influential portion was Presbyterian. A minister soon came to them. In August, 1821, two months before the sale of lots, the first Presbyterian sermon was delivered. The service was held under a large black walnut tree near the southwest corner of Washington and Mississippi Streets, the underbrush having been laboriously cleared away for the occasion. It may be worth while to attempt a reproduction of the scene. Dr. Isaac Coe, James Blake, Caleb Scudder, and James M. Ray were the acknowledged leaders. Coe, by virtue of his talents, zeal, and ecclesiastical experience, was, then and afterward, foremost. He was as sound a stick of Calvinism as ever grew. He came from sturdy stock. The first of the name who emigrated to America was Robert Coe, from Ipswich, Suffolkshire, England, with seventy-four other pilgrims, in the ship *Francis*, captain John Cutting, in the year 1634. He resided first at Watertown, Mass., and afterward at Stamford, Conn. The grandfather of this first emigrant, of the same name, suffered martyrdom in Suffolkshire in September, 1555. He was burned by Queen Mary and is mentioned in Fox's "Book of Martyrs." Dr. Isaac Coe came from Virginia to Indianapolis, by Madison, in May, 1821. He was a man of mind, educated, thoroughly settled in the highest principles of morality, and a competent guide in all Christian affairs. Blake, whose cheerful energy in days of war and peace was itself an inspiration, had before him a long and prominent career of usefulness. Scudder, in a quiet sphere, illustrated the value to a young community of mature and modest virtue. Ray surviving until March, 1881, was permitted to teach another generation what serenity and strength religion can afford for days of darkness.[1] Brought together under the big tree on that memorable August day, these four men

---

[1] For notices of the pioneers of the town see Ignatius Brown's "Historical Sketch," Holloway's "Indianapolis," and Nowland's "Early Reminiscences of Indianapolis."

were destined in yet closer bonds to toil side by side for many a year.

The preacher at this first service, a stout, florid man, with a great voice and a big wart on his forehead, was the Rev. Ludwell G. Gaines, of Ohio, an itinerant sent to the field by the Assembly's Committee of Missions. James M. Ray writes:

> He was a robust man, earnest in impressing the value of religion and good morals in our young community, and was listened to with interest and quietly by about two hundred and fifty of the settlers (as we called each other then). His forcible appeals tended to strengthen those among the first comers who wished to have Sunday kept from the beginning in the future capital of the state and to have the day rescued from the indulgence in shooting game and fishing then general in the West.

Licensed by Miami Presbytery April 5, 1821, immediately after his Indiana tour, Mr. Gaines was in October appointed to the charge of Hopewell and Somerset in Ohio. He died February 6, 1861. "He was a man of deep piety and earnest devotion to his Master's work."

It was some time before this community of Presbyterians again heard a sermon from one of their own ministers, though late the same autumn,[1] on his way to Missouri, whither the Connecticut Missionary Society had sent him, young David Choate Proctor passed through Indiana and Illinois. The lack of a minister was in part supplied by the diligence of Isaac Coe, who opened a Bible class, February 20, 1822, at the house of Lismund Basye.[2] Two or three months later, returning homewards from the Mississippi, Mr. Proctor spent a week during the month of May at Indianapolis, on several occasions preaching to the

[1] Cf. "Life and Times of Stephen Bliss," pp. 56-9. (It was after, not before, the occasion alluded to by the biographer of Bliss that Proctor's service at Indianapolis began.)

[2] Cf. Greene's "Historical Sketch of the Origin and Progress of the Indianapolis Sabbath Schools," p. 5.

people. An effort was made to detain him permanently, and four hundred dollars were subscribed for three fourths of his time for one year from the first of the ensuing October. The remaining Sabbath of each month was to be given to Bloomington. Meanwhile the Rev. Isaac Reed visited the congregation about the first of June ; and finally, according to the previous arrangement, Mr. Proctor in October assumed charge of the parish, and thus became the first settled minister at the capital. During this early period the extemporized pulpit was for the summer in Caleb Scudder's cabinet-shop, and through the winter at the residence of Judge McIlvaine.

On Friday, March 7, 1823, the first number of the *Western Censor and Emigrants' Guide* contained the following :

PUBLIC NOTICE :—The Presbyterian congregation will meet on Saturday, the 22d day of March, inst., at one o'clock, at the schoolhouse in the town of Indianapolis, for the purpose of incorporating themselves, agreeably to an act of the legislature, and electing trustees. It is particularly requested that all persons who subscribed for building a meeting-house and for the support of Mr. Proctor will attend.

The subscription for the meeting-house had already reached the sum of twelve hundred dollars. The second number of the *Censor*, March 19, says :

We understand that the establishment of a Sunday-school is in contemplation in this town. We hope for the benefit of society that it will be successful. The advantages that have been derived from these institutions in many parts of the United States have already had a very considerable effect upon society.

On April 2, the same paper continues :

We are requested to state that the Sunday-school will hold its first meeting on Sunday morning, the 6th inst., at Mr. Scudder's cabinet-shop.

According to appointment the school did meet amidst the saws and the shavings. James M. Ray was elected superintendent and thirty scholars were enrolled, of whom some came six miles. Thus began the march of that grand army for so many years marshalled, each Fourth of July, by Colonel James Blake, to hear the Declaration of Independence and eat gingerbread in the State-House Square. One of the original members of the first school says :

> Fifty years ago to-day I entered that school, a boy eight years old, and did not know one letter of the alphabet, nor do I believe that among the ten or twelve boys present there was one who could spell his own name, or would know it should he see it in print. The incidents of that day were calculated to make a lasting impression on the young mind. The Sunday-school had been the topic of conversation with the boys of the village for some time. We thought it a great innovation upon our personal rights. We thought that Messrs. Coe, Blake, and Ray, who organized the school, were assuming power they had no right to. I was assigned to the class of the late James Blake, who taught me the alphabet, as well as to spell and read. In Mr. Blake's class I learned to repeat the Catechism, Lord's Prayer, and Ten Commandments. I remained in that school some nine or ten years and there learned many useful and instructive lessons. The rules at first were most rigid, and delinquency on the part of the scholars was severely reprimanded and reported to their parents. One of the rules required that we should attend church on the Sabbath; hence Sunday was a day of rest to the ground squirrels and rabbits. Birds were left uninterrupted to build their nests.[1]

Thus far there was only the Sabbath-school—a union school, heartily supported by Presbyterians, Methodists, Baptists, and New Lights, who for five years wrought harmoniously together.[2] But by the Sunday-school is

---

[1] Letter of J. H. B. Nowland in Greene's pamphlet, p. 16.
[2] The separate Methodist school was not established until April 24, 1829. That of the Baptists was organized in 1833.

sure to grow the church. Accordingly says the *Censor* newspaper, June 18, 1823:

> We are requested to give information that a Presbyterian church will be formed in this place and the sacrament attended on the first Sabbath in July. The service on this occasion will commence on the Friday preceding at two o'clock.

This arrangement was afterward slightly changed, and the *Censor*, July 9, announced that

> On Saturday, the 5th inst. (July, 1823), a Presbyterian church was constituted in this town. Fifteen members were received into communion. The Rev. Mr. Proctor, the resident minister, was assisted on the occasion by the Rev. Mr. Martin, the Rev. Mr. Reed, and the Rev. Mr. Day, who went away pleased with the conduct and orderly deportment of our citizens.

So early had the backwoods capital established a reputation for propriety and order.

For the Saturday service the congregation found the usual shelter in the cabinet-shop. Thither the fifteen persons who were to compose the society, with their friends, made their way through the thickets and along the cow-tracks. The next day, for the first communion season, they were to have a grander welcome. The twelve-hundred-dollar meeting-house was not complete, but could be occupied. Thirty-four by fifty-four feet it was, on Pennsylvania Street, just north of Market. There assembled the Sunday congregation with eloquent "Father" Martin, ubiquitous Isaac Reed, and Ezra H. Day, so near the end of his short career, to assist Mr. Proctor in the administration of the sacrament. That day's work, setting up God's altars in what was to be the most populous and important community of the state, was one well worth the toilsome journeys from Livonia, from the "Cottage of Peace" in Owen County, and from New Albany. To complete the picture it is necessary to sketch the career and character of the central figure of the occasion, who for a few months longer was to remain in charge of the flock.

DAVID CHOATE PROCTOR, born in New Hampshire in 1792, a graduate of Dartmouth and of Andover, was licensed by a Congregational Association, and in 1822, having received ordination, came to the West, under appointment from the Connecticut Missionary Society. He crossed the Wabash about March 1st, and on the 5th of the same month organized the first Presbyterian church in Edwards County, Ill.[1] He visited Indianapolis in the following May and concluded his engagement with the congregation there for one year from the subsequent October. From Indianapolis he removed to Kentucky in the fall of 1823 and took charge of the Springfield and Lebanon churches. His services at Lebanon were highly acceptable,[2] but in 1826 he was called to the presidency of Centre College at Danville, a position which he held from the resignation of Dr. Chamberlain until the election of Dr. Blackburn in the ensuing year. Upon his marriage he settled upon the venerable plantation near Shelbyville. When the education of his children required it he transferred his residence for four years to New Haven, Conn., having previously disposed of his estate. Returning to Kentucky, he purchased a farm near Frankfort, where he died of pneumonia January 18, 1865.

In person Mr. Proctor was of medium height, of dark complexion, and of attractive presence. He was of a social disposition, fond of anecdotes, and devoted to his horse. Later in life he cultivated a marked decorum of manner and of speech. In reply to an ordinary question about the probabilities of the weather he would be likely to say: "Really, sir, I cannot affirm." To his friends he was

[1] "Life and Times of Stephen Bliss," pp. 56–9.

[2] "Historical Discourse Preached at Lebanon" by the Rev. A. A. Hogue, Louisville, 1859, pp. 9, 10.

strongly attached and was accustomed to "use hospitality." "I reckon Kentucky would suit him," said one who knew his early characteristics and the cordiality of southern society. "A real Yankee he was in some things," is the recollection of another who had in mind his minute and sagacious advice to seamstresses and cooks. In business affairs his precision and order became proverbial, these qualities also appearing in the carefulness of his toilet. His thrift was extraordinary. "There was not a man in Shelby County whose judgment about a horse would be more valued." Dr. Thomas H. Cleland speaks of his recollection of names and faces : "He knew every chick and child." One who was long associated with him writes :

He was a well-educated minister. His preaching was sound and useful, though not particularly attractive in the manner of utterance. Very few of our ministers in Kentucky have done so much gratuitous labor in feeble churches and destitute regions. If he had given himself wholly to the work he would have done more, but he was exceedingly sensitive and rather than be dependent on anybody he chose to "labor with his own hands" and preach without compensation. I think he misjudged in his plans of life and usefulness, but I confess to an admiration for his generosity and independence.[1]

[1] MS. letter of the Rev. Dr. Edward P. Humphrey, dated June 27, 1876.

CHAPTER X.

EXTENSION TOWARD THE NORTH.

1822.

THUS far the labors of Protestant missionaries had been almost wholly confined to the southern half of Indiana. That vast northern tract of swamp and forest which with characteristic acumen and enterprise the French priests had explored and seized upon two hundred years before, until now had continued to be the happy hunting ground of Indians. Wallace, a Presbyterian chaplain, had at an early day gone with the troops to the junction of the St. Joseph and the St. Mary,[1] but the church sent no successor after him. There was indeed too scanty a white population to require a stated ministry. Not until 1821, when the surveys for the capital were completed, did the conditions annexed to the treaty of St. Mary's expel the red man from these ancient haunts of duck and deer. Their enforced departure was the signal for moving the line of settlements northward. With the settlers promptly came a missionary of the General Assembly. In December, 1822, John Ross, who afterward attained a longevity entirely unique in our annals, preached the first Presbyterian sermon to the residents of Fort Wayne. From May, 1820, to the time of Mr. Ross's visit, the Rev. Isaac McCoy, of the Baptist Church, had resided there, preaching the gospel and maintaining a mission school for the benefit of the Indians. In August, 1822, a Baptist society was organized, consisting of the mission family, two Indian women, and one

[1] See Chapter IV.

black man.[1] Mr. Ross found at the settlement about one hundred and fifty persons, including French and halfbreeds, mainly engaged in the Indian trade. The nearest village was at Shane's Prairie, forty miles distant. Except as the trace was dotted with occasional cabins, a day's journey apart, all northwest of Piqua was a wilderness.

The missionary, who at the time was pastor of a church in the New Jersey settlement on the Big Miami, opposite Franklin, took passage in a light two-horse wagon, with Matthias Griggs, of Lebanon, Ohio, afterward a member of the church at Fort Wayne and now about to visit that place on a trading expedition with hats and dried fruits. In a letter dated November 26, 1859, Mr. Ross describes the peril and exposure of the journey; how their first night's encampment in the woods, a few miles north of Dayton, was made memorable by the howling of wolves on every side; how the snow-storm afterward met them in the wilderness with intense cold, which froze fast in the mud the wheels of their wagon; how, failing to strike fire from the flint, the woodsman's last hope, they were compelled to leave their conveyance under guard of a faithful dog; how, by walking and leading their horses, the cold being too severe to ride, they reached Fort Wayne at a late hour on a wintry night; and with what kindness he was received by Samuel Hanna, afterward long an honored elder in the Fort Wayne church. Mr. Ross says:

The next day being the Sabbath, I preached in the fort morning and afternoon, because there was no other convenient place to preach in. . . . I visited the place five times from 1822 to 1826. I was once sent out to Fort Wayne by the Synod of Ohio. In all my visitations I preached in St. Mary's, Shane's Prairie, and Willshire, and scattered religious tracts and Bibles. There was no place that appeared to me so unpromising as Fort Wayne. . . . There was no Sabbath kept, but on the part of a few.[2]

[1] Williams's " Historical Sketch," pp. 12, 13.
[2] Williams's " Historical Sketch," pp. 13-5. It was not until November, 1829, that any further missionary work was attempted at Fort Wayne. The A. H. M. Society

JOHN ROSS, who assisted so prominently in laying the foundations of Christian society at Kekionga, had a remarkable career. He was born of Roman Catholic parents in Dublin, Ireland, July 23, 1783. Early made an orphan, he went to Liverpool when about eighteen years of age, and became a shoemaker's apprentice. He was three times impressed into the British service, the third time just as he had completed his apprenticeship. Sent to the West Indies, he finally effected an escape with six comrades, and concealing himself in an American vessel landed at New London, Conn., hatless, shoeless, and penniless. For a time he was employed at his trade, but experiencing conversion began a course of study for the Protestant ministry. Graduating from Middlebury College and from Princeton Seminary at the age of thirty-four, he was married at Stonington, Conn., and labored as a missionary in Philadelphia. He was settled at Somerset, Pa., and successively at Gallipolis, Ripley,[1] and the Jersey settlement in Butler County, Ohio, coming from the latter parish to Richmond, Ind., in the year 1824. During a pastorate there of five years he removed to a farm near the town, where he resided for sixteen years, supplying vacancies as he was able, and until financial reverses compelled his removal. Again becoming a laborious itinerant, his last

then sent out the Rev. Charles E. Furman, in response to an appeal from Allen Hamilton, the postmaster, who represented that there were five hundred people there and no preaching within eighty miles. Mr. Furman continued his labor in the place for about six months. In June, 1831, the Rev. James Chute, of the Presbytery of Columbus, visited Fort Wayne, and on the first of July following organized the first Presbyterian church, consisting of seven members, Smalwood Noel and John McIntosh being ruling elders. In September, under appointment of the A. H. M. Society, Mr. Chute took up his residence in the place. He was born at Boxford, Essex County, Mass., November 15, 1788; graduated from Dartmouth in 1813; studied divinity under the tutelage of Dr. J. L. Wilson, of Cincinnati; and died at Fort Wayne, December 28, 1835. Cf. "Memoir of the Rev. James Chute," privately printed, 1874.

[1] Mr. Ross was succeeded at Ripley by John Rankin of "underground railroad" fame. A son of the latter recollects that the people of the parish used to illustrate the amiable unworldliness of Father Ross by narrating how, though without a horse, he bought up sets of harness because they were cheap, and in his garden diligently pulled up the big corn to give the weaker stalks a chance.

settlement was at Burlington, Ind. Overcome finally by the infirmities of age, he found a home under the roof of his daughter at Tipton, where he lingered until March 11, 1876, having nearly completed his ninety-third year. He was a faithful minister of the New Testament and showed through all his public life a trust in providence which early perils and deliverances had been well calculated to develop.[1]

While the new ground in the extreme north was being broken the more familiar region along the Ohio was at the same time receiving attention. In the church at New Albany, too long neglected, hope was rekindled by the coming of a pastor.

The plat of the city of New Albany had been drafted in 1813. Five years later than that, however, large trunks of trees which had been felled but not removed lay over most of the town.[2] But the place had "a steam saw-mill, several stores, mechanics' shops, and a boat yard for the building of steamboats." Joel Scribner, a prominent landowner and one of the first settlers, was a Presbyterian. On the 19th of February, 1816, a church was organized at Jeffersonville, composed of members residing there and at New Albany, which was called "The Union Church of Jeffersonville and New Albany." Thomas Posey, governor of the territory, and his wife, John Gibson and his wife, James M. Tunstal, James Scribner, Joel Scribner, Phebe Scribner, Esther Scribner, and Anna M. Gibson constituted the membership. Thomas Posey and Joel Scribner were chosen elders. Subsequently Mary Merriwether and Mary Wilson were admitted to the communion. On the

---

[1] At the semi-centennial celebration of the Synods of Indiana, October, 1876, it had been hoped that "Father Ross" might be present. But with "Father Johnston," the only other representative of the Northern Synod whose service reached back to the commencement of the Synodical history, he was summoned hence in March of that year. One died on the day of the other's burial.

[2] "Christian Traveller," p. 86.

7th of December, 1817, all the members residing at Jeffersonville having removed to other churches, the Union Church held a meeting at New Albany, with the Rev. D. C. Banks as moderator, at which it was resolved that the name be changed to the First Presbyterian Church of New Albany. At the same time four new members were received, making the whole number nine. Isaac Reed, the first minister of the society, beginning his service September 1, 1818, continued as pastor for fifteen months. Shortly after his settlement Orin Fowler found him there, busily and usefully engaged. Upon Mr. Reed's removal the pulpit long remained vacant and the feeble church almost died, the comfortable meeting-house having been destroyed by fire. It was not until November, 1822, that the Rev. Ezra H. Day came to their aid. When inviting him to the field the session represented that it was "highly important that some effort be made speedily to save this wreck of the church and to collect this scattered flock." The pastor's arrival at once restored their courage, but almost immediately their prospects were darkened again by his sudden death.[1]

EZRA H. DAY was probably a native of Morristown, N. J. He was a member of Westchester Presbytery, New York. "His modest unassuming manners, his sound judgment and evident piety endeared him," says Dickey, "to the few friends who were favored with his acquaintance." It was, however, the will of God that he should fall at his post just as he had proven his peculiar fitness for it. A bilious fever, which at the time was prevalent in the neighborhood, terminated his life September 22, 1823. He was of medium height, not stout, and of fair complexion. "Gentle, grave, and serious in his walk he made the impression upon all that he held close fellowship with

[1] Hovey's "Historical Sermon" in the *New Albany Ledger*, November 25, 1867, and MS. "History of Presbyterianism in New Albany," by the Rev. S. Conn, D.D.

the skies." At the time of his death he was about thirty-eight years of age. He left a wife and three children, who returned to New Jersey. He was buried in the old Lower First Street Cemetery, but the grave cannot be identified.

It was in 1822 that WILLIAM GOODELL also reached Indiana upon his agency for the A. B. C. F. M., which had sent him out to the churches to awaken an interest in the cause of missions and to raise funds for the work of the society. Dr. Rufus Anderson was afterward accustomed to say that "Goodell cut a swath through all that region," so steadily did contributions flow into the treasury from the neighborhoods which had felt his power. He was then a fervid young candidate for the foreign mission service. Those who heard him on this western tour were not surprised that he afterward became a learned linguist, a translator of the Bible, an apostle of the New Testament pattern, the fragrance of whose life, like a garden of spices, is known throughout the Turkish Empire. His biographer says :

Traveling westward into the states of Ohio and Indiana, he found in many places an unexpected interest in the cause of missions to the dark portions of the world, the result of a gracious outpouring of the spirit upon the churches of that comparatively new region of country ; but in other places there was literally a famine for the bread of life, and the gospel message which he carried to them was heard with gladness. He wrote at the time (February 18, 1822): "There are but two settled ministers, of the Presbyterian or Congregational order, in the whole state of Indiana.[1] I preached in one place where some of the people said they had heard but three sermons from Presbyterians there before."[2]

Besides Ross and Day, separated in their work by

[1] This was far from correct, but only proves how scanty were the means of information even for the most diligent and competent observers.

[2] "Memoirs of Rev. William Goodell, D.D.," by his son in-law, Dr. E. D. G. Prime, pp. 68, 69.

nearly the entire length of the state, and separated, too, by that striking diversity of providence which called one immediately from his earthly task and kept the other here until more than half a century had been completed ; and besides Goodell, the witty, impassioned, and devoted friend of the new foreign missionary enterprise, there came another from the East to Indiana, a pioneer of the pioneers, a missionary of the missionaries, a Hebrew of the Hebrews, Charles Beatty's son Charles, who, from his father, one of the founders of the church in western Pennsylvania, had inherited the evangelistic spirit, and was hindered only by an event which suddenly changed his whole course of life from permanently identifying himself with the Indiana settlements.

DR. CHARLES C. BEATTY writes :

I was commissioned by the Board of Missions to labor as a missionary in Indiana and adjacent parts of Illinois, commencing in Wayne County, Ind. This I did the first of November, 1822, and arriving at Indianapolis toward the close of the week, was induced by friends there to spend the Sabbath, and preached twice for Mr. Proctor. On Tuesday evening I preached across the river on my way to Bloomington, preached at that place Wednesday night, and left the next day, expecting to reach Mr. Scott's, near Vincennes, by Sabbath. But in consequence of a delay at the river I preached Friday night at a small place this side and got to Carlisle, where I spent the Sabbath, preaching in the meeting-house. On Monday I went on to Mr. Scott's, from whom I received valuable information as to my field up the Wabash on both sides. He was *the* preacher on the Wabash, missionated much and had the care of the churches. I met him afterward on all my visits to that vicinity, Vincennes being one of my preaching points. I established a kind of circuit, and went round about three times in my four months' tour, closing it at Shawneetown early in March. Thence I passed into Kentucky, preaching on across to Shelbyville and Louisville, from which I crossed to Indiana, visiting Corydon, Washington, and Salem, and going thence back to Parke County, where I had organized two churches on the Raccoon.[1] These congregations

---

[1] Shiloh church was organized, with seventeen members, December 17, 1822. Ebenezer church was organized, with nineteen members, January 9, 1823.

made out a call for me and I made arrangements to settle, going down with the elder to the Presbytery of Louisville, which met at Charlestown, Ind., and passing by Spencer, in Owen County, where I assisted the Rev. Isaac Reed in administering the Lord's Supper. From there I passed to Bloomington, where I preached, and so on to Presbytery. Here I got intelligence of my father's death, which ultimately changed my plans. My journal and all my papers were left on Raccoon and were never recovered.

During my four months' service I organized three churches[1] and rode over all that western region. My farthest points north were Crawfordsville[2] and the mouth of Vermillion. Mr. Balch, who had brought an emigrating church from east Tennessee to Sullivan County, had died before my visit. I knew his children and people and held a communion at Turman's Creek church with blessed results. At Vincennes I always had large congregations, and they wished me to settle there; but there was no church, or church members, though I trust my ministry there had some fruits. At Terre Haute but few attended. Some were gathered at Turman's Creek, at Raccoon, and across in Illinois.

My field of labor was very new and rough, but the people were kind and always gave me the best. I was a constant singer, and I believe my singing made me more acceptable—popular than my preaching. I found but two places on my whole circuit where I could have a room to myself to study, and accordingly wrote no sermons, and but few briefs. I studied as I could. I should have been very willing to spend my life in a log cabin on Raccoon and live on the common fare of the country. I liked the people and the work; but it would have soon used me up. All the ministers were agreeable and at the meeting of the Presbytery of Louisville at Charlestown, which I attended, April, 1823, it was decided to ask the Synod to set off the new Presbytery of Salem ; which was done, and I was then expected to be the most remote member of it.[3]

[1] The third was Union church, Vigo County, organized January 8, 1823.

[2] Here Mr. Beatty solemnized the first marriage in Montgomery County, Samuel D. Maxwell, afterward first mayor of Indianapolis, being the groom.

[3] Letter dated October 9, 1876. Dr. Beatty was present at the semi-centennial celebration at Indianapolis, October, 1876. Except the Rev. Ravaud K. Rodgers, D.D., of Athens, Ga., and the Rev. Samuel G. Lowry, of Oakland, Minn., he was at that time the only survivor of all the Indiana missionaries whose service preceded the Synodical organization.

CHAPTER XI.

THE SHADOW OF SLAVERY.

1823.

AMONG the missionary appointments to Indiana for 1823 appears in the records of the Assembly the name of NICHOLAS PITTINGER from Ohio. This year brought also to the state Joseph Trimble and John Finley Crowe, of whom the one was permitted to give almost fifty years of toil to the Indiana church, while the other came only to die.

JOSEPH TRIMBLE, a licentiate of Carlisle Presbytery, Pennsylvania, was commissioned to service in the West by the General Assembly. He was tall, straight, and of rather full habit. At college his fellow-students observed the soundness of his judgment and his strong common sense. His considerable talents and engaging manners, together with the maturity of his piety and zeal, gave pleasing promise of usefulness. Reaching Madison in June, 1824, during the following month he received a call to the pastorate there. On the 10th of August the Presbytery met in special session to ordain and install him, but he was already prostrated with a bilious fever and on the day following he died. His co-presbyters assembled at his bedside, and with prayer and the singing of a hymn commended him to God—a service which is still recalled as one of the deepest pathos and solemnity. The doubly afflicted church laid him to rest near the beloved and accomplished Searle. Upon the modest tombstone is the following inscription :

In memory of Joseph Trimble, who departed this life August 11, 1824, in his 30th year. Mr. Trimble was a graduate of Jefferson College, Pennsylvania, and studied theology at Princeton Seminary; in 1823 he was licensed to preach the gospel and visited Indiana as a missionary; in 1824 he was chosen pastor of the Presbyterian church of Madison, but on the very day appointed for his ordination was called from his labors on earth to his reward in heaven. With talents and accomplishments above mediocrity, he was distinguished for his industry and energy, piety, entire devotedness to his Master's service, and the success which attended his labors. For him to live was Christ, to die was gain.[1]

A very different career was destined to be that of JOHN FINLEY CROWE, the founder of Hanover College, who had previously crossed from Kentucky into Indiana for missionary service,[2] but now came to reside within the boundaries of a free state. Born in Green County, Tenn., June 16, 1787, his early boyhood was spent amidst the privations of frontier life. The proximity of hostile savages sometimes summoned his father to the camp. In 1802 the family removed to Belle Vue, Mo., where for six years young Crowe[3] led a careless and irreligious life. But a few Presbyterian families in the neighborhood having established a prayer-meeting, his conscience was awakened and he entered upon a Christian career. He was now twenty-one years of age and soon began a course of study in preparation for the ministry. His opportunities for obtaining knowledge had been few, but he had read with avidity all the books in his father's little library and all he could borrow from others. At the age of twenty-two he left home for Danville, Ky., expecting to enter a school there, but upon his arrival he found that the school had been disbanded. In this emergency the Rev. Samuel

[1] The place of Searle's and Trimble's sepulture is likely to be abandoned to less sacred uses at no distant day. The graves are neglected. The freestone slabs are weather-beaten, moss-grown, and discolored, so that the inscriptions are scarcely legible.

[2] He had organized Corydon church, Harrison County, January 2, 1819.

[3] "Crow" was the orthography in all his own earlier correspondence.

Finley, pastor of two churches near Lexington, received him into his family and gave him instruction. In 1812, becoming a student at Transylvania University, he there remained for nearly two years. Returning in September, 1813, to Missouri, he was united in marriage to Miss Esther Alexander. The young couple soon bade adieu to their friends, packed their worldly goods into their saddle-bags, and started on horseback toward Kentucky. The whole distance was traversed, through almost unbroken forests, without fear or accident. Both had excellent voices and often made the wilderness rejoice with hymns of praise. After securing for Mrs. Crowe a home in the family of a Kentucky friend, the candidate for holy orders, still riding his horse, proceeded to Princeton to complete his studies in divinity.[1] After a year in the seminary, he was licensed, in 1815, by the Presbytery of New Brunswick.

Upon the return of Mr. Crowe to Kentucky he supplied the churches of Shiloh and Olivet in Shelby County. He afterward removed to Shelbyville, where, in addition to pastoral labors, he had charge of a female seminary. In each of these spheres of labor he was both diligent and successful. But the significant feature of his character appeared in the fact that at this same period he was editor of the *Abolition Intelligencer*, a bold and prudent opponent of slavery upon Kentucky soil. While Dickey and Martin, his future friends and companions, had already made their escape from the intolerable shadow of the peculiar institution, he remained beyond the Ohio. It was not, however, to be presumed that even the most cautious defense of man's inalienable rights could at that period in Kentucky long continue to be either agreeable or safe. It was therefore a happy relief to be summoned by providence to other duties, north of the fatal border-line.

[1] "During Mr. Crowe's connection with the seminary at Princeton he resided in the family of Colonel Beatty and was private tutor to his children, especially his son Charles, preparing him for college. C. C. B."

In 1823 Mr. Crowe received a call to the church at Hanover, and soon removed with his family to that place, just in time to be one of the original members of the first Indiana Presbytery, now shortly to be convened. In this new field he at once entered assiduously upon missionary labors, seeking, in coöperation with his brethren, to carry the gospel to the whole surrounding wilderness. "He manifested great interest in securing laborers for this territory," wrote the Rev. James H. Johnston,[1] "and was instrumental in doing much for the accomplishment of this object." It was the lack of laborers, daily pressed upon his attention as he rode among the multiplying settlements, that from the first unconsciously urged him toward the enterprise which became the distinguishing incident of his career. If ministers enough could not be gotten from abroad, was it not possible to make them here at home? This problem burned in his bones. It never let him rest. It was the quiet but constant passion of his subsequent life, enabling him without the endowments of genius and in the use of such scanty and homely materials and methods as the frontier offered, to project and achieve an enterprise of the greatest utility.

On the first of January, 1827, he opened a school for boys in a log house on his own premises. Before the close of a week six students were enrolled, and this little school was the beginning of Hanover College and of Indiana Theological Seminary, now the McCormick Seminary at Chicago. Through manifold vicissitudes and perils he continued to guard and aid this child of his faith and prayer for more than thirty years. In connection with the school he held the pastorate of the church until 1832, when he began to devote himself exclusively to the college, either as instructor or financial agent. In 1838

[1] In a letter to Professor Joshua B. Garritt, whose own MSS. have greatly aided the preparation of this sketch.

he again assumed charge of the church, retaining it until 1847, when once more he gave all his time to the college. He continued in its service until laid aside from active duties by a stroke of paralysis in January, 1859. From this stroke he recovered in a great measure, and was able to occupy himself with the preparation of a history of the institution, in founding which his own instrumentality had been so conspicuous.[1] Finally, January 17, 1860, in the seventy-third year of his age, he fell asleep.

The qualities which marked Dr. Crowe, and admirably fitted him for his task, were conscientiousness, industry, and perseverance. In early life he enjoyed few of those facilities for intellectual culture which are now common, and it was not until his majority had been reached that he turned toward a professional career. Yet he became an instructive preacher; as a teacher he secured in a high degree the respect and affection of large numbers of intelligent pupils; while his undoubted sincerity and uniform courtesy and dignity everywhere enhanced his influence. Says one of his Hanover students:[2]

> Tall, symmetrical in form, stately and dignified in appearance, kind and paternal in manner, Dr. Crowe was my beau ideal of a Christian gentleman. He was my first preceptor and spiritual guide, after my own father, and next to my father I learned to love him.

Dr. Edwards adds:

> There have been more profound scholars; there have been more brilliant popular preachers; there have been few kinder, more courteous gentlemen, few more consistent Christians.[3]

Among the services rendered by Dr. Crowe must also be emphasized his continued advocacy of the principles

---

[1] The MS. has not been printed.

[2] The Rev. William M. Cheever.

[3] Dr. J. Edwards's " Address at the Dedication of the Chapel and Library of the Seminary of the Northwest," p. 11.

THE SHADOW OF SLAVERY. 161

of civil freedom. The ministers of the old Synod of Indiana, coming in the main from the Southern States, were most intelligent and positive in their opposition to slavery, and consistent in their efforts for its removal. The constitutional prudence of Dr. Crowe did not prevent frequent references to the subject upon public occasions. At the meeting of Synod in October, 1827,

a memorial on this subject, addressed to the General Assembly of the Presbyterian Church, which had been prepared by Rev. J. Finley Crowe, was presented for our adoption and received the ready and cordial concurrence of the entire Synod. This was but nine years after the adoption by our General Assembly of those noble resolutions of 1818 in which that body had declared by a unanimous vote: "We consider the voluntary enslaving of one part of the human race by another as a gross violation of the most precious and sacred rights of human nature, as utterly inconsistent with the law of God, which requires us to love our neighbor as ourselves; and as totally irreconcilable with the spirit and principles of the gospel of Christ, which enjoins that all things whatsoever ye would that men should do to you, do ye even so to them." . . . The object of the memorial adopted by our Synod, at the meeting referred to, was simply to call the attention of the Assembly to those strong and decided utterances made but nine years before, and to urge the importance of such action on the part of the Assembly, from year to year, as would prove that those were made in sincerity and truth.[1]

The fate of this document was like that of many similar deliverances of those stormy days. It was deftly deposited in the waste-basket by the Rev. Dr. Leland, of South Carolina, chairman of the Committee on Bills and Overtures.[2]

[1] Johnston's "Ministry of Forty Years in Indiana," pp. 12, 13.
[2] See Johnston, pp. 15, 16.

CHAPTER XII.

THE FIRST PRESBYTERY.

1823, 1824.

THE origin of the oldest Indiana Presbytery is described by Dickey in his "Brief History."[1] He says:[2]

Previous to October, 1823, the churches in the state of Indiana within the bounds of the Synod of Kentucky were under the care of the Louisville Presbytery, which generally met in the fall in Kentucky and in the spring in Indiana. By an act of the Synod, October, 1823, all that part of the state of Indiana which lies west of a line due north from the mouth of the Kentucky River was constituted into a new Presbytery, denominated the Salem Presbytery, which at its formation consisted of the following members, viz.: William Robinson, John Todd, Samuel T. Scott, William W. Martin, John M. Dickey, John F. Crow, and Isaac Reed. In October, 1824, all that part of the state of Illinois belonging to the Synod of Kentucky, which lies north of a line due west from the mouth of White River, was added to this Presbytery. At the same time that part of the state of Indiana which lies south and west of the following lines, viz.: beginning opposite the mouth of Green River, running due north twenty miles, thence northwesterly to the mouth of White River, was attached to Muhlenburg Presbytery. The Salem Presbytery held its first meeting at Salem in April, 1824. All the ministers belonging to the Presbytery were present except one, who was prevented by age and infirmity.[3]

The following is a transcript of the records of the first meeting of Salem Presbytery:

Salem, April 1, 1824. The Salem Presbytery met agreeably to

---

[1] For the earlier ecclesiastical relations of the Indiana Presbyterians see Appendix II.
[2] Pp. 19, 20.
[3] The absentee was William Robinson.

a resolution of the Synod of Kentucky and was opened with a sermon by the Rev. Samuel T. Scott on Ephesians iv.: 3, 4, and was constituted by prayer. Members present: Samuel T. Scott, John Todd, John M. Dickey, William W. Martin, Isaac Reed, and John F. Crow, ministers; with Lemuel Ford, Alexander Walker, William Reed, John Holme, James McPheeters, James Carnahan, Thomas N. White, Jonathan E. Garrison, William Alexander, Peter Ryker, John Martin, Samuel S. Graham, and Andrew Weir, elders. Absent, the Rev. William Robinson. Mr. Crow was chosen moderator, and Mr. Dickey clerk. Messrs. Todd, Dickey, and Alexander were appointed a committee to prepare a standing docket. Messrs. W. W. Martin, Dickey, and White were appointed a committee to prepare a narrative on the state of religion, and Messrs. Scott, I. Reed, and Ford were appointed a committee to prepare a Presbyterial report.

Resolved, That the rules appended to the new edition of the Confession of Faith be adopted as general rules for the government of this Presbytery.

Resolved, That William W. Martin, Isaac Reed, and Samuel S. Graham be a committee to prepare a system of by-laws for this Presbytery. A call having been presented to the Louisville Presbytery by the Salem congregation for one half of the ministerial labors of the Rev. Wm. W. Martin, which business properly belongs now to the Salem Presbytery, therefore

Resolved, That the installation of Mr. Martin be the order of the day for Saturday at 11 o'clock; and that Mr. Scott preach the sermon, and Mr. Dickey preside and give the charge. Rev. William Martin and Lemuel Ford, an elder of the Charlestown church, were appointed commissioners to the next General Assembly.

Mr. Tilly H. Brown presented himself to Presbytery as a candidate for the gospel ministry and requested to be taken under its care.

Resolved, That the request of Mr. Brown be attended to to-morrow morning, 8 o'clock. Petitions for supplies were made by the churches of Jefferson, Shiloh, Washington, Graham, Blue River, Dartmouth, and Bloomington. Presbytery then adjourned till to-morrow morning, 8 o'clock. Concluded with prayer.

April 2. Presbytery met according to adjournment and was constituted with prayer. Members present as on yesterday. The minutes of the last session were then read and Presbytery proceeded to the consideration of Mr. Brown's request.

WHEREAS, Mr. Brown has been under the care of the Louisville

Presbytery and examined on experimental religion and his motives for seeking the sacred office, likewise on the Latin and Greek languages, geography and astronomy, which examinations were sustained, and he was directed by the Louisville Presbytery to prepare a lecture on Matthew v.: 17-20, and a sermon on 1st John ii.: 2 ; but while attending to the above parts of trial he was dismissed at his own request on account of ill health ; therefore

Resolved, That Mr. Brown be received agreeably to his request and that he prepare a lecture and a sermon on the subjects assigned him, against the next meeting of this Presbytery, and that he attend also to theology and other studies under the direction of Mr. Crow, with a view to his licensure.

The committee to prepare a standing docket presented their report, which was approved and adopted and is as follows: 1st. The choice of a moderator and clerk. 2d. The reading of the general rules and by-laws. 3d. The reading of the minutes of the last stated sessions. 4th. Calls and supplications. 5th. The appointment of committees : (1) to examine the sessional records ; (2) to prepare a Presbyterial report ; (3) to prepare a narrative on the state of religion ; (4) to settle with the treasurer ; (5) to report to the Board of Education. 6th. An inquiry into the state of religion within our bounds. 7th. An inquiry respecting education of youth for the ministry. 8th. A call for sessional records. 9th. A call for congregational reports. 10th. Unfinished business of last Presbytery. 11th. Appointment of commissioners to the General Assembly. 12th. A call for monies collected (1) for the education fund; (2) for the commissioners' fund; (3) for the missionary fund ; (4) for the Presbyterial fund ; (5) for the theological seminary. 13th. Appointments to supply. 14th. The time and place of the next meeting of Presbytery.

William W. Martin was chosen stated clerk of Presbytery and John M. Dickey treasurer. The committee to prepare a system of by-laws made their report, which was amended and adopted and is as follows: 1st. The Salem Presbytery shall have two stated sessions in the year, one in April and one in October, and these shall be in rotation in the churches. 2d. Presbytery shall carefully inquire into the state of the churches under its care and particularly that church in the bounds of which the Presbytery may meet. 3d. Presbytery shall establish a fund to defray its incidental expenses, to which at each stated meeting each member shall contribute fifty cents. 4th. The Presbytery shall take measures to defray the expense of their commissioner to the

General Assembly, and shall require the churches under its care to take up collections and forward the money to the spring meetings of Presbytery. 5th. The Presbytery enjoins it on all the churches under its care to make some pecuniary compensation for missionary labors spent among them or occasional supplies sent them by Presbytery. 6th. The sacrament of the Lord's Supper shall be administered at each stated meeting of Presbytery, under the direction of the moderator with the sessions of the church where the Presbytery may meet. 7th. Presbytery shall spend a part of the first day of its meeting, if convenient, in stated prayer to God for the outpouring of his spirit on the churches, for unanimity and harmony in the efforts of the Presbytery in promoting the divine glory by the salvation of souls; and the moderator shall direct in these exercises. 8th. This Presbytery shall use vigorous exertions to educate poor and pious youth for the gospel ministry, and in this way endeavor to supply the vacant churches with the means of grace. 9th. Presbytery shall require the churches to forward their congregational reports to the spring meetings of Presbytery and their sessional records and reports to the fall meetings. 10th. Presbytery shall at each spring meeting consider the expediency of addressing a pastoral letter to the churches under its care. 11th. A missionary sermon shall be preached at each stated meeting and a collection for the purpose of missions within our bounds shall be taken up. 12th. Presbytery shall require the churches under its care to assemble regularly for social prayer on vacant Sabbaths, under the direction of the ruling elders of the several churches. To this profitable exercise the Presbytery call the attention of their beloved people. 13th. Presbytery most earnestly recommend to the elders of vacant churches to attend to catechetical instruction of the youth of the congregation and that they particularly impress on professing parents to pray in their families and to bring up their children in the nurture and admonition of the Lord.

Resolved, That each member take a copy of the two last articles of the by-laws and that the stated clerk furnish with a copy the churches not represented at this meeting.

Received for the commissioners' fund from the church of Indianapolis $4; from Bethany church, $3; from Bloomington, $4.25; from New Lexington, $2.50. Received from the members for the Presbyterial fund, $7.50.

Resolved, That the committee on the state of religion also prepare a pastoral letter to be addressed to the churches and that the Rev. Isaac Reed be added to that committee.

Presbytery then proceeded to a free conversation on the state of religion within the bounds of the Presbytery. Mr. Henry Rice, an elder in the church of Corydon, appeared in Presbytery and took his seat. Adjourned till to-morrow morning at 8 o'clock. Concluded with prayer.

April 3d. Presbytery met according to adjournment and was constituted by prayer. Members present as on yesterday. The committee to make a narrative of the state of religion reported, which was approved and adopted. The committee to prepare a Presbyterial report reported, which was approved. The stated clerk was directed to forward the Presbyterial report and the narrative of the state of religion to the stated clerk of the General Assembly in due time, and also to the Society of Inquiry in Princeton Theological Seminary.

Messrs. Crow, Dickey, W. Reed, Walker, and Ford were appointed a committee of education to devise ways and means for the education of poor and pious youths for the ministry, and that they report at the spring meeting of Presbytery. The committee to prepare a pastoral letter was ordered to have it printed and sent to the churches in the bounds of this Presbytery.

Mr. Scott was appointed to supply one Sabbath at Washington, one at Carlisle, and one at Hopewell; Mr. Todd, three Sabbaths, one in New Albany, one in Graham church, and one in Mr. John Martin's neighborhood; Mr. Dickey, one Sabbath in Nazareth church; Mr. Martin, one Sabbath in Corydon, one in Bloomington, and one in Terre Haute; Mr. Reed, one Sabbath at New Albany, one at Indianapolis, one at Crawfordsville, and one in Shiloh church; Mr. Crow, one Sabbath at Dartmouth, one at Bloomington, one at Washington, and one at Jefferson church.

Resolved, That Presbytery aid as far as possible Samuel Gregg and James Crawford at the Princeton Seminary, now prosecuting their studies, and that contributions be made in the churches for that object.

Mr. Martin was appointed to preach the missionary sermon at the next stated meeting of Presbytery.

Saturday, 11 o'clock, Mr. Martin was installed pastor of Salem church. Presbytery then adjourned to meet at Charlestown the second Friday of October, 12 o'clock. Concluded with prayer.

JOHN F. CROW, Moderator.
JOHN M. DICKEY, Clerk.

These are the records of a small beginning indeed, but every line has life in it. There is only a handful of people, but the men are good and true, and the great harvests that have grown from the seed they sowed will surprise no intelligent student of Christian history.

TILLY H. BROWN, the young man who at this first meeting of the first Presbytery applied for licensure, and whose studies had already been delayed by feeble health, never sufficiently recovered his strength to endure the hardships of the frontier ministry. A native of Fitchburg, Mass., he was licensed October 9, 1824 (the first Presbyterian licensure in Indiana); was ordained and installed over Bethlehem and Blue River churches June 25, 1825; served them one year, found his health again failing, engaged in teaching, and died in 1849, at the age of fifty-four. He showed a remarkable degree of conscientious devotion to the Master's work.

JOHN T. HAMILTON, in 1823 receiving licensure from Muhlenburg Presbytery, came to Indiana in July of the year following and connected himself with Salem Presbytery, October, 1826. He was another of the Presbyterians preordained to teach a school, but on alternate Sabbaths until February, 1828, he also occupied the pulpit of the New Albany church. This society had suffered greatly since the death of Mr. Day in September, 1823. They were in a condition to receive gratefully even a partial dispensation of the Word. "During this period it is worthy of being recorded to the praise of God's grace that the members of the church were generally bound to each other in Christian love, liberal in their contributions, active in the promotion of benevolent associations, and considerably regular in their attendance on religious meetings, both public and social."

While engaged at New Albany Mr. Hamilton for two years gave a part of his time to the Charlestown congregation. In the following note to the pastor at Madison, dated Charlestown, September 30, 1826, he briefly alludes to a "peril" which St. Paul must have omitted from his famous catalogue only because he had never encountered it:

Dear Brother: I have appointed a sacramental meeting in this place on the third Sabbath in October and I earnestly desire your assistance on that occasion. Since I made the appointment I have taken the fever and ague, and am unable to do anything. My family are all sick. Do come if possible.

Near the close of his term of service at New Albany Mr. Hamilton removed his family to Louisville, where he engaged in teaching. He was dismissed to Louisville Presbytery April 4, 1828. "The members of the church were much distressed after his departure, and while they sought in various ways to obtain assistance they gave themselves unto prayer that God would succeed their endeavors and send them a minister of his own choosing."[1] "A modest, retiring man he preached the truth in the love of it, and the congregation was warmly attached to him."[2]

[1] Cf. "Records of New Albany Session."
[2] Conn's MS. "History of Presbyterianism in New Albany."

CHAPTER XIII.

HELP FROM PRINCETON.
1824.

WITH the establishment of Salem Presbytery a new and more hopeful prospect opens. Thus far the work had been too transient and uncertain. A considerable number of men, thirty-five or forty in all, had come and gone as itinerants. Of the actual settlers Baldridge had removed to Ohio, Proctor to Kentucky, and Balch, Hickman, Searle, Day, and Trimble, more than one third of the entire company of residents, had died. All except the first of these in youth or early manhood had yielded to the violent maladies of the new country. Of the seven remaining to form the Presbytery, two, Scott and Robinson, were near the end of their journey. John Ross was settling at Richmond just about the time of the Salem meeting, but he was east of the Presbyterial limit, within the bounds of Miami.

The little band immediately received, however, most valuable accessions. With the exception of SAMUEL TAYLOR, sent to Morgan County by the Assembly's committee, those who arrived in 1824 became residents. Tilly H. Brown and John T. Hamilton have already been mentioned. The remaining five constitute a remarkable company of enthusiastic Princeton fellow-students. Bush, the commentator; Hall, first principal of the Bloomington State Seminary; Williamson, from Cumberland Valley, Pa.; Young, an early victim of the prevailing disease; and Johnston, for Indiana the most notable name of all.

GEORGE BUSH was a scholar whom the world now claims. Born in Norwich, Vt., June 12, 1796, educated at

Dartmouth, whence he graduated in 1818[1] with the highest honors, completing the theological course at Princeton ; serving as tutor in Princeton College ; licensed by the Presbytery of New York,[2] preaching for a time at Morristown, N. J., he came to Indiana, taking charge of the congregation at the capital. At Dartmouth, Dr. Marsh, subsequently of the Vermont University, Professor Thomas C. Upham, of Bowdoin, and Rufus Choate had been his classmates, the latter his roommate and friend. Mr. Bush brought with him from Dartmouth and Princeton not a little distinction for classical and oriental scholarship, and for graces of style in literary composition,[3] a reputation which his subsequent career fully justified.

On the 9th of July, 1824, Mr. Bush arrived at Indianapolis, having obtained a commission apparently from the Assembly's Committee of Missions.[4] He at once began to preach in the court-house, the meeting-house being still incomplete. September 6 the congregation "voted unanimously by ballot that they are desirous to settle Mr. Bush as their pastor,[5] and appointed Daniel Yandes, Obed Foote, and Isaac Coe a committee to circulate a subscription for his support." At the schoolroom in the church, Saturday afternoon, September 18, at 3 o'clock, a meeting of the society, of which the Rev. Isaac Reed was modera-

[1] David C. Proctor, his predecessor at Indianapolis, was a classmate.

[2] " Minutes Salem Presbytery," Vol. I., p. 16. Dr. Coe's MS. " History of the First Church, Indianapolis " agrees with the above. According to Dickey's history (p. 16) Mr. Bush was a licentiate of New Brunswick Presbytery.

[3] See an appreciative notice of Bush in Griswold's " Prose Writers of America," pp. 354–6.

[4] This is the statement in Coe's MS. It seems to be implied in Gillett's reference to the matter, Vol. II., p. 409. The next year his commission was from the United Domestic Missionary Society of New York, " for twelve months from May 16, 1825."—" Fourth Annual Report of U. D. M. S.," p. 25.

[5] The congregation had previously, after Mr. Proctor's removal, made unsuccessful overtures to the Revs. Samuel D. Hoge and Wm. W. Martin, the latter, however, not receiving the invitation from the irregular post until months had elapsed and negotiations with Mr. Bush had begun.

tor, formally extended him a unanimous call, and Isaac Coe, Caleb Scudder, James Blake, Alexander Frazer, William W. Wick, and James M. Ray were directed to sign the call for the congregation. Mr. Bush was accordingly ordained[1] and installed by Salem Presbytery, March 5, 1825, his examination and trials having been unanimously, and, as the record suggests, with unusual cordiality, sustained. Crowe, Dickey, and Reed conducted the service. Immediately after Mr. Bush returned to the East, to attend the General Assembly, bringing back with him in July his newly-married wife, an accomplished daughter of the Hon. Lewis Condict, of Morristown, N. J.

The settlement of such a man in the aguish little hamlet, surrounded by bogs, overshadowed by the "forest primeval," and overgrown with dog-fennel, was a great event. He immediately drew about him the most thoughtful and prominent citizens. He easily made friends. Tasks laid upon him by the Presbytery he cheerfully assumed. Frequent calls for aid at "sacramental meetings" he willingly accepted. The literary work that controlled his later activity was already taking possession of him. Under his leadership the prospects of the Indianapolis flock seemed most flattering.

It could not be expected, however, that his original and erratic genius would long be satisfied with the old paths. Some of the more intelligent listeners occasionally heard a sentence that startled them. The session, representing a good deal of Scottish fervor and possibly a very little Caledonian obstinacy, were alarmed. About December 1, 1826, Mr. Bush declared from the pulpit that there was not a shadow of scriptural authority for the Presbyterian form of church government.[2] This led to numerous conferences

[1] This was the first Presbyterian ordination in Indiana. Reed's " Christian Traveller," p. 200.
[2] See Coe's MS. history.

between the pastor and the elders, and Mr. Bush presented in writing a statement of his opinions concerning the questions in dispute. This statement refers to eight separate points, as follows :

(1) . . . It is not clear that there is any other visible church besides this on the earth. I cannot therefore at the present time agree to the definition of the church given in the confession, as it would seem to exclude all who have not made a profession though they may all belong to the spiritual body of Christ.

(2) The great objection I have to the Presbyterian scheme lies in this, that it holds forth a vast visible body which is said to be in the order of nature prior to single or particular churches, . . . with jurisdiction over the component parts. I object to it because I do not find Scripture warrant for the existence of such a body, and moreover because I perceive it is precisely on that foundation that the kingdom of anti-Christ was erected. For if the united body of Christ is to be considered as visible, it will naturally lead to a visible head, the fountain of church power, and whether this be in the shape of a pope or General Assembly the principle is the same, and for aught I can see the consequences will be likely to be the same. Both are opposed to the supreme headship of Christ; not but the Presbyterian system may be carried on for a length of time without any very great abuses, but I conceive the tendency is such as I have intimated.

(3) I hold to associations of churches and pastors for purposes of mutual edification and coöperation in advancing the interests of truth and godliness. But I object to them being regarded as stated tribunals, and would abolish such terms as "courts" and "judicatories," as tending insensibly to beget wrong ideas of the true nature of such councils of Christ's servants ; neither would I have them organized in several grades.

(4) I object to that feature of the confession which insists so strenuously on complete uniformity in this respect ; nor does it appear to be consistent with other parts of the system, as may be shown.

(5) It appears that the Presbyterian view of the visible church leads to great laxness in the admission of members, this right of admission not being grounded upon the evidence of reality of conversion, but upon a profession of it.

(6) As to a single church I hold that the government is vested in the proper officers of the church, which are elders and deacons, although I consider that it is the duty of the whole church to judge of any important business in the church, and that every affair of moment should be done with their knowledge and concurrence, and generally in their presence.

(7) I hold that in every rightly constituted church there should be a plurality of elders, that these constitute what is properly called the "eldership" or "presbytery" of a church, which I conceive is all the presbytery spoken of in the Scriptures. These elders I regard as all pastors, whose duty it is to feed the flock of Christ and to rule in it by his word, not lording it over God's heritage, but being ensamples; that they are all of equal authority; that they are all equally the clergy; that the title "lay elder" is improper; that although the officer is the same, yet there are different departments, among which "laboring in word and doctrine" is the principal, and entitles the incumbent to pecuniary support. Though cases might occur in which even all the elders in a church might properly receive maintenance from the church. All that is here asserted I conceive may be fairly proved from the word of God, and also that the practices and notions now prevalent respecting the elder's office may be traced to the ambition of the clergy.

(8) I hold that ordination confers no office power whatever, but merely recognizes such power or character already conferred by the Holy Ghost. Hence the presbytery of a single church might lawfully ordain an elder without the concurrence of any other person. Although I would esteem it most prudent and becoming, whenever it was practicable, to obtain such concurrence.

This statement was not calculated to reassure the minds of sturdy Presbyterians. They thought Mr. Bush's system "agreed with no other on earth, was erroneous in theory and unattainable in practice, as well as inconsistent with itself."[1] They thought it, however, desirable to retain their minister, if he would refrain from the public expression of his peculiar opinions. This, of course, Mr. Bush would not consent to, and the negotiation was terminated where it began by the departure of Mr. Bush

[1] Dr. Coe's manuscript.

for the East in April, 1827, to attend the Assembly and to advocate in that region the claims of the Home Missionary Society.[1]

He writes to a friend from Princeton, June 3, as follows:

As our session, that of the Assembly I mean, has just closed, and I have a little leisure, it will not probably be unacceptable to receive a little sketch of our proceedings. . . . And, imprimis, the petition of the Synod respecting the boundary line between us and Ohio failed. . . . The next matter of moment is the business of the Western Seminary. This is to be located at Allegheny and Dr. Janeway is to be professor; at least he is chosen, though he has not signified his acceptance. There was a strong pull and a strong vote for Walnut Hills, and if the vote had been taken again, an hour after it was, Walnut Hills would have got it. The votes were 44 to 42. I gave my voice for Allegheny on the ground that it would be better supported at that place than the other. The grand objections to Allegheny were that it was not central and that it would interfere with Princeton—serious difficulties, I acknowledge, but I am not sure that we want such a seminary as is contemplated any farther west, and therefore did not plead hard for Charlestown,[2] which would have stood no chance against the formidable bids of the other two sites. . . .

And now a few words for myself. It is uncertain whether I return to the West. This I say, not because I have secretly resolved not to return, but to pre-intimate to you not to be surprised in case I should openly resolve in this way. You will at once inquire, What has happened to make it uncertain? I answer, Nothing new. The old sore still runs and the symptoms are worse. Shall I return to Indianapolis merely to tear a peaceful church to pieces, and stand in such a peculiarly unpleasant relation to my former brethren, whom I dearly love, but who could not act with me on any other ground than that of strict Presbyterianism? What shall I do? I am willing to go to the West and live and die there. But I could not live at Indianapolis except as a Presbyterian, and where else in the state would you as a friend

---

[1] At the first anniversary of the society, in May, he presented one of the resolutions in an important address. See first report of A. H. M. S., p. 6.

[2] Clark County, Ind., would seem to be rather a feeble rival of Allegheny and Walnut Hills, as a site for a divinity school. There was no audacity of faith of which these pioneers were incapable, however. And three years later they sent off Dr. Crowe to Virginia for Dr. Matthews, and successfully opened the Theological School at Hanover.

advise me to go? How am I racked with a troubled mind. And among the worst of all thoughts is this, that you and others will think the cause insignificant. But whether little or great, it is with me purely a matter of conscience, and its dictates I must follow. Pray let me hear from you. Direct to Morristown. My work[1] is now in the press at this place. The system and plan of the questions is highly approved, so far as it has been examined. As to my agency[2] I am thinking of setting out immediately or of getting released.

The following day from New York he writes to a member of the session,[3] and after alluding again to the possibility of remaining in the East, and assuring his correspondent that it is "not from any dissatisfaction with the place or country," he continues:

I am perfectly willing to live and die in Indiana. I am strongly attached to the dear people with whom I have lived and labored. Indeed I knew not till since I have left them how much I loved them. But the reason of my hesitation about returning is I cannot hope to serve God according to those rules which I conscientiously believe he has laid down in his word for the government of his people. I wish, therefore, to be placed in a situation where I can act upon those principles of church order which the great Head of the church has instituted and enjoined. In several important points I do not regard the Presbyterian polity as being that which Christ has established, or which I can properly countenance even by the slender influence of my example or practice.

The grand features of the scheme to which I principally object are the authority claimed by their courts, for which I find no warrant in Scripture; and the admission, expulsion, and discipline of members being carried on without the presence and concurrence of the body of the believers. Not that all are officers by any means; the exclusive performance of these duties belongs to the proper officers whom Christ hath appointed. But this power is to be exercised in the body and not out of it. . . .

Such are briefly my views on this point, and from all that is past have I not every reason to believe that I could not return and

[1] This was the germ of his commentaries.
[2] For the American Home Missionary Society.
[3] Mr. Ebenezer Sharpe.

endeavor to have the church modelled on these principles without tearing it to pieces? And in its present infant state would it be wisdom or duty to think of such a thing? Let me say, however, I do not wish to set up entirely another church, nor would my principles lead to any such consequences; but all I wish is to keep as close as possible to the New Testament model, for I should then feel safest and have most hope of the presence and blessing of Christ. And I have learned that there are many churches in the Presbyterian connection which deviate still more widely than I propose from the authorized platform. I submit these views of the matter to your candid and Christian consideration, and as I began by saying that I now feel somewhat uncertain whether I shall return to remain permanently in Indiana, I wish, however, to hear from you as soon as practicable, as your answer will probably govern my final decision.

On receiving a reply to the foregoing Mr. Bush wrote, August 23, 1827, from Morristown :

I am willing to refer the matter to the Presbytery or Synod. Let either of these bodies be selected as judges, and if they upon a fair representation of the case declare that I cannot act conscientiously as a Presbyterian pastor, and that it would be improper and unfavorable to the interests of religion that your church should employ me, I will submit to the decision, withdraw from the connection, and endeavor to serve God and my generation some other way.
. . . On mature consideration I am not clear that my opinions of church government are unequivocally hostile to the confession when rightly understood. Therefore, it seems to me that so long as I do nothing and say nothing contrary to the true intent of the acknowledged standards of the church I ought not to be excluded from a post of usefulness which I have made great sacrifices to attain.

Late in the summer Mr. Bush returned to Indiana. But other clouds gathered about him. Theological debate was for the time abruptly closed, and all hearts were touched with sympathy by the severe illness of the pastor's accomplished and amiable wife. On the ninth of November she fell asleep. On the occasion of her funeral[1]

---

[1] Mrs. Bush lies buried in Greenlawn Cemetery, Indianapolis. The following is the inscription on the native stone: "Sacred to the memory of Mrs. Anna B. Bush, con-

the Rev. William Lowry, whose lamented death in the swollen Whitewater occurred soon after, delivered a discourse remarkable for its beauty and power.

The conflict, however, of a mind like that of Mr. Bush with the Presbyterian system, and with every fixed and rigorous system, was inevitable. Sorrow might interrupt the debate, but it could not solve the problem. Indeed it is more than likely that the wise influence of Mrs. Bush upon her husband had delayed his erratic course and prevented a much earlier divergence from the old paths.[1] At any rate, events were rapidly precipitated after the wife's hand had been withdrawn.

On the 25th of February, 1828, Mr. Bush addressed a letter to the session setting forth the terms, under three particulars, on which he was "willing to live and if it (should) be the Lord's will to die among the people of his charge." The three particulars were: (1) that the brethren have the privilege of being present at all meetings of the session; (2) that he might consider himself to have the hearty concurrence of the session in his privilege of talking, writing, publishing, or preaching, relative to the constitution, laws, and order of the church, whatever, whenever, wherever, and in what way soever he might think proper, if consistent with his general duty to Christ; (3) that three hundred dollars be provided annually for three fourths of his time, and as much more be paid him as might be raised.

This communication was succeeded by a lengthy and tedious correspondence, in which not the slightest progress was made. It was the old meeting between "two irresistible forces"—a mind so independent that it first

sort of the Rev. George Bush, and daughter of the Hon. Lewis Condict, M. C., of Morristown, New Jersey. She died strong in the Christian hope, November 9th, 1827, aged xxvii. Precious in the eyes of the Lord is the death of his saints."

[1] The hiding of Glass's "Works" from her husband was one of the wifely expedients recalled by an Indianapolis friend.

imagined chains and then chafed under them, and a half dozen Virginia and Kentucky Calvinists representing the venerable and symmetrical system of our church. The congregation was finally convened, March 10, 1828; Dr. Coe presented an elaborate defense of Presbyterian polity, and after considerable discussion and an adjournment till evening, application was made to Wabash Presbytery for a dissolution of the pastoral relation. The petition was granted at a special meeting at Indianapolis June 22, 1828. Mr. Bush brought the subject before Synod by complaint, and that body, with but two dissenting voices, sustained the Presbyterial action, at the same time declaring, however, that said action "should not be understood to imply that (Mr. Bush's) private sentiments are so heretical that he ought to be disclaimed by the Presbyterian connection."[1] Synod also recommended to the session of the church to "use for the present all possible forbearance" and appointed a committee to visit the church and promote its harmony.[2] The tenor of this action of Synod induced the session to go, by complaint, to the court of last resort. Meanwhile the local excitement was greatly promoted by the preaching of Mr. Bush in the courthouse to a separate congregation and his appointment of a stated prayer-meeting at his own house, after the dissolution of the pastoral relation. This arrangement continued until March, 1829, when Mr. Bush finally withdrew and returned East.[3] It does not appear, however, that he ever transferred his connection from Wabash to any other Presbytery of our church.

[1] "Minutes Synod of Indiana," Vol. I., pp. 75-7.

[2] "Minutes Synod of Indiana," Vol. I., p. 83.

[3] The Rev. John R. Moreland had been called to succeed him in the pastorate October 27, 1828. Mr. Moreland had spent the earlier years of his life as a boatman on the Ohio, and had enjoyed but small opportunities to obtain an education. His style of preaching was somewhat rough, but full of warmth and energy and often productive of the deepest impressions. His pastorate was terminated by his death, October 13, 1832.

On the 29th of the following April he writes from Cincinnati :

You perceive by my date that I am still in this city of "bustle, brick, and business." I have concluded to make an effort to get my books into circulation, or at least into notice, and as they are not yet out of press, I shall probably be compelled to remain here till the latter part of May. In the mean time, in order to keep straight with men and things, and not grow poor myself while aiming to make others rich, I have embarked for a few weeks in the editorship of the *Pandect*, which without special efforts will not live.

Although I have not seen Mr. S. I am in hopes to get him to take out twenty-five copies of my pamphlet on "Ezekiel's Vision," which I will thank you to sell. . . .

Messrs. Campbell and Owen have been the great topics of talk recently. The two disputants have been seen, within a day or two, walking arm in arm through Main Street, so that the inference is, that though not both Harmonists, they are still harmonious.

At the opening of the following year he is again in his old haunts at Princeton, and writes :

When we last met, or rather when we last parted, I had little thought that my next communication would be dated Princeton, N. J. Yet here I am, the wheel of providence having rolled round and landed me where I was six years ago. I came to this place about three months since with the design of spending the winter in the prosecution of scriptural studies, with the valuable aid of the libraries and the learned society here to be enjoyed. You will probably think this a strange movement, yet if I as a conscientious man can justify it to myself, and be fattening in this green pasture while so many strayed sheep are wandering upon the mountains, you of course will be satisfied. I confess I have little hopes of making my steps plausible, and not any great anxiety to do it, but as I have always dealt freely and candidly with you, I will say that it is purely out of conscience that I am not employed at this time as a preacher and pastor. I can no more act in the Presbyterian connection than I can in the Roman Catholic.[1] For my soul I dare not do it. . . .

[1] It will be seen how gradually but certainly his mind had drifted from his earlier beliefs. This was 1830. In 1827 he had said : " I am not clear that my opinions of church government are unequivocally hostile to the confession when rightly understood."

God has graciously, I believe, rewarded the stand I have taken against human usurpations with giving me an insight into his prophetic oracles that is most enrapturing. O how astonishingly have my views of heaven, the judgment, the resurrection, altered in two years' time. Yet the world, even the professing world, cannot, will not, receive it, and I shall as certainly be accounted a dreaming enthusiast as I am a living man. . . It will finally be beyond dispute that in the great fundamental principles of my construction of the word of God, I am right. No thanks to me; for I acknowledge sovereign grace in every step. . . . I am delivering lectures weekly in the church on the Apocalypse. Dr. Alexander attends regularly—has declared himself well satisfied, and even more. May possibly publish hereafter. . . . I think much of Indiana, and should be happy to sit down at your table or your fireside, but am only able, sitting at my own, to assure you of the continued friendship and fellowship of your brother in the gospel.

In 1831 Mr. Bush was elected to the professorship of Hebrew and Oriental Literature in the University of the City of New York, and thus was afforded the best advantages for prosecuting those investigations for which his genius and learning qualified him. His first important publication was the "Life of Mohammed," which appeared in 1832. It was succeeded the year after by a "Treatise on the Millennium," and subsequently by "Scriptural Illustrations."[1] In 1835 his "Hebrew Grammar" was issued, a second edition having been called for three years later. The publication of his commentaries on the Old Testament was commenced in 1840. The *Hierophant*, a monthly magazine, began its career in 1844. The same year he published his "Anastasis," replying to his critics in a kindred work on the "Resurrection of Christ."

It was in 1845 that Professor Bush openly accepted the doctrines of Emanuel Swedenborg, after which time he devoted himself to their defense. He translated Swedenborg's diary from the Latin; published with notes others of

[1] Harper's *Family Library*, Vol. X.

his writings; made a "Statement of Reasons for joining the New Church," and became editor of the *New Church Repository*. In 1847 he published a work on "Mesmerism," and in 1857, "Priesthood and Clergy unknown to Christianity." Much study impaired his health and he died at Rochester, N. Y., September 19, 1859. He was at the time pastor of a small Swedenborgian congregation there.

During his long residence in New York City his Indiana friends had opportunities to renew the old fellowship, which he welcomed as warmly as they. He also for a long time maintained a correspondence with some of them. Two of his letters of that period so fully reveal the tendencies of his mind and the kindliness of his heart, and are withal so characteristically expressed that they have more than local interest.

NEW YORK, September 1, 1831.

My Dear Friend: After a long, very long season of silence, I propose to become once more vocal, or at least significant, and to disturb the dormancy of speech; a signal, I hope, for your doing the same thing. That I have not for nearly a year heard by letter the least syllable of news, good or ill, from Indianapolis I attribute in some measure to my own neglect; for I doubt not my friends there would have had something to say to me had they known where to direct, or been at all certain that their written missives would have hit the mark. It has indeed so happened for the most part during the last two years and a half that my mode of life has been as unsettled as an Arab's, and even up to this hour I must say with Paul, "I have no certain dwelling-place." My anchor, however, for the present is cast in this haven and I am in hopes not to be under the necessity of weighing it again for a long time to come. At any rate my friends may be sure that any communications addressed to this place will safely reach their destination.

I have had several opportunities, and such too as most wandering Levites would consider eligible, to fix myself in a permanent location; but there has almost invariably been some vexatious condition about them that grated too harshly on my liberty-loving cords, and I of course refused them. I am still a sworn enemy to conditions, terms, pledges, vows, promises—to everything in fine that fetters the exercise of the most unlimited freedom both in opinion and action. And because all sects in religion are pestering the world with these miserable nuisances, I am an anti-sectarian, as warm a one as Richard Rush is an anti-Mason; and then, lastly, because I am an anti of this description, I find favor and friendship next to nowhere. This has prevented my settlement. But my opinions on the subject of religious liberty are fixed, and I am ready, if needs be, to become a martyr to them. I know they will, they must, finally prevail. They may possibly be permitted to starve me and a few others to death before they eventually triumph, but their success is certain. The day of human creeds is drawing toward its sunset, to be followed by a long bright day of pure Bible law, the approach of which all good men will hail from the bottom of their hearts.

But, not to moralize, my present location is extremely pleasant. I have a nook monastic in the lower part of Greenwich Street, near the Battery, where I am pretty constantly employed pondering my polyglots and plying my pen.[1] My brother is an inmate under the same roof. I have matters forthcoming of which the speaking time is not quite arrived. One advantage of my present residence is that it affords me the opportunity of visiting my dear child at Morristown. . . . He talks a great deal about his

[1] This picture agrees with one presented by the *Providence Journal* soon after his decease, and referring to a period a little subsequent to the above. The *Journal* says: "The professor was twice married, the second time ten or twelve years ago, when his circumstances were somewhat improved. For several years he occupied a very small room in the fourth or fifth story of a building on the corner of Beekman and Nassau Streets, in New York, the walls of which were lined with old books, Hebrew, Greek, Latin, and German preponderating. On the floor, too, were piles of huge volumes in vellum—Bibles, commentaries, and lexicons in the oriental languages. A pine table, two or three wooden chairs, a small stove which retained its place the year round, and a cot bed, constituted his furniture. For years neither brush nor broom disturbed the accumulated dust of this secluded retreat, and here the professor wrote those translations of and learned commentaries on several books of the Old Testament which have made his name widely known among theologians of Europe and America. On his second marriage this sanctum was abandoned and he removed his books to his dwelling-house in Howard Street, where he lived many years. Professor Bush was particularly fond of attending book auctions. It gave him a little harmless excitement, brought him in contact with literary men, who, like himself, were ever mousing about for rare and choice books, and enabled him to procure the books he wanted at low prices. Indeed it may be said that nine tenths of his books were purchased at auction; besides as there were few competitors for the literature he sought, he often got Latin, Hebrew, German, and various oriental books for a mere song. After using his books a few years, and getting from them all he required, he would send them to auction to make way for others."

mother, and when I showed him a ring that was hers he kissed it most affectionately two or three times. . . .

I wish you would favor me with a letter filled full of all manner of news—personal, domestical, political, theological, statistical, topographical, biographical, and so on. I wish to know how your town prospers and promises and what important changes have taken place latterly among the inhabitants, such of them as I know.

To the same :

NEW YORK, June 18, 1836.

The return of Mr. Sullivan, who has visited me several times, offers an opportunity too favorable to be lost of at least sending a greeting of friendship. It is pleasant thus just to hail each other, while sailing in our respective courses on the ocean of time, and gratefully hear the "All's well" returned from either party. May we ever be able to give this response mutually while voyaging onward to our final haven, and then have it exchanged for the "Well done" of our Lord and master.

. . . I am still mainly employed in the line of book-making, of which I send you a little specimen. My works have never as yet been very popular or profitable, but on the whole are perhaps looking up. I am now *totis in illis* in preparing a set of notes on the Old Testament, precisely on the plan of Barnes on the New. The first volume will probably be published next fall. I shall commence with Joshua and publish on the Pentateuch afterward.

As you may possibly have heard, I am now connected as literary editor with the American Bible Society. My duties are to superintend the text of all our editions, and to correspond with foreign translators. The work is pleasant and at present easy, but likely to become laborious by and by.

. . . I am yet single, but not despairing of duplication. But, however enumerated, I beg you to set me down as your cordial and abiding friend and brother in Christ.

P. S.—My old friend, so to speak, Dr. C. is now in this region and visits me every once in a while, probably both glad of an opportunity to exercise toward each other certain Christian graces that would no doubt have lain dormant had we been otherwise affected toward each other in ancient times.

The personal allusion in the last sentence discloses a rare gentleness and goodness—qualities which characterized the man throughout his career. From the brief account of it one may readily perceive that the long and warm discussion of vital questions at Indianapolis had on both sides been conducted with an uncommon degree of patience and charity. Both parties were determined and conscientious. The young pastor was born to seek out new ways; his session was predestined to love remorselessly the old paths. They could not be harmonized. It is not often that such a conflict is closed with so successful a defense of the public interests and so small and so transient an injury to private character and personal friendship. Those who knew Professor Bush in the early days of battle will cordially unite in bearing testimony to "the extent and variety of his learning, his rare courage, the unpretending simplicity and the kindness of his manners, his fervent and trustful piety."[1] In his odd story of Indiana life Professor Hall introduces Mr. Bush as "Bishop Shrub," and describes with the warmth of friendship these same characteristics.[2] "I never saw him but once, within my recollection," writes another whose parents knew and loved him well; "that was in New York City, when he made a long and affectionate call upon my father. He was a delightful talker, and, I suppose, in all his feelings, and in his treatment of others, a gentle, Christ-like man."

A volume of "Memoirs and Reminiscences of the late Professor George Bush" was published in Boston the year after his decease.

BAYNARD RUSH HALL was the son of Dr. John Hall, an eminent surgeon[3] in Philadelphia. Dr. Hall was a man of wealth. He died, however, when the son was but four years of age, and the property, except a small portion

[1] Griswold's "Prose Writers of America," p. 356.
[2] "The New Purchase," p. 224.
[3] The father's profession and residence readily explain the son's middle name.

of it, never came into the possession of the rightful heir.[1] The latter was born in Philadelphia, in 1798, and commenced his collegiate studies at the College of New Jersey, completing them, however, at Union College, New York, from which institution he graduated with honor in the class of 1820. His friends wished him to study law, but his own inclination was for the ministry and he entered the seminary at Princeton in the autumn of the same year. On leaving the seminary, having received licensure from the Presbytery of Philadelphia,[2] he set out for the West.

He had married several years before, at the age of twenty-two, a lady whom he had formerly known in Philadelphia and whose family had removed to Danville, Ky.[3] From his own chatty pen, through a thin veil of fiction, we are led to the substantial truth as to his settlement in Indiana.

It was mere accident that turned our folks to their location in the New Purchase. The Seymours at the close of the last war with Great Britain resided in Philadelphia. Like others they risked their capital during the war in manufactories; and like others, when peace was proclaimed the Seymours were ruined. John Seymour, familiarly known among us as Uncle John, on his arrival from the South, where, during a residence of many years, he had acquired a handsome fortune, found his sisters, Mrs. Glenville and Mrs. Littleton, in great distress, their husbands being recently dead; and having not long before his return buried his wife, who had, however, borne him no children, he immediately took under his protection the two widowed ladies, his sisters, together with the four children of Mrs. Glenville. Fearing his means were not sufficient to sustain the burden providentially cast upon him, at least in the way that was desirable, he resolved to remove to Kentucky. Accordingly the new-organized family all removed to the West, with the exception of Miss Eliza Glenville, who was left to complete her education with the excellent and justly celebrated Mr. Jandon.

[1] Index volume of the *Princeton Review*.
[2] Dickey's " Brief History," p. 16.
[3] Reed's "Christian Traveller," p. 111.

With this amiable and interesting creature, the young lady, Mr. Carlton, who somehow or other always had a taste for sweet and beautiful faces, became acquainted . . . and was married. It had been part of the arrangement that Mr. and Mrs. Carlton should join the family in Kentucky, and that we should establish a boarding-school for young ladies; but now came a letter from John Glenville, that Uncle John, unfortunate, not in selling a very valuable property at a fair price, but in receiving that price in worthless notes of Kentucky banks, which, like most banks, every twenty or thirty years had failed, had with his remaining funds, as his only resort, bought a tract of government lands in the New Purchase; and that, if I could join him, with a few hundred dollars, in a little tanning, store-keeping, and honest speculation, we might gain, if not riches, at least independence. He added that maybe something could be done in the school line.[1]

Thus allured to "Glenville," a little settlement not far from the present Gosport, Mr. Hall became, early in 1825, the principal of the State Seminary, located in 1820 upon the state lands adjoining the town of Bloomington, which were now for the first time opened. He says:

Nearly south of Glenville was the grand town—our Woodville.[2] And nearly west, some eight or nine miles and a piece, was Spiceburg,[3] at least in dry times, for the town being on the bottom of Shining River was, in hard rains, commonly under water, so that a conscientious man dared not then to affirm, without a proviso, where Spiceburg was precisely. Northeast from us, some fifty long lonesome miles, was the capital of the state, Timberopolis,[4] the seat of the legislature and of mortality.[5] South of Woodville and in the very edge of the forest were at this time two unfinished brick buildings, destined for the use of the future university. As we passed to-day in our vehicle the smaller house was crammed with somebody's hay and flax, while the larger was

[1] Hall's "New Purchase," pp. 84-6.
[2] Bloomington.
[3] Spencer.
[4] Indianapolis.
[5] "New Purchase," p. 83. It is considerately added concerning "Timberopolis" that "death in later times there domineered less."

pouring forth a flock of sheep—a very curious form in which to issue college parchments.[1]

In connection with the care of the school at Bloomington Mr. Hall at once undertook the labors of the pulpit. Having been received by Salem Presbytery, in March, 1825, he was ordained and installed over the Bloomington society the month following.[2] Though this relation was dissolved one year later he continued to preach to the congregation until early in 1830. Meanwhile the young State Seminary had got into stormy seas, the rivalries of political parties and ecclesiastical sects seriously threatening its existence. In the effort to establish it upon a collegiate basis it was thought necessary to distribute the professorships among the combatants, and Mr. Hall retired. He had certainly not been "the very first man since the creation of the world that read Greek in the New Purchase,"[3] though he had no doubt been one of the best classical scholars there. His experience as a teacher had also prepared him for the profession which he was to prosecute during nearly all of his later life.

Leaving Indiana in 1831, he became pastor of the church in Bedford, Pa., the following year, where he remained, at the same time conducting a school, until

[1] "New Purchase," p. 68. This, and other "New Purchase" descriptions, intended as suggestions of the small and rude beginnings of that day, must be taken, so far as the details are concerned, " with a grain of salt."

[2] In this year there were six ordinations in the Presbyterian Church in Indiana. "Four of these I attended and took a part in them," says the Rev. Isaac Reed. ("Christian Traveller," p. 146.) "At the first, which was the installation of the Rev. George Bush at Indianapolis as moderator, I gave out the appointments to the others, and took the address to the congregation on myself. At the second, which was this at Bloomington, I preached the sermon. At the next, the ordination of the Rev. Alexander Williamson as evangelist, I was not present. At the fourth, the settlement of the Rev. Tilly H. Brown over the Bethlehem church, I preached the sermon. At the fifth, the ordination of Rev. Stephen Bliss, which took place at Vincennes, I gave the charge to the evangelist."

[3] See " New Purchase," p. 153. He could justly claim the distinction of bringing the first piano to Bloomington.

1838.[1] He then became successively the principal of academies at Bordentown and Trenton, N. J. (at the latter place also having charge of the recently organized Second Church[2]), and at Poughkeepsie and Newburgh, N. Y., and in 1852 removed to Brooklyn and became principal of the Park Institute.[3] The last few years of his life he spent in preaching to the poor, a portion of the time under the direction of the Reformed (Dutch) Church. He died January 23, 1863, and was laid to rest in the cemetery of the Evergreens, a beautiful spot two or three miles east of Brooklyn, and overlooking the bay. He left a widow and two children in destitute circumstances, but three years after the last member of his family followed him. None of his near relatives survive.

In 1842 the degree of A. M. was conferred upon him by the College of New Jersey, and in 1848 the degree of D. D. by Rutgers College. His first publication was a "New and Compendious Latin Grammar." In 1842 an article from his pen on "Theories of Education" appeared in the *Princeton Review*. Twelve years after leaving Indiana he published "The New Purchase, or Life in the Far West" and "Something for Everybody." The following year, in 1847, "Teaching, a Science; the Teacher an Artist," and "Frank Freeman's Barber Shop" appeared. His cliosophic address at Princeton in 1852 was printed.[4] His writings were not unsuccessful. "The New Purchase," a story founded on his experience in Indiana, reached a third revised edition in 1855, its two volumes in one. The book has many readers still, especially in the region where its amusing scenes are laid.[5] Extracts from it already

---

[1] Gillett's "History of the Presbyterian Church," Vol. I., p. 494.

[2] See Dr. John Hall's "History of the First Church in Trenton," p. 118.

[3] See index volume of the *Princeton Review*.

[4] Dr. John Hall's "History of the First Church in Trenton," p. 118.

[5] An intelligent reader will easily detect some of the localities and characters partially obscured by their *noms de plume*. Perhaps, however, a glossary will be welcomed. The

quoted will sufficiently indicate its style. Too diffuse and familiar, it still has elements of strength. The narrative is often racy, and sometimes admirably preserves the vernacular of the region and the time. There was a degree of offensive personality in the first edition which did not multiply the author's friends among those at all sensitive to sarcasm. This feature of the book was removed from the revised issue and we may all thank the lively pen, never dipped in gall, for its familiar trifling with our household gods.

During his residence in Brooklyn Dr. Hall occasionally ventured into the lecture field, and with success. In these efforts, as in his writings, wit sometimes had too sharp an edge. The "hits were admirable," but cut too deep. "In his long struggle with poverty, finding himself distanced in the race of life by many who were greatly his inferiors, both in mental power and intellectual attainments, it is no wonder that he sometimes gave way to melancholy and permitted a bitter tone."[1] He had lost his father in early childhood, and thus was deprived of a friendship admirably suited to help and educate a boy. His considerable patrimony he had not been permitted to receive and enjoy. By nature well endowed and in the best schools thoroughly trained, his refined faculties found his circumstances discordant. The high but wearisome task of the schoolmaster, even when joined to ministerial work, failed to yield a sufficient support, and he was

Carlton and the Rev. Mr. Clarence, of the book, are the author; Rev. James Hilsbury is Rev. Isaac Reed; Dr. Bloduplex, Dr. Wiley; Rev. Mr. Shrub, Rev. George Bush; Woodville, Bloomington; Spiceburg, Spencer; Sugartown, Crawfordsville; Sproutsburg, La Fayette; Timberopolis, Indianapolis; Big Shiney, White River; Slippery River, Eel River. Mrs. Glenville, Chap. XXXII., is the mother of Mrs. Hall, Mrs. Isaac Reed, and " John Glenville "; Dr. Sylvan is Dr. Maxwell; and the leader of the party described in Chap. XLIV. is Williamson Dunn, father of the Hon. McKee Dunn. Harwood is Harvey, at his death, a few years since, editor of the *Louisville Democrat*. Lawyer Cutswell afterward became Governor Whitcomb.

[1] MSS. of the Rev. J. Edson Rockwell, D.D., who kindly communicated the facts of Dr. Hall's later life.

forced to frequent removals. It was a long struggle for bread, most honorably maintained by one who doubtless reflected that he had been wronged, and that his wife and his children were suffering needlessly. We must gratefully remember the man who in his earliest enthusiasm so gaily bore for us the heat of the day, and in the "Cottage of Peace" with "Bishop Hilsbury," and at "Timberopolis" with the "Rev. Mr. Shrub," showed qualities so genial, generous, and strong.

By one who saw him at Bloomington in the winter of 1830–1[1] he is remembered as "a short, heavily-built man, with long, light hair." The lithograph prefixed to his principal book, and representing him as he was twenty years later, shows a noble, finely-chiseled face, marked deeply with lines of sorrow. In the portrait the story of his life is accurately told.

ALEXANDER WILLIAMSON was born in Cumberland County, Pa., September 17, 1797. He graduated from Jefferson College, Cannonsburg, in 1818. Having entered Washington College early in 1816, he was there converted under the ministry of Dr. M. Brown, but afterward became a student at Jefferson. He studied theology at Princeton and graduated in the class of 1822. Licensed by the Presbytery of Carlisle, on account of delicate health he accepted a missionary appointment for two years in Mississippi. Thence he came to Indiana, settling at Corydon, and after eight or nine years removing to Delphi, Carroll County, and to Monticello, White County. In these fields he remained for ten years, when, his health and his mind becoming impaired, he removed to Corydon, about two years before his death, which occurred July 14, 1849. For some years he was able to do but little in the ministry, but, though he took gloomy views of himself, he was,

---

[1] The Rev. Dr. Henry Little.

HELP FROM PRINCETON. 191

says Dr. C. C. Beatty, his classmate at Princeton, "eminently a man of God."

At the meeting of Synod, Indianapolis, September, 1849, formal record was made of his fidelity. "No ordinary cause," says the memorial, "would prevent him from fulfilling his appointments, however distant, and it is believed that the exposure he thus endured brought on the disease which disabled him and finally terminated his life. . . . He was eminently a man of prayer. His delight was in the law of the Lord."

CHAPTER XIV.

Two Fellow-Travelers.

1824.

OF the Princeton quintet referred to in the previous chapter, Young and Johnston made the journey westward in company. The latter lived to a good old age, enduring half a century of most honorable toil. His friend, smitten by the poisonous fogs of the Wabash, scarcely survived to complete the brief term of his first commission.

JOHN YOUNG spent the early years of his life in Springfield, Otsego County, N. Y., graduated from Union College in 1821, and studied divinity at Princeton. He came West in 1824, reaching Madison, Ind., December 9. His commission, from the Assembly's Committee of Missions, was for six months. Remaining in Madison eight weeks, he supplied the vacant pulpit there. He was present at the ordination of Mr. Bush at Indianapolis, March 5, 1825.[1] After a few weeks' labor along the White River in the vicinity of Indianapolis he went to the Wabash. He was at the meeting of Presbytery in April at Washington. Crossing into Illinois, he gave most of his time until July 15 to the congregation of Paris, Edgar County, and New Hope, partly in Vigo County, Ind., and partly in Clark County, Ill. The term for which he had been commissioned had already expired and he had turned toward home. Arriving at the house of the Rev. S. T. Scott, near Vincennes, he delayed his journey eastward in order

[1] See "A Funeral Sermon, occasioned by the early death of Mr. John Young . . . by Isaac Reed, A. M., Indianapolis, printed by Douglass and Maguire." Cf. "Christian Traveller," pp. 149, 150, 209, 210.

to attend the third anniversary of the Indiana Missionary Society. On the 2d of August he preached at Princeton what proved to be his last sermon. He was at that time suffering from illness. Returning on the 3d to Vincennes, symptoms of fever appeared, but on the two following days he was able to attend the meetings of the Presbytery and the Missionary Society. On the latter occasion he addressed the assembly with singular solemnity. But he soon withdrew to the house of a good physician of the town, and lying down, sank steadily until near midnight, August 15, when he died. He had expected soon to be in the home of his childhood again, but another welcome was prepared for him. His little property he bequeathed to the Domestic Missionary Society of New York, the American Bible Society, and the Tract Society.[1]

Mr. Young was small in stature, of a well-formed person and fine countenance. His manners were grave. He was "a man of ardent piety and earnest zeal."[2] In the churches of Paris and New Hope he was greatly loved.[3] "He did much in little time." His early death caused "great lamentation," and especially grieved the little company of Princeton fellow-students[4] who had chosen the same field of labor. Baynard R. Hall[5] says:

We visited the grave of a young man who, unavoidably exposed to a fatal illness in discharging his missionary duties, had died at Vincennes in early manhood and far away from his home. Deep solemnity was in the little company of his classmates as they stood gazing where rested the remains of the youthful hero. Dear young man, his warfare was soon ended, and there he lay among the silent ones in the scented meadow-land of the far West.

A faded letter of Mr. Young's, dated "Washington,

[1] Letter of the Rev. Samuel T. Scott in Reed's "Funeral Discourse," p. 12.
[2] Johnston's "Forty Years in Indiana," p. 28.
[3] See *Indiana Journal* of September 6, 1825.
[4] Bush, Hall, Williamson, Johnston.
[5] "New Purchase," p. 280.

April 9, 1825," contains the following references to his work in Indiana :

You will perhaps have some curiosity to know where I have been and what doing since I saw you. (1) I have been in Indiana, in the mud, in log cabins, in the woods. (2) After you left me at Indianapolis I took a tour up White River and preached one Sabbath at a Mr. Mallory's. Visited the falls of Fall Creek.[1] Preached one sermon in the prison of that place. I spent some time conversing with those poor unhappy murderers.[2] Found them free to converse. The two old men are from all accounts bad. The young man appears truly penitent. He frankly confesses the whole transaction. . . . After visiting these unhappy wretches I returned to Indianapolis ; spent one Sabbath there ; then left for Illinois. From Indianapolis to the Wabash I had a rather gloomy, unpleasant time. The greater part of the way is woods.

JAMES HARVEY JOHNSTON was of goodly parentage. His grandfather, the Rev. William Johnston, was born in Dublin, Ireland, in 1713. He had received a thorough education at Edinburgh University, spending four years in the literary and three in the theological department.[3] He came to this country when a young man and married Miss Cummins, an English lady of education and rare accomplishments. She was annually in receipt of £150 from England, which after the Revolution, however, was not transmitted. "Dominie" Johnston, having previously resided in the vicinity of Albany and Schenectady and at Curry's Bush[4] and Warren's Bush, settled in Sidney Plains, N. Y., arriving there May 10, 1772. He was the pioneer of that town. He came on foot, with his son Witter, subsequently known as Colonel Johnston, driving a cow from the neighborhood of Cherry Valley. The son remained during the winter, his father returning in the

[1] Now Pendleton.
[2] Cf. Oliver H. Smith's "Indiana Trials," pp. 51-3.
[3] See " The Sidney Centennial Jubilee," p. 28.
[4] Now Florida, Montgomery County, N. Y.

autumn to Curry's Bush for the remainder of the family, who reached Sidney Plains the following June. A tract of land consisting of 520 acres was secured, and upon this homestead the Johnstons enjoyed comparative quiet until November 11, 1778, when occurred the fatal Cherry Valley massacre under Captain Walter Butler and the Mohawk Indian, Brandt. The family, warned by "Hughy," the younger son, escaped only to see their house in flames. They fled to the vicinity of their former residence, where they remained until after the war. The "Dominie," who died in 1783, never returned to his estate.

Colonel Witter, father of the subject of this sketch, continued in the service of the colonies until peace was secured, when he returned to Sidney Plains and successfully sought from the legislature a title to the homestead, the former title having been found worthless and the whole property, really held by a loyalist, having been confiscated. Colonel Johnston was a man of great force of character, though not possessed of a robust frame or vigorous constitution. While an officer in the army of the Revolution his pay was the chief support of the family. In later life, when in prosperous circumstances, he was accustomed to lead in all public enterprises. His firmness and self-reliance were characteristic. He died in October, 1839, at the age of eighty-six.

James Harvey Johnston was born at Sidney Plains, October 14, 1798. When about fourteen years of age he heard his pastor preach on "the unpardonable sin," and such was the impression the sermon made upon him that he could not study and in the schoolroom was continually weeping. The teacher, a woman, sent him home, advising him to make his case known to his mother. It is probable that then, under his mother's sympathy and instruction, the life of faith began.

It was the wish of his mother that he should have an education, and his studies were now directed to prepare him for a collegiate course. Before he had reached the age of seventeen he taught school at Unadilla to obtain means to prosecute his studies, and in 1816 he entered the freshman class at Hamilton College. Albert Barnes was his classmate, and remained through life a warm friend.[1] Mr. Johnston graduated in 1820, with the first honors of his class. Having spent a year in teaching at Utica he went to Princeton Seminary, and there completed the course in divinity. He was licensed to preach at the opening of the last year at the seminary, and concerning that event the following entry in his diary appears, under the date October 24, 1823 :

> I last week attended the Columbia Presbytery, to which I had previously attached myself, and having sustained the examinations, and passed through the trials required, was only licensed to preach the gospel. My licensure took place on the 14th day of this month, my birthday, I having on that day completed my 25th year. In this entering upon the high and holy work of the gospel ministry I trust my mind has been in some measure impressed with a sense of its importance. . . . May I never be guilty of doing the work of the Lord deceitfully. May I never neglect or abandon it. As I hope that this work has not been undertaken from mere worldly motives, for the purpose of obtaining a temporal support, I pray God that in prosecuting it my aim and my conduct may never become mercenary. Though the laborer is worthy of his hire this direction is given to govern those to whom the gospel is preached, rather than to be insisted on by preachers themselves. My motto should be, " A necessity is laid upon me; yea, woe is me if I preach not the gospel wherever providence may call me."

The diary continues:

> *Princeton, July 1, 1824.* The time allotted to my theological

---

[1] Upon the death of Mr. Barnes Mr. Johnston preached, February 26, 1871, in the Centre Church, Crawfordsville, Ind., a memorial discourse, containing extracts from a long correspondence. It forms a beautiful and just tribute to his distinguished friend. The sermon was published, Philadelphia, 1874.

course is rapidly drawing to a close. I have now entered upon the last session at this seminary. The last two months have been spent on a missionary tour. My field of labor was in Montgomery and Albany Counties in New York. I preached almost daily and was constantly employed in visiting from house to house. As opportunities presented did all in my power to promote Sabbath-schools. My traveling, during the tour, which would average from ten to fifteen miles per day, I performed on foot. This tour was to me a very interesting one. Took much satisfaction in discharging the duties incumbent upon me. Saw much to convince me of the need of missionary labor in the region which I visited. The means enjoyed by the people limited; ignorance great; errors abounding; vices prevailing. Was treated with much kindness and with much respect for my work's sake. A pleasing attention was generally manifested to the preaching of the Word. One or two hopeful conversions under my preaching. Was solicited to remain in two different places. In either place my station would have been obscure and my sphere limited, but I felt willing to remain if it appeared to be God's will.

Sidney Plains, October 28. God has mercifully restored me once more to my father's family, but it is in circumstances different from any in which I formerly visited home. I am this day to bid adieu to my friends and direct my course to the far distant West. Previous to leaving Princeton I thought it my duty, after much prayerful deliberation, to take a mission for the state of Indiana. An engagement to spend a year in that state as a missionary was entered into, with the Domestic Missionary Society of New York, before I reached home. Some intimation of such an intention had some weeks before been given to my friends at home in a letter, but no explicit avowal had been made till after my commission had been obtained.

On arriving at home and declaring my purpose my father and other friends opposed me. They had expected me to settle nearer them. They cannot even now be convinced that duty requires me to move so far. Their opposition renders the trial of parting still more severe, but, happy as I should be to comply with their wishes could I consistently do it, my views of duty remain unchanged. The wants of the church and the prospects of usefulness in the region assigned me by my commission I believe to be greater than in the vicinity of this place, or anywhere in my native state. It appears clear to me, notwithstanding the arguments which my friends have used and the wishes they have expressed, that I ought to go to the field which I have engaged to visit. This is the day appointed for my departure. The separation about to take place, the distance to which I am destined to go, the responsibility of the undertaking, my ignorance of the character of the people whom I may visit, and of the circumstances in which I shall be placed, the privations and hardships which I shall experience, and the dangers to which I shall be exposed, all these combine to fill my mind with anxious and painful feelings. But my trust is in the Lord; in his strength I will go forward.

Madison, Indiana, December 9, 1824. Agreeably to my expectation, on the 28th of October I left home and commenced my journey on horseback to this state. Mr. John Young, another missionary for Indiana, had agreed with me before leaving Princeton to bear me company on the journey. We were to meet at Geneva. The first Sabbath after leaving home I spent at Hamilton College; the second at Geneva. At that place I found that Mr. Young had waited for me for some days, but had left for Canandaigua. On Monday the 8th of November I proceeded to the latter place, hoping to overtake him, but he had left about three hours before my arrival there. I pursued my journey alone to Buffalo, where I had the pleasure of overtaking Mr. Young. In his company I proceeded to Chautauqua County before the next Sabbath. In that county we both spent the Sabbath. The following Sabbath was spent near Cleveland in Ohio, the Sabbath succeeding near Worthington in the same state, and the next Sabbath in Harrison and vicinity, on the borders of Indiana. This day we have reached Madison.

I feel bound to render humble thanks to God for his goodness in rendering my journey so pleasant and prosperous. He has preserved me from sickness and from death, has permitted no accident or harm to befall me. We have met with a very kind and apparently cordial reception from the people of this place. I am greatly pleased with the appearance of the town and of the people. The recent affliction the church has experienced in the loss of their minister, the Rev. Joseph Trimble, renders their case still more interesting.

Thus began what was to be the longest period of continuous service ever accomplished by a Presbyterian minister in Indiana—eighteen years at Madison and nearly a half-century of active labor in the state.

The work was initiated by an extensive tour of exploration, Mr. Young having undertaken for a time the supply of the Madison pulpit. Mr. Johnston was engaged for nearly three months upon this missionary journey. He makes the following reference to it in his journal:

Madison, March 10, 1825. The intervening time has been spent in itinerating through the southeastern section of the state. I have traveled about five hundred miles and preached about fifty times. Have enjoyed good health, been prospered in my journey, been kindly received, and as well accommodated as the circumstances of new settlements would permit. Have received as a compensation for my services since leaving here five dollars and twenty cents, and have expended in traveling the same sum.[1]

[1] A loose leaf of the journal contains the following interesting record: " Arrived within ye bounds of Indiana on ye 7th of December, 1824. Arrived at Madison on ye 9th. Preached at Madison on ye eve of ye 10th from Heb. ii.: 3. Preached on ye Sabbath at Sam'l Ryker's from Rev. iii.: 20. On Thursday eve., 10th, at Madison from Luke xv.: 11-24. On Sabbath, 19th, at Madison, from 1 Peter i.:8, Eccl. xii.: 1, and Matt. v.: 6. On Wednesday eve., 22d, at Vernon, from Eccl. xii.: 1. Thursday eve., 23d, at Mr. Clapp's, Heb. ii.: 3. Friday eve., 24th, at Columbus, Matt. v.: 6. Sab. morn., 26th, at Mr. Young's, Rev. iii.: 20; eve., at Mr. King's, Franklin, Luke xv.: 11-24. Wed. eve., 29th, at Indianapolis, Eccl. xii.: 1. Tues. eve., Jan. 4, at Mr. Smock's, Matt. v.: 6. Wed. eve., 5th, at Mr. Morgan's, on Sugar Creek, Rev. iii.: 20. Thur. eve., at Shelbyville, Heb. ii.: 3. Sat. eve., 8th, at Greensburgh, Rev. iii.: 20. Sab., 9th, Rom. vi.: 23, Luke xv.: 11-24. Mon. eve., 10th, at Mrs. Hamilton's, Isa. lv.: 6. Tues. eve., at Wm. Threp's, Heb. ii.: 3. Thurs. eve., 13th, at Mr. Donnell's, Matt. xxv.: 1-13. Frid. eve., 14th, at Mr. Antrobus', 'The rich man and Lazarus.' Sab. morn., 15th, at Cyrus Hamilton's, 1 Peter i.: 8; eve., at Mr. Collins', 2 Peter iii.: 18. Thur., 12 o'clock, at Rushville, Heb. ii.: 3; eve., Luke xv.: 11-24. Sab. eve., Jan. 23, 1 Peter i.: 8. Mon. eve., 24th, at Mr. Brownlee's, Matt. xxv.: 1-13. Tues. eve., 25th, at Connersville, Rev. iii.: 20. Wed., 12 o'clock, at Mr. Bell's, Matt. v.: 6. Wed. eve., at Dunlapsville, Heb. ii.: 3. Thur. eve., 27th, at Bath, Matt. xxv.: 1-13. Frid. eve., 28th, at Mr. Sering's, Isa. lv.: 6. Sat. eve., 29th, at Mr. Murphy's, Amos iv.: 12. Sab. morn., 30th, Bath, Eccl. xii.: 1; eve., at Mr. Simonson's, Cedar Grove, Luke xv.: 11-24. Monday, 31st, at Mr. Gouday's, 2 Peter iii.: 18. Wed., Feb. 2d, 12 o'clock, at Esq. Cox's, Amos iv.: 12. Thur., 3d, at 12 o'clock, at Mr. Bell's, Rev. iii.: 20. Sat. eve., 5th, at Rushville, Rev. iii.: 20. Sab., 12 o'clock, Eccl. xii.: 1. Sab. eve., Matt. xxv.: 1-13. Wed. eve., 9th, at Cole's settlement, 1 Peter i.: 8. Sab. eve., 13th, at Indpls, 1 Peter i.: 8. Tues., 12 o'clock, 15th, at Franklin, Matt. xxv.: 1-13. Wed., 16th, 12 o'clock at Edinburgh, Heb. ii.: 3. Sab. morn., 20th, at Bloomington, 1 Peter i.: 8. Thurs. eve., 24th, at Mr. Steele's, Rev. iii.:20. Sab. morn., 27th, at Mr. Reed's place of worship, Heb. ii.:˙3. Mon. eve., 28th, at Speuser, Amos iv.: 12. Sab. eve., Mar. 6th, at Mr. Smock's, 'Ye Rich Man and Lazarus.' Mon. eve., Mar. 7th, at Franklin, Matt. v.: 6. Tues. eve., at Columbus, Rev. iii.: 20. Wed. eve., 9th, at Vernon, 1 Peter i.: 8. Preached from the time that I left Madison to ye time that I returned fifty times. Traveled about 500 miles in all."

Monday, October 3d. After having spent a number of months in a very pleasant manner, preaching to this people, the church and congregation have this day made out a unanimous call for me to become their pastor. I know no place where I would more willingly take up my permanent abode and no people to whom I would more cheerfully become united in the endearing relation of pastor.

Thursday, October 20th. This has been to me a most solemn and interesting day. Salem Presbytery convened here yesterday, and having received me under their care, attended to the requisite examinations and trials, and to-day they have installed me as pastor of this church.[1] Rev. John Finley Crowe preached the sermon; Rev. John M. Dickey presided and gave the charges to myself and to the congregation and also offered the consecrating prayer; Rev. Alexander Williamson and Rev. Tilly H. Brown were also present and united in the imposition of hands.

April 17, 1826. I am this day to set off on a journey to the East for the purpose of visiting my friends and attending the meeting of the General Assembly at Philadelphia.

July 28. After a long absence from my people I have this day been permitted to return. I have visited my father's family and other relatives and friends, and attended as I expected the General Assembly.[2] Found one of my sisters on a bed of languishing and death. Before the close of my visit I witnessed her decease. It is my earnest prayer that I may be as well prepared for death as she appeared to be. My visit, though on many accounts interesting, has not afforded me so much enjoyment as I anticipated. My mind dwelt much upon the dear people of my charge. The interest I feel in their spiritual welfare I found to be greater when separated from them than I was aware of when with them. Madison appears to me the dearest place on earth.

The missionary, now fully established upon his field, found opportunities for useful labor rapidly multiplying. The Indiana Missionary Society, at first auxiliary to the Assembly's Committee of Missions, but at the fourth annual meeting, August 4, 1826, made tributary to the American Home Missionary Society, on Mr. Johnston's

---

[1] He was at the same time ordained.—" Minutes Salem Presbytery," Vol. I., p. 36.

[2] The petition from Salem Presbytery for a division into three Presbyteries he successfully presented to the Assembly.—" Minutes Salem Presbytery," Vol. I., pp. 33, 34.

arrival in the state, placed him upon the executive committee. He also became the society's secretary. Missionaries from the East were instructed to report to him, and were by him apprised of the fields selected for them.[1] He was thus required to assume the burden of an extensive correspondence and to acquaint himself by frequent explorations with the whole territory. Large packages of letters received from students in the seminaries, and from missionaries recently arrived, together with official communications from every quarter, show the high esteem in which he was held and the conscientious assiduity of his service.

The more we study the spirit and purposes of the men who founded our church in Indiana the more we are compelled to admire their zeal, their faith in God, and the wisdom and breadth of their plans for God's kingdom. But there is a painful sense of the extreme poverty of the means at their command. The effort to systematize missionary operations in the state was attended with severe sacrifices on the part of all our oldest and most useful men. But besides the Missionary Society they undertook the establishment of state benevolent societies in behalf of the Bible, the tract cause, temperance, etc. They fostered education and wrought unitedly for the Hanover Academy. A theological department was founded and professors were secured. In all these far-reaching plans Mr. Johnston was prominent. When, in addition, the publishing of a religious newspaper as the organ of the Indiana Missionary Society was contemplated, he, in consideration both of his qualifications for the trust and of his convenient location, was by all approved for the editorial chair. To this latter undertaking he makes the following reference in his diary:

[1] The missionaries of the A. H. M. S. upon this field were "located" by the Indiana society. See Johnston's "Forty Years in Indiana," p. 9.

June 27, 1828. Have this day commenced the publication of a religious periodical. What will be the result of this undertaking and how long it will be prosecuted is very uncertain. I have engaged with no very sanguine hopes of success. Have been influenced by the advice of a number of my brethren. Through God's blessing religion may be subserved by this humble periodical.

The *Indiana Religious Intelligencer*, started without capital, with no support but the faith of a few missionaries whose annual income reached all the way from fifty to four hundred dollars, without a single salaried assistant, was published in the wilderness for eighteen months, and in a modest sphere was useful. With such scanty resources it was impossible, however, to maintain a rivalry with old and well-supported journals. The last and seventy-first number appeared January 29, 1830. No doubt the work of the printers, at first C. P. J. Arion and afterward Arion & Lodge, had often to be in great part a labor of love. "It is now my desire and determination," observes Mr. Johnston, "to devote myself more exclusively and more zealously than ever to the work of the ministry."

Meanwhile, March 26, 1829, he had been united in marriage with Mrs. Eliza Ann McChord, and had again visited his early home in New York. When the organization of a second church was effected in Madison he continued there as pastor of the new flock. For a single year he exchanged labors with the Rev. Henry Little, agent of the American Home Missionary Society. As stated clerk of Synod during the sad period of strife within our church he was required to assume grave responsibilities, and then exhibited qualities which won the admiration of opponents and friends.

Finally, in 1843, he removed to Crawfordsville and for eight years was pastor of Centre Church. In 1851 he became principal of the female seminary at Crawfordsville, continuing in that position for about four years. From 1854 to the summer of 1866 he led a laborious life of missionary service, statedly preaching at Perrysville, Covington, Eugene, Newport, Brown's Valley, and Parkersburgh, and frequently accepting calls for labor in yet other localities. In 1866 Centre Church, Crawfordsville, secured his services and during the succeeding winter nearly one hundred names were added to the roll. "As if to give a peculiarly splendid crown to his long period of service God blessed his ministry with the most remarkable revival ever experienced in the town." In August, 1867, he became pastor *emeritus*, retiring from active duty in the ministry. Having three years before preached for the last time, after a slow and peaceful decline he fell asleep March 8, 1876, and two days later, on the fifty-first anniversary of the commencement of his labors as pastor at Madison, he was laid to rest in Oak Hill Cemetery.

In person tall and slender, of a grave countenance and demeanor, Mr. Johnston united great gentleness with unusual firmness and force. Not insensible to argument, his opinion when intelligently formed was with difficulty shaken. He inherited Colonel Witter Johnston's steadfastness. "He is well remembered by the older residents of Sidney Plains as an amiable young man, remarkable for his diligence in the pursuit of knowledge, his freedom from the frivolities and excesses of youth, and perhaps more than all for his strictly conscientious deportment and exemplary religious character, which dates back almost to his earliest childhood."[1]

Ex-President Woolsey of Yale College writes:[2]

Mr. Johnston and I were classmates at Princeton in 1821, 1822, and 1823. In the last-mentioned year I left Princeton to be a tutor in Yale College. I have had a little correspondence with him

[1] "Sidney Centennial," p. 90.
[2] MS. letter dated June 30, 1876.

since then by letter, but I believe that we have never met since that time. I esteemed and respected Mr. Johnston more perhaps than any other of my classmates. I had entire confidence in his character as a Christian man, and respected his manliness and soundness of judgment. We agreed then in our theology, and I always thought him cut out, as it were, to be a minister. It is now fifty-two years since our Princeton days, and the impression he made on me was so positive that I have never failed or abated in my respect for him. His traits of mind and character, as they presented themselves to me, were great soundness of judgment in practical matters, an uncommon amount of principle, and a solidity of character on which I could entirely rest. We all thought highly of his abilities, though he had nothing brilliant about him. He was a model to the class.[1]

What Mr. Johnston was in youth, and later in his student days, that he continued to be in old age, perhaps growing in mellowness and cheerfulness as the years increased.

I have just been calling [says President Tuttle] on the venerable patriarch of our church in Indiana, the Rev. James H. Johnston. There was no special reason for the call beyond the pleasure it brought the visitor himself. To-day I find him as cheerful and even hilarious as he ought to have been when so many years ago he dismounted in that pretty town on the Ohio for the first time. I have not heard a merrier laugh in many a day than his, as he told me of the inquiries made by himself and his traveling companion for a suitable stopping-place at Rising Sun, when on his first journey westward. They were told of a Major Jelly as keeping a sort of "ministers' tavern," and asked their informant if the major was a pious man. "He's only middling," was the reply. After his hearty laugh Mr. Johnston added, "We found the major was not a church member, but his wife was, and they gave us a cordial welcome."[2]

[1] To an official letter dated: "Office of the A. H. M. S., 87 Nassau Street, January 4, 1827," and signed, "Absalom Peters by T. D. Woolsey," the following postscript is appended: "My dear friend, I know not that I should have fulfilled my promise made in the spring, of writing to you, if I had not been called to do it in this official manner. I am at present performing the duties of an assistant secretary of the A. H. M. S. until an individual can be found to take the place permanently and am happy that it has fallen to my lot to correspond with you. Ever yours, T. D. W."

[2] A communication dated December 9, 1872, and printed in the "Sidney Centennial Volume," pp. 90, 91.

February 5, 1865, Mr. Johnston delivered at Crawfordsville an historical discourse describing "A Ministry of Forty Years in Indiana." The sermon was published, and not only preserves many valuable facts but unintentionally proves how large a part he himself was of the early days. Yet he says :[1]

It is but an humble part I have borne. But I have great cause for thankfulness for the uniform health and strength that have been vouchsafed. Few, indeed, have been the Sabbaths, throughout this whole period, on which I have been prevented from preaching by bodily indisposition. And with the exception of four years, in which my duties in connection with Crawfordsville Female Seminary required my whole attention, I have seldom failed to preach on the Sabbath from any cause. The wonder is that I have been permitted to labor so long. Scott and Martin and Matthews and Dickey and Crowe, and very many others much younger than they, have passed away. Of the eight ministers that were present at the first meeting of the Synod of Indiana in 1826, I am the only one now living, and of the fifteen that constituted the whole number of Presbyterian ministers in the state in 1825, all are in their graves but myself.

But now, perhaps, the fellowship alluded to in a letter addressed to him by Albert Barnes has been attained, and not with his college friend alone, but also with his fellow-laborers upon this western field.

I showed you yesterday the spot where I shall soon enter on my long, last sleep, and it is not improbable that my eyes will be closed in that long slumber before they will look on you again. Yet we shall not sleep in the sense that we shall, in no respect, be awake and conscious. In that spirit world of which we talked, and of which we felt that we knew so little, I trust we may often meet, before the archangel's trump shall awake the slumber of our graves.[2]

[1] "Forty Years in Indiana," pp. 27, 28.
[2] Johnston's "Sermon on the Death of Albert Barnes," p. 13.

CHAPTER XV.

A Period of Increased Missionary Zeal.

1825.

NEW and more earnest discussions of the problems of domestic missions were just now prominent in influential circles of religious thought throughout the older states. Especially were the young men and the professors in the theological seminaries aroused. It has been seen what Princeton had done for Indiana alone during the year 1824. There was the same wise enthusiasm at Andover. An important result of the missionary revival was the attempt to concentrate and thus to economize effort, and the consequent establishment of a national organization—the American Home Missionary Society.[1] There had thus far been a great variety of small local societies[2]; there was now to be a system of labor for the whole land. In this enterprise the Presbyterians were largely and for the time happily united with the Congregationalist, the Reformed (Dutch) Church, and other evangelical Christians.

Growing out of the awakened interest in domestic missions at least six young men in the senior class of Andover Seminary
had already decided to devote themselves to missionary labors in the western or southern portions of our country. These were Hiram Chamberlain, Augustus Pomeroy, Lucius Alden, John M. Ellis, Luther G. Bingham, and Aaron Foster. In looking about for some society under whose patronage and commission they might go forth, Mr. Bingham applied to the Connecticut Mission-

---

[1] For a valuable though not altogether dispassionate account of the origin of the A. H. M. S. see *The Home Missionary*, Vol. XLIX, No. 1.

[2] Cf. Appendix I.

ary Society; under the advice and agency of Rev. Dr. Porter, Mr. Foster made application to the Charleston (S. C.) Domestic Missionary Society, and the others to the United Domestic Missionary Society of New York. Upon request of this latter society, as suggested by Rev. Dr. Porter, four of the above-named young men—namely, Pomeroy, Alden, Ellis, and Bingham—on the evening of the day after the anniversary, that is the 29th of September, 1825—were ordained as missionaries by a council called for the purpose in the Old South Church, Boston. . . . Mr. Chamberlain, being a member of Rev. Dr. Spring's church in New York, received ordination from a Presbytery. Mr. Foster, in connection with two or three other classmates, found it convenient to be ordained, October 19, 1825, in Rutland, Vt. And agreeably to an understanding with the executive committee in New York— who had agreed to take three of these young missionaries under their patronage—a request was made by said executive committee that a council should be called in Boston for their ordination. As this occasion was new, so it was one of great interest, and "was attended by persons interested in the prosperity of Zion from various parts of the United States." Rev. Matthias Bruen, of New York, preached the sermon from 1 Cor. iv.:1; Rev. Brown Emerson, of Salem, Mass., offered the ordaining prayer; Rev. Samuel H. Cox, D.D., of New York, gave the charge; and Rev. Justin Edwards, of Andover, presented the right hand of fellowship.

Thus set apart for the missionary work, Mr. Alden went to Indiana, Mr. Ellis to Illinois, Mr. Pomeroy to Missouri, where, in St. Louis, he met his friend, Rev. Hiram Chamberlain, under commission likewise from the United Domestic Missionary Society of New York. Rev. Mr. Bingham went to Ohio, under the patronage of the Connecticut Missionary Society, and for several years was pastor of the church at Marietta. Rev. Mr. Foster went to South Carolina, and was for a while pastor of the Presbyterian church in Pendleton.[1]

LUCIUS ALDEN had been one of the committee of six appointed by the "Society of Inquiry" at Andover, April 12, 1825, to foster the interest in domestic missions throughout the Christian community. He received his first commission from the U. D. M. S.

[1] *The Home Missionary*, May, 1876, p. 4.

One hundred dollars was granted him as an outfit to bear his expenses to the field of his contemplated ministry, with the expectation that he would locate himself where the principal part of his support would be paid by the people. We are now happy to state, from the reports of Mr. Alden, that after a tour of about eight weeks, in which he seems to have embraced, with great fidelity and zeal, every opportunity of subserving the cause of Christ, he became located on the 8th of January, 1826, in the town of Aurora, Dearborn County, Ind., where his prospects of extended and increasing usefulness are such as to satisfy this committee that he has been wisely directed to that as the field of his future labors. Our missionary has been received with great cordiality by the people of that place and vicinity, and there is a prospect that they will be able to sustain a large portion of his support. With the exception of one Dearborn is the most populous county in the state and previous to the arrival of our missionary had no Presbyterian minister within its bounds.[1]

Reference is made to Mr. Alden in the official records of the two subsequent years:

His labors appear to have been acceptable to the people and highly useful in the places above named [Lawrenceburgh and Aurora] and in several of the neighboring congregations, particularly in Cæsar-Creek township, Broome County, Ky., where he has preached occasionally. As Lawrenceburgh is the seat of justice and Aurora the seat of a flourishing school, which has grown up under the fostering care of our missionary, these are regarded by the committee as very interesting and important locations.[2]

The reports from these congregations [says the society the following year] have been interesting. Our missionary has been instrumental in forming four Sabbath-schools with libraries, one of which has one hundred scholars and eighteen teachers, and all of which are flourishing.[3]

With his other work Mr. Alden was able also to give some attention to the Hopewell church, near Dillsboro.[4]

[1] Fourth Report of U. D. M. S., p. 22.
[2] Report of A. H. M. S., May, 1827, p. 12.
[3] Report of A. H. M. S., May, 1828, p. 11.
[4] Stewart's "History of Whitewater Presbytery," p. 23.

In 1830 his field was "Rising Sun, Cæsar Creek, and vicinity," and on July 7th of that year he writes to the secretary of the Indiana Missionary Society as follows:

> Within this field of labor are three small churches of the Presbyterians. We have one place of worship completed and arrangements are making to erect two others. We have a temperance society of one hundred and fifty members which has effected much good, diminishing the sale of ardent spirits three fourths in about six months, and some intemperate persons have been, we hope, thoroughly reformed. We have a tract society and have expended about twenty dollars for tracts. Considerable has been done to supply the destitute with Bibles. Our Sunday-schools prosper and generally have libraries. A seminary of learning for the higher branches has been established, and considerably well sustained. Yet almost all here is yet to be done. A little preparatory work, however, has been accomplished. I am now to visit the East, and leave this people only with the prospect of occasional supplies from Presbytery.

Princeton Seminary also continued its benefactions to the West, furnishing this year three new men to Indiana. LEWIS MCLEOD came from the U. D. M. S., having obtained his commission a few days earlier than Mr. Alden.

> One hundred dollars was granted him as an outfit, with the expectation that he would be able to select a location where his support after reaching the field of his labors would be derived principally from the people. Our missionary writes us from Harrison in that state[1] under date of March 13, 1826, that having visited several places in Indiana, which present very interesting and important fields for missionary enterprise, he has at length concluded to spend the summer on the White Waters, chiefly in the county of Dearborn. This he has found to be a very destitute region, and one which presents great encouragement to the faithful labors of a minister of Christ.[2]

After traveling extensively in the state Mr. McLeod, however, finally located himself at Augusta, Ky.

[1] Harrison was in Ohio.
[2] Report of the U. D. M. S., May, 1826, p. 34.

JAMES STEWART served the Rushville church for a few months, and for a similar brief period labored in the southwestern part of the state.

SAMUEL GREGG, a licentiate of New Brunswick Presbytery, was a Tennessean by birth, tall, spare, bent, with thin cheeks, a good man, and a good preacher. After five months of horseback service in Bartholomew, Shelby, and Johnson Counties, he was ordained by Madison Presbytery, October 7, 1826, and installed as pastor of Jefferson church.[1] Here he remained for about ten years, when he returned to his native state and took charge of the Mt. Zion and Meadow Creek churches. Once more taking a parish in Indiana he connected himself with the Presbytery of Crawfordsville, but his health soon failed and his name appears upon the obituary roll presented to the Assembly (N. S.) of 1843.

"Mr. Gregg was a frequent and most welcome visitor at my father's house," says an aged member of the Shelbyville congregation, "and invariably he took the Bible and gathered us children around him, and taught us a chapter in an impressive and attractive manner. The first religious conversation I ever had was with him." He organized the first Sunday-school in Shelby County.

WILLIAM NESBIT, formerly pastor of the Hopewell congregation in Hartford Presbytery, Synod of Pittsburg, was sent this year to Perry and Spencer Counties.

STEPHEN BLISS is a name that belongs especially to Illinois, but his ordination by Salem Presbytery, August 6, 1825, his intimate association with ministers of the Synod of Indiana, and his occasional labor on the eastern bank of the Wabash require some reference to him here. Born in

[1] Dr. Henry Little, during his first Indiana journey, saw him there, and on the same occasion found the father of the Rev. Henry L. Dickerson ardently exercising his gifts as music-master.

Lebanon, N. H., March 27, 1787, prepared for the junior class in college under the tuition of his uncle, the Rev. Dr. Samuel Wood, of Boscaween, a graduate of Middlebury in 1812, a student of theology for two years in his uncle's parsonage, he applied in 1814 to the Hopkinton Association for licensure, but was rejected on account of what were deemed defective views of the person and work of the Redeemer. He turned to the Yankee boy's unfailing resource, and had charge successively at Greenbush, Milton, and Utica of important schools, where his reputation steadily increased, securing to him from Hamilton College the complimentary degree of Master of Arts. Consumption, the scourge of his family, compelled him, however, to seek a change of climate, and in September, 1818, he set out on horseback, with his friend May, for the West. He traversed Ohio and Indiana, crossed the Wabash at Vincennes, and purchased a small farm on Decker's Prairie. April 11, 1819, the two friends opened what was perhaps the first Sunday-school in Illinois. In the autumn of 1820 he traveled back to New Hampshire, and was married, April 7, 1821, to Miss Elizabeth, daughter of the Rev. Dr. Noah Worcester. Returning with his bride to the log house on the Illinois prairie, Sabbath "reading meetings" were soon instituted, Mr. Bliss conducting the service. The Hopkinton Association, through the influence of Dr. Wood, in 1822 reviewing its action with regard to him, sent him a license, and he began in an informal way to preach in his own neighborhood, gathering the little flock which he was long to lead, and which, as the Wabash Presbyterian Church, still reveres his memory. What was the estimation in which the people held him is shown by his unsolicited election in October, 1824, to the senate of the state. Returning from the first session of the legislature in Vandalia he went, with his elders, Danforth and Gould, to

Washington, Ind., where occurred his ordination by Salem Presbytery. Of the work thus at last prepared by providence there was no serious interruption until the death of the pastor, December 6, 1847.

Mr. Bliss was a man of substantial abilities, great kindness and modesty, uncommon perseverance, evangelical character, and permanent usefulness. Though not impassioned in utterance, as a public speaker he was both instructive and impressive. Except in a period of strife his theological views would perhaps not have been criticized, and his mature opinions occasioned him no embarrassment among the "Old-school" Presbyterians of Illinois.[1]

SAMUEL G. LOWRY was born March 26, 1800, in Washington County, Tenn., and received his education at Washington College in his native state. Licensed by Ebenezer Presbytery October 6, 1821, and ordained by the same Presbytery December, 1822, he came to Indiana in December, 1825, and was received by Madison from Cincinnati Presbytery October 5, 1826. For seven years he labored in Decatur County in charge of Sand Creek (now Kingston) church, and during four and a half years of that period also cared for the church at Greensburgh, which he himself organized May 2, 1826. Supplying the pulpit of Poplar Spring church, Putnam County, for two years from 1832, an agent of the A. H. M. Society from 1834 to 1839, during a part of which time he was likewise engaged as agent of Wabash College, preaching for nearly eight years at Rockville from July, 1839, his last charge in Indiana comprised the Bainbridge and New Winchester congregations, over which he was installed in February, 1848. While at Bainbridge he gave a portion of his time to the churches of Parkersburgh and Waveland. Resigning his position in November, 1856, he removed to Minnesota

[1] See "Life and Times of Stephen Bliss," by Samuel C. Baldridge, Cincinnati, 1870.

in the spring of 1857, where he remained until his death, at Austin, September 26, 1886. Of all the Indiana pioneers settled previous to 1826 he was long the solitary survivor. The Rev. Thomas S. Milligan wrote :

Mr. Lowry spent more than thirty years of his ministry in Indiana and performed much hard labor for the churches, besides enduring a great amount of physical toil in providing for a numerous family.[1] His amiable manners, practical wisdom, his familiar acquaintance with ecclesiastical law, his soundness of doctrine and wide experience made him useful in an eminent degree.[2]

[1] This was an incident frequently emphasizing the necessity of applications to the missionary treasury. The Sand Creek church in its request for aid wrote to the A. H. M. S., September, 1825: "Our proposed minister is a young man with a rising family, who has expended his small patrimony in preparing himself to preach the gospel." Report, May, 1826, p. 69.

[2] See also Sluter's "History of the Shelbyville Church," pp. 10, 11.

CHAPTER XVI.

ORGANIZATION OF THE SYNOD OF INDIANA.

1826.

WHAT Indiana was in 1826 we may learn from one whose observation was uncommonly intelligent and whose pen was singularly graceful. It was no doubt George Bush who wrote from Indianapolis, November 30, his impressions of his western field :[1]

The state of Indiana presents at this moment a field both of action and contemplation in the highest degree interesting. Possessing a territory of which the beauty of its visible aspect is equaled only by the amazing fertility of the soil, a soil unmoistened by the sweat or the tears or the blood of the slave, it must soon, from its local relations and its internal resources, rank with the most populous states of the Union. It is now teeming with the hordes of emigration, and the progress of improvement is inconceivable. The earlier inhabitants, in viewing or describing the changes which ten or fifteen years have effected in the state of this immense forest (as it was at that time), can scarce refrain from bursts of astonishment. Though the trees, wherever you travel, bear the marks of the Indian tomahawk, and the very poles and the crisped barks which formed their temporary camps are still to be seen, yet farms are everywhere opening in the wilderness, the resounding axe is heard as often and as far as the yells of wild beasts, the nimble deer feed among the domestic herds, and every twenty or thirty miles the spire of a handsome court-house of brick rises amidst the deadened trunks of the poplars, walnuts, and oaks.

From living in a central part of the state, on a road that forms the great thoroughfare from the East to the West, I am situated favorably for observing the flow of emigration. During the autumnal months, nothing is more common than to see ten,

[1] See Report of A. H. M. S. for 1827, pp. 93-5.

fifteen, or twenty wagons passing in a single day, carrying the little all of the families, which pass in groups by their sides. As many as thirty of these loaded wagons have been known to camp for the night at the same spot in the wilderness. The destination of the great body of emigrants that pass through the center of the state is the tract of country bordering along the Wabash, particularly from the point where this river falls in with the eastern boundary line of Illinois, upward toward its source. This region is becoming the garden spot of Indiana ; and the rate at which population is augmenting in that quarter exceeds belief. And truly, from the acquaintance I have gained, during a recent tour to the Wabash, with that part of the state, I am ready to believe that, were a stranger to the peculiar features of the Mississippi Valley to be suddenly set down in any of the prairie tracts which adorn that noble stream, he could not but wonder that the wisdom and goodness of providence should have so long withheld such enchanting regions from the possession of civilized men.

Such is the natural character of a very considerable portion of a country, of which its moral aspect forms a mournful reverse to the sketch now given. The Canaanite is yet in the land ; its clusters are the clusters of Sodom. Not that the body of the population are entirely regardless of any form of religion. On the contrary, there is an abundance of what is called the preaching of the gospel ; much of a disposition to hear ; much of a certain kind of zeal and of the form of godliness. But alas ! there is little, little of the true evangelical dispensation of the word of life, or its appropriate fruits.

This dark view, however, we are happy to state, is relieved by many grateful facts of a different kind. The Lord has a chosen seed scattered here and there over this barren land. And the lonely missionary who turns aside to tarry for a night in the humble cabins of the wilderness will often find himself delighted and refreshed by the pious conversation and prayers of a venerable father or mother in Christ. These are they who are pining for the bread of life, who are turning their anxious eyes to the proffered aid of your society. They are few in number and weak in means ; but could the gospel once be stately fixed among them, their prospects would be enlightened, as it is well ascertained that there is scarcely any settlement in the country containing a few pious families but the number would be speedily increased by emigrants were there only a certainty that the privileges and ordinances of the gospel awaited their arrival. How then shall this seed become productive of a future harvest without cultivators? And where are the cultivators to be found? They are not in the field; nor are they rearing up in the midst of us. In the Presbyterian connection there are not three candidates for the ministry in the whole state. Whence then shall we look for Pauls and Apolloses to tend the husbandry of God but to your society?

Our population at present is rated at between 200,000 and 300,000; and we have only twelve resident Presbyterian ministers in the state. The Presbytery to which I belong embraces a range of territory nearly 200 miles in length and 80 in breadth; in which we have only four members with charges, though we number nineteen congregations. I am stationed in the center of a large body of population, yet my nearest clerical neighbor lives at the distance of 50 or 60 miles. I was this year obliged to travel 140 miles to attend Presbytery.

The scarcity of ministers and missionaries forms the burden of our lamentation. Few are they who are found ready to devote themselves to the blessed apostolical work of seeking the wandering sheep; fewer, no doubt, than they would be, could those who have abundance be persuaded to bestow a part of it toward furnishing the laborer with his well-earned hire. "The Lord's sheep are scattered because there is no shepherd; yea, his flock are scattered upon all the face of the earth and there is none to search or seek after them." Most earnestly therefore do we request that shepherds may be sent among us, those who shall "seek that which is lost, and bring again that which is driven away, and bind up that which is broken, and strengthen that which is sick."

The needed "shepherds" came slowly. TRUMAN PERRIN, however, of the Royalton Association of Vermont, arrived this year, having been summoned to take charge of the Presbyterian seminary at Vincennes. He was also helpful in the pulpits on both banks of the Wabash, but did not formally connect himself with Presbytery. As a corresponding member he was present in the Synod of Indiana at its first meeting, and again the subsequent year.

JAMES CRAWFORD, a Princeton graduate, "was appointed as a missionary in Indiana" by the A. H. M. S., August 14, 1826. He reached the state December 1, and labored in Jennings County, "in a circuit embracing Paris, Vernon, and Dartmouth." In northern Indiana his usefulness extended through many years.[1]

SAMUEL E. BLACKBURN, a licentiate of Louisville Presbytery, was received by Salem Presbytery, and on December 1, 1826, was ordained at Jeffersonville.

JAMES DUNCAN, a minister of the kirk of Scotland, a man of force and scholarship, coming to America had settled in the neighborhood of Steubenville, Ohio. He was received by Madison Presbytery October 5, 1826. Already an old man, and afflicted with dropsy, he preached irregularly. He frequently visited the family of Mr. Alexander Gordon, at Shelbyville, where he occupied his leisure upon the manuscript of a volume of sermons which he afterward printed.[2]

On his foot-journeyings through the state [says James M. Ray[3]] he preached several times in the Indianapolis church. He was a well-built, broad-shouldered, sturdy traveler, a scholar of the olden days, having the paragraphs of his sermons duly numbered, and taking his periods so leisurely that his stopping at times to cut a chew of tobacco with his jack-knife from a plug from his pocket would only cause him to say to us, "Well, well, as I was stating under my last head." He was the father of Congressman Duncan, from Cincinnati. Among the scraps of memories of his preaching I still have hold of one in which he manifested to his own satisfaction, and doubtless to all those who had kept awake

[1] See *The Home Missionary*, Vol. I., pp. 116, 183; Vol. II., pp. 63, 176; Vol. III., p. 134; Stewart's "Recollections of Carroll County," and Ranney's "History of the Presbyterian Church, Delphi, Carroll County."

[2] A copy of this rare volume was presented to the Franklin church, at its semi-centennial, by Judge Fabius M. Finch.

[3] MS. "History of the Early Days of Presbyterianism at Indianapolis." Cf. Judge Banta's "Historical Address" at Franklin, pp. 18, 19.

in a summer day, that slavery was a breach of every one of the Twelve Commandments.

Among the missionaries of the Assembly this year were ISAAC A. OGDEN in Union, Franklin, and Fayette Counties, and JOSEPH ROBINSON in Bartholomew and Shelby Counties.

The event of the year, however, was the organization, by an act of the General Assembly on the 29th of May, of the Synod of Indiana, consisting of the four Presbyteries of Salem, Madison, Wabash, and Missouri, and including, besides nearly the whole of Indiana, vast regions in Missouri and Illinois. To the Indiana congregations and ministers, thus far required to contemplate annually a long, toilsome, and perilous journey across the Ohio to the Kentucky Synod, it occasioned most welcome relief to see the center of ecclesiastical power transferred to their own borders.

Old Vincennes was appropriately designated by the Assembly as the first place of meeting. Baynard R. Hall, who was present, has described the horseback ride from Bloomington.

Uncle John had been appointed lay delegate from the Welden Diocese to attend an ecclesiastical convention about to meet early this fall at Vincennes ; and he now, before our return to Woodville, obtained my promise to accompany him. Accordingly, a few days after our return, he, and with him Bishop Shrub, called on me, and we three set out for the convention, or—as all such gatherings are there called—the Big Meeting.

The weather was luxurious, and the ride across the small prairies was to me, who now for the first time saw these natural meadows, indescribably bewitching ; indeed, this first glimpse of the prairie world was like beholding an enchanted country. . . The bosoms of these grassy lakes undulate at the slightest breeze, and are sprinkled with picturesque islets of timber, on which the trees are fancifully and regularly disposed, suggesting an arrangement by the taste of an unrecorded people of bygone centuries for pleasure and religion. The whole brought back delusive

INDIANA SYNOD ORGANIZES. 219

dreams—we felt the strange and half celestial thrill of a fairy scene.

. . . This Protestant assembly was a gathering of delegates principally from the land of Hoosiers and Suckers, but with a smart sprinkling of Corn-crackers and a small chance of Pukes from beyond the father of floods, and even one or two from the Buckeye country. These were not all eminent for learning, and polish, and dress, wearing neither *doane* gowns nor *cocked* hats ; although some there were worthy seats in the most august assemblies anywhere and however distinguished for wit, learning, and goodness. Most of these Protestants, indeed, carried to excess a somewhat false and dangerous maxim—"Better wear out than rust out," since it is better to do neither. And worn, truly, were they, both in apparel and body, as they entered the town on jaded horses, after many days of hard and dangerous traveling away from their cabin-homes, left far behind in dim woods, beyond rivers, hills, and prairies.

. . . Truly it was a House of Bishops, if not of Lords ; if by a bishop is meant one that has the care of many congregations, an enormous parish, abundant religious labors, and a salary of one or two hundred dollars above nothing. In the midst of so fraternal a band of ministers and brothers, I was constantly reminded of an old saying, " Behold how these Christians love one another." What could exceed their cordial and reciprocal greetings at each arrival? What their courtesy in debate? What the deep interest in each other's welfare, the lively emotions excited by their religious narratives and anecdotes? And then their tender farewells ! To many the separation was final as to this life.[1]

Of this interesting meeting, the first Indiana Synod, the following full abstract from the records is taken :

The Synod of Indiana convened at Vincennes on the 18th day of October, 1826, agreeably to the appointment of the General Assembly. Rev. William W. Martin, the person appointed to preach the opening sermon, being absent, Synod was opened with a sermon from Rev. John M. Dickey on Genesis xviii.:19. Constituted with prayer.

Present: From Missouri Presbytery, Mr. Salmon Giddings,

[1] See "The New Purchase," 3d. ed., pp. 271, 272, 278, 279. The thin veil of romance in these descriptions is easily penetrated. Cf. Chapter XIII.

minister, and Mr. James McClung, elder; from Salem Presbytery, Mr. Tilly H. Brown, minister, and Mr. James Young, elder; from Wabash Presbytery, Messrs. Samuel T. Scott, George Bush, and Baynard R. Hall, ministers, and Messrs. James Scott, John Orchard, Frederick Dey Hoff, John Holme, James Carnahan, Robert Taylor, Thomas Gold, Samuel Peery, and James McKee, elders; from Madison Presbytery, Messrs. John M. Dickey, John F. Crow, and James H. Johnston, ministers, and Alexander Walker, elder.

Absent: From Missouri Presbytery, Rev. Messrs. John Matthews, Charles S. Robinson, Thomas Donnell, John Brich, William S. Lacy, and John S. Ball; from Salem Presbytery, Rev. Messrs. William W. Martin, John Todd, John T. Hamilton, and Alexander Williamson; from Wabash Presbytery, Rev. Messrs. Isaac Reed and Stephen Bliss; from Madison Presbytery, Rev. Messrs. William Robinson, James Duncan, Samuel G. Lowry, and Samuel Gregg.

Mr. Dickey was appointed moderator, Mr. Johnston clerk, and Mr. Brown assistant clerk.

Rev. Truman Perrin, from the convention of Vermont, being present, was requested to take his seat as a corresponding member.

Resolved, That Synod adopt the General Rules for Judicatories, recommended by the General Assembly, as the general rules of this Synod.

Messrs. Samuel T. Scott, Crow, Giddings, and Dickey were appointed a committee to prepare Permanent Regulations and a Standing Docket. Messrs. Crow and Dey Hoff were appointed a committee to examine the records of Missouri Presbytery. Messrs. Samuel T. Scott and Carnahan, a committee to examine the records of Madison Presbytery. Messrs. Giddings and Holme to examine the records of Salem Presbytery. Messrs. Johnston and Walker to examine the records of Wabash Presbytery. Messrs. Crow and Bush were appointed a committee to prepare a Synodical report. Messrs. Samuel T. Scott, Bush, James Scott, and Holme were appointed a committee of Bills and Overtures, to meet at this place to-morrow morning at 8:30 o'clock and afterward on their own adjournments. Messrs. Crow, Hall, Brown, McKee, and Gold were appointed a committee for judicial purposes, to meet at this place to-morrow morning at 8:30 o'clock and afterward on their own adjournments.

Presbyterial reports were presented from Missouri, Salem, and Madison Presbyteries, all of which were accepted.

INDIANA SYNOD ORGANIZES. 221

On motion, *Resolved*, That Synod meet to-morrow morning at 6:30 o'clock to spend a season in special prayer that a spirit of union and harmony may be granted during its deliberations. Adjourned. Concluded with prayer.

October 19th. Synod met agreeably to adjournment. Constituted with prayer. Members present as on yesterday. Minutes of yesterday were read. Synod spent a season in social prayer.

. . . *Resolved*, That Synod proceed to the election of a stated clerk and treasurer. Whereupon Mr. Johnston was appointed stated clerk and Mr. Crow treasurer.

. . . An overture was presented requesting Synod to form a new Presbytery in the state of Illinois, making the boundaries of the state the boundaries of the Presbytery. . . . After some discussion it was resolved that this business be indefinitely postponed.

An overture was presented requesting Synod to appoint a committee to prepare a petition to the General Assembly, to make the Ohio River our boundary on the south and the eastern line of Indiana our boundary on the east. This overture was now taken up and Messrs. Johnston, Crow, and Giddings were appointed said committee.

. . . An overture was presented requesting Synod to consider whether some plan may not be adopted to put a stop, in some measure, to the growing evils resulting from the intemperate use of spirituous liquors and the profanation of the Sabbath within our bounds.

Resolved, That this overture be now taken up and a committee be appointed to report on the subject before the close of the present session of the Synod. Messrs. Giddings, Hall, and Crow were appointed said committee.

An overture was presented requesting Synod to consider what exertions ought to be made by this body to secure the location of the Western Theological Seminary at Charlestown in Indiana.

Resolved, That this overture be now taken up and a committee be appointed to report on the same before the close of the present sessions of Synod. Messrs. Giddings, Bush, Hall, Crow, and Johnston were appointed said committee.

The following Preamble and Resolutions were presented for the consideration of Synod, viz.:

WHEREAS, Salem Presbytery at its spring session in 1825 appointed a committee to prepare a succinct history of the churches under its care, which history was not completed until after the division of said Presbytery and the formation of the Synod of Indiana, therefore

Resolved, That a committee be appointed to examine said history and report to Synod what disposition shall be made of it. Messrs. Giddings, Hall, and Carnahan were appointed a committee agreeably to the above resolution.

Resolved, That Mr. Bush be appointed to preach the missionary sermon at the next meeting and that Mr. Hall be his alternate.

Resolved, That Mr. Scott be appointed to preach the "Concio ad clerum" at the next meeting and that Mr. Crow be his alternate.

. . . . .

October 20th. Synod met agreeably to adjournment. . . . The committee appointed to report on the growing evils of intemperance and Sabbath breaking presented a report which was accepted and adopted and is as follows, viz.:

The committee appointed to inquire what can be done to remedy the evils arising from the intemperate use of ardent spirits and the profanation of the Sabbath beg leave to report,

1. That Synod recommend to each minister to preach a sermon on the subject of intemperance.

2. That Synod procure one hundred and fifty printed copies of a memorial to Congress, praying for an excise upon spirituous liquors, to be distributed among the members of Synod.

3. That Synod recommend to its members to use their exertions to obtain subscribers to this memorial, to secure the coöperation of other denominations, and to forward the memorial as soon as practicable to our representatives, at the ensuing session of Congress.

4. That Synod enjoin upon its members to pay particular attention to the recommendation of the General Assembly on the profanation of the Lord's Day contained in the 29th and 30th pages of their minutes for 1826.

Mr. Hall was appointed to superintend the printing of the memorial above referred to.

The committee appointed to prepare a petition to the General Assembly respecting boundaries presented a report which was accepted and adopted and is as follows, viz.:

The committee appointed to prepare a petition to the General Assembly submit the following: To the Rev. Moderator of the General Assembly:

Rev. Sir: Permit us through you to lay before your body the following resolution of the Synod of Indiana passed at its sessions in Vincennes at its first meeting, viz.:

Resolved, That a committee be appointed to prepare a petition to the General Assembly to make the Ohio River our boundary on the south and the eastern line of the state of Indiana our boundary on the east. In support of the above petition we would respectfully offer the following considerations :

1. We deem it very desirable that the boundaries of our respective Synods should be so obvious and notorious that there can be no difficulty in ascertaining them and consequently no conflicting claims to congregations. That a case of this kind occurred in respect to Sand Creek church will be seen by referring to the minutes of the General Assembly of 1825.

2. The boundaries of the state of Indiana seem to be the natural boundaries of the Synod of the same name.

3. As the Presbytery of Missouri is attached to the Synod of Indiana, and the state of Illinois seems naturally to belong to the same Synod, it appears improper for the jurisdiction of the Kentucky Synod to extend north of the Ohio River.

4. The convenience of the churches within the specified limits requires that they should all be attached to the same Synod.

5. The desire of the churches that would be affected by the proposed alterations has been expressed, to a considerable extent at least, decidedly in favor of these alterations.

Resolved, That the above petition be signed by the moderator and forwarded by the stated clerk to the General Assembly.

Resolved, moreover, that the stated clerk be directed to write to the stated clerks of the Muhlenburg, Cincinnati, and Miami Presbyteries, and inform them of the measures adopted by Synod on this subject and request the coöperation of their respective Presbyteries.

. . . The following overture was taken up, viz.: "Is it right for ministers of our order to invite ministers of the Cumberland Presbyterian order to assist in the administration of the sealing ordinances?"

Resolved, That this business be indefinitely postponed.

. . . The following overture was taken up and adopted, viz.:

WHEREAS our Synod presents a great missionary field which ought to be occupied, and inasmuch as our people are more ready to contribute for missionary exertions within our bounds, therefore,

Resolved, That the General Assembly be requested to permit this Synod to manage its own missionary concerns and that the stated clerk be directed to forward this resolution to the General Assembly.

. . . Synod adjourned to meet at Salem on the third Thursday of October next. Concluded with prayer and the Apostolic Benediction.

JOHN M. DICKEY, Moderator.
JAMES H. JOHNSTON, Clerk.

Having now traversed the first period of our Indiana church history, concluded in the establishment of the Synod, the limit of these studies has been reached. What we have seen may well satisfy our pride. The roll-call of pioneers in any presence may be listened to with gladness and gratitude. Their labors were prodigious. Their success was abundant. Their reward is assured. It will be our duty not to forget what they heroically and wisely did to lay the foundations of that Christian society whose privileges remain for us and for our children.

The five good men who came in 1827 have all passed from earth. CALVIN BUTLER, from Andover and the A. H. M. Society, was for twenty years eminently useful at Princeton, Evansville, Washington, Booneville, and other points.[1]

The two following letters, addressed by Mr. Butler to the secretary of the Indiana Missionary Society, are better than a biography :

ANDOVER THEOLOGICAL SEMINARY, June 22, 1827.

Rev. and Dear Sir: I learn from the first Report of the A. H. M. S., of which the Rev. A. Peters is the corresponding secretary, that the Rev. James H. Johnston is the corresponding secretary of the Indiana Missionary Society. I have agreed to go as a missionary to Indiana under the patronage of the A. H. M. S. The report of the Executive Committee of that Society runs thus : " Your appointment, therefore, is for twelve months from your

[1] See McCarer's " Memorial Sermon "; A. H. M. S. Reports, 1828-1835; *The Home Missionary*, Vol. I., p. 11; Vol. II., p. 195; Vol. III., p. 200.

arrival on the field of labor, to labor in such place or places in the State of Indiana as shall be advised by the Indiana Missionary Society." The object of my writing is that you, as Cor. Sec. of your Society, would write me, as soon as possible, designating the field to which I shall bear my course immediately after leaving this Seminary.

I wish to state explicitly the situation in which I am going. I am going with a companion ; not, however, with a feeble, sickly thing, unaccustomed to any place except the parlor. The health of my intended companion, like my own, is at present perfectly good. We both have firm constitutions. I am to receive my support, including what I may obtain from the people there, from the A. H. M. S. I am going with the expectation of staying there, and of settling, when it shall be convenient and best. I am going without any property, except it be a good library, but am owing more than the value of that ; but I think I know the meaning of the old adage —" Necessity is the mother of Invention," and I hope I am not ignorant of another of a superior kind—" For we walk by faith, not by sight."

I have been thus explicit because Mr. Bush from Indianapolis, who is here at present, told me that there were many places to which he should not recommend a man to go with a companion ; but there were others where he should. I have no particular choice, except it be to go where there is a fair prospect of enjoying good health and of doing the most good. If there were two places equal, as it regards these, the one lying on the river Wabash and the other in the country, probably I should prefer the former. Mr. Bush mentioned some places which he considered the most important, viz. : Terre Haute, Crawfordsville, Raccoon, Franklin County, and Bartholomew County. Still he said you would decide it.

I hope to start from New England about the middle of October next, and I wish to know the field of labor as soon as possible, in order to make the necessary preparations.

I am requested to make a similar inquiry for a definite field of labor for Brother Cobb, a classmate, who is going to labor under the patronage of the same society. I will give you the vote of the Ex. Com., viz. : Voted to commission Mr. Leander Cobb, to labor twelve months in such place or places in the State of Indiana, or Illinois, as shall be advised by the Indiana Missionary Society. Mr. Cobb will go out single, but wishes to know where his field of labor is as soon as possible. Mr. Bush mentioned Fountain and

Tippecanoe Counties, Vermillion, Putnam, Owen, and Morgan Counties as inviting fields for Brother Cobb.

PRINCETON, Nov. 30, 1827.

Rev. and Dear Sir: After the trials of a long and tedious journey I have at last arrived at what I shall call the place of my destination. Myself and companion were mercifully preserved in perfect health and without accident through the whole way. When we arrived at Indianapolis we were somewhat disappointed to learn that Terre Haute was preoccupied. Our minds had been fixed upon that place ever since I received your letter last summer and for some time before; but I doubt not that it was all ordered for the best. I was still further disappointed not to find according to your letter—"a copy of instructions ready for me at Indianapolis," but still shall hope 'tis all for the best. I was told there that my place of location was to be at Washington and that I was to labor in Washington, Paoli, and Princeton. I went to Washington and Mr. Carnahan told me that I was to locate myself in either of the places, and was to labor in the vicinity of the place I should choose, and not in the other two places. I thought he must be correct as he was personally interested. I accordingly went to Paoli, and made some inquiries, and went to see Mr. Martin, supposing that he would know all about it. He told me as he understood the business it would be proper for me to select any place within the bounds of the Salem Presbytery, or in Washington, etc. I then went to Princeton, and made what inquiries were necessary, and called on Mr. Scott as I returned to Washington, where I had left my wife. He thought I was to labor in Washington and Portersville and that no other places were assigned. I then concluded to make my own selection, according as I thought the path of duty marked out, after I had made all necessary inquiries; and accordingly came to this place. I thought it would be eventually more for the interest of Christ's kingdom to come here than to stay in Washington, because the principal part of the inhabitants are not professors of any denomination, and still they are very anxious to have a Presbyterian minister reside among them. They have also a fine institution just coming into existence which they wish to have patronized in such a manner as to make it valuable to the cause of education. At Washington they are mostly professors of some denomination. They have also a Cumberland minister among them and although they have a large church and are anxious that I should stay, still I thought it more for the interest of the cause to come to this place, which is larger and unoccupied.

LEANDER COBB, also from Andover, labored long in Clark and Washington Counties, returning to Massachusetts in 1841.[1] WILLIAM LOWRY, a Princeton graduate of unusual promise and maturity, was drowned in the Driftwood, near Columbus, February 11, 1828.[2] WILLIAM HENDERSON was received from Ebenezer Presbytery, but in a few months died. JAMES THOMSON, eldest son of John Thomson, of Springfield, Ohio, licensed by Cincinnati Presbytery, October 5, 1826, and ordained October 3, 1827, came to the wilderness where Crawfordsville has been built and was prominent in the penniless quintet of missionaries who, a little later, established Wabash College. He died at Mankato, Minn., October 4, 1873.

Our review closes just as a second generation of noble men, some of whom are still among us, appears to prosecute the Master's work. The last name recorded naturally suggests a brief consideration of what was accomplished by Presbyterians for the cause of education in Indiana, during these first years.

[1] See A. H. M. S. Reports; "Salem Presbytery Reporter"; *The Home Missionary*, Vol. I., pp. 11, 63, 98, 182; Vol. II., pp. 81, 141; Vol. III., pp. 60, 119, 201.

[2] See an obituary notice in Report of A. H. M. S., 1828, p. 31. The water-stained Confession of Faith found in the saddle-bags of the missionary after his death is an interesting relic of the "perils of waters" in the early days.

CHAPTER XVII.

INDIANA PRESBYTERIANS AND EDUCATION.

PRESBYTERIANS build schoolhouse and church side by side. In all their history and in many lands they have been educators. Upon American soil this characteristic tendency has noticeably appeared. Of Indiana it is almost literally true that there were no schools until the Presbyterian minister arrived. Nearly without exception the first ministers were school-teachers also, and when an exception did occur the minister's wife usually was competent and willing to take upon herself what had come to be regarded as a feature of the ordinary pastoral work. Scott at Vincennes, about 1803, and Baldridge at Lawrenceburgh, as early as 1811, started schools. Who in Indiana taught Greek and Latin before them?[1] Their immediate successors in the pulpits—Robinson, Dickey, Todd, Martin, Reed—all followed them into the schoolroom too. Bible and spelling-book as civilizers helped each other, and tuition fees made a grateful though slight addition to the precarious and scanty income. In the early schemes to establish permanent institutions of learning, there was, however, a different and stronger motive, the desire to obtain for the new West a competent, indigenous ministry.

[1] In "The Schools of Indiana" a statement is made which requires modification. "The pioneer teachers," says the writer, "were generally adventurers from the East, or from England, Scotland, or Ireland, who sought temporary employment during winter while waiting for an opening for business." This may be largely true of the second generation of school-teachers whom Mr. Hobbs remembers. But there were others of a different sort, twenty or thirty years before them. It is believed that the best pioneer school work in Indiana was done by Presbyterian ministers, and that they were the literal pioneers in that work, with the sole exception of two or three Catholic missionaries like Father Rivet. Cf. "The Schools of Indiana," pp. 53, 54.

Of the oldest Indiana college, the State Institution at Bloomington, the origin is to be traced to national legislation. But in its beginnings, the work, though undenominational, fell upon the Presbyterians.[1] The first instructors were all Presbyterian ministers and the board of trustees was largely Presbyterian. This predominance, fairly won at first, naturally disappeared in time from an institution adopted and fostered by the state, and might probably with advantage have been yielded with less delay.

In 1802 the national Congress had made a grant of a township of land in Gibson County for the support of an institution of learning, and encouraged by that act the territorial legislature in 1807 incorporated the Vincennes University. When in 1816 Indiana was admitted into the Union, Congress granted an additional township for college purposes, and under that act Perry township in Monroe County was designated. Thereupon, the Vincennes University being regarded as a lifeless scheme, the legislature in 1820 appointed the trustees of the Indiana Seminary, and the board having met in the following June at Bloomington, selected the site of the future university. Steps were taken toward the erection of a building, the contracts being let in March, 1822. Two years were consumed in the work, which was still incomplete when, in the spring of 1825, with about twenty students, Baynard R. Hall, who had come West for that service, opened the school. He had entire charge of the institution until May, 1827, when John H. Harney became associated with him, as professor of mathematics, natural philosophy, and astronomy. Early in 1828 the legislature chartered the school as a state college, and the Rev. Andrew Wylie, D.D., president of Washington College, Pennsylvania,

[1] On an ill-considered page an Indiana writer, describing the origin of the first schools, ventures to attribute to unworthy motives the natural prominence in the work of education of the few men on the field who were themselves educated. See " Indiana Methodism," p. 317.

was summoned to the head of it. There he remained until his death, November 11, 1851, for twenty-three years successfully conducting its affairs through many perils and conflicts.[1] The school was greatly embarrassed by its poverty. By and by serious disagreements arose in the faculty. The jealousies of the sects made trouble. In 1854 nearly everything visible belonging to the college was destroyed by fire. And finally the Vincennes University, supposed to have been long comfortable in its grave, successfully asserted before the courts its claims to the proceeds of the Gibson County lands, which had been expended at Bloomington. By the timely intervention of the legislature, the state, rather than the college, was made the sufferer, the judgment against it amounting to sixty-six thousand five hundred and eighty-five dollars. The institution was thereby rescued from what had looked like irretrievable disaster. In recent years a generous attitude toward its child has been maintained by the General Assembly, and the State University now honorably occupies the place it has bravely conquered for itself. With regard to its aims, its methods, and its success Indiana Presbyterians can never be indifferent, having borne so largely all the responsibilities of its early career.

It was in the establishment of HANOVER COLLEGE, however, the oldest of the denominational schools, and only a little less ancient than the institution at Bloomington, that the earliest energies and affections of the church were directly engaged. The lack of Christian laborers was a daily burden upon the hearts of the faithful men who were toiling in these swamps and forests.[2] Few recruits could be expected from the older communities.

[1] See "Address on the Life and Character of Andrew Wylie, D.D.," by Theophilus Parvin, M.D., Indianapolis, 1858.

[2] See Dr. Crowe's account of the origin of the college, Johnston's "Forty Years in Indiana," pp. 21, 22. Cf. Cressy's "Appeal in Behalf of the Indiana Theological Seminary," pp. 7, 9.

Some who did venture away from the more luxurious conditions of society in the East were feeble and useless as frontiersmen. There must be a way devised to educate the Christian young men already on the ground. How could that object be secured? The problem was a constant theme of lonely thought, and of long debate in Presbytery, by cabin back-logs and on horseback journeys, considered too with an intensity of feeling, a fixedness of purpose, and a solidity of judgment in every way remarkable. The names of the men most conspicuous in these negotiations are happily not forgotten. They were chiefly John Finley Crowe, John McElroy Dickey, and William W. Martin. Into their circle was fully admitted, upon his arrival in 1824, James H. Johnston, whose position at Madison, and as secretary of the Indiana Missionary Society, made him painfully familiar with all the necessities of the field. Dickey had carried the burden longest. Martin was already training ministers and ministers' wives in his own Livonia log house. Crowe, the pastor at Hanover, years before a successful teacher in Kentucky, a man of admirable discretion and persistence, was steadily pushed forward by providence until, laying down a few first bricks, he found that he had "builded better than he knew," and had become the founder of a college.

No sooner had Salem Presbytery come together at the first meeting than they began to confer about the means of Christian education.[1] The theme so promptly introduced was never allowed to rest in Presbytery or Synod until provision had been made for a complete classical and professional training. At the meeting of Presbytery in the autumn of 1825 a committee was appointed to perfect a scheme for a Presbyterial academy and to determine its location. The committee's report at a subsequent meeting

[1] Cf. Chapter XII.

favored the village of Hanover as the seat of the academy and a committee was designated to obtain a teacher. Already as a preparatory step a private school had been opened at Hanover by a gentleman invited thither by Mr. Crowe. But the search for a permanent instructor proved unsuccessful, and finally, in 1826, the Presbytery[1] formally laid the whole work upon Mr. Crowe, requesting him to organize the academy and take charge of it until other arrangements should be made. Accordingly "in a log cabin on Dr. Crowe's grounds, near the Presbyterian Church, on the first of January, 1827, the school was organized with prayer."[2] Thus at last was planted in Indiana the germ of a Presbyterian college.

The first pupil of the school, the Rev. William M. Cheever, has furnished an account of his earliest Hanover experiences:

> My father,[3] who was teaching school in Paris, Jennings County, Indiana, was prevailed upon by Rev. John Finley Crowe to remove in 1825 to South Hanover and open a school in the old stone meeting-house, which was to become in part a sort of feeder to the classical academy which Mr. Crowe intended to open at no distant day. Though a mere lad, I attended my father's school, studying under him the Latin grammar. Two years after, in 1827, when between eight and nine years of age, I started to Mr. Crowe's Classical Academy, which was opened in his old loom-house. I remember vividly that first day. It was quite an epoch in my life. Besides, my father, who was deeply interested in this "young school of the prophets," as he termed it, often afterward alluded to the events of that day and they became fixed in my memory. He used to tell me that I had this preëminence, if no other, "I was the first student on the ground the day when Dr. Crowe opened his academy." I have seen and heard a

---

[1] The first steps were taken by *Salem* Presbytery, at the time the only Presbytery in the state. Upon the organization of the Synod in 1826 the academy was included in the territory of *Madison* Presbytery, which conducted its affairs until they were committed to the Synod.

[2] "Semi-Centennial Sketch," by George C. Heckman, D.D., pp. 4, 5.

[3] Joshua Cushman Cheever, a native of Vermont, a student, though not a graduate, at Brattleboro, a good classical scholar and lifelong teacher.

variety of statements as to those early days, none of them being absolutely correct. Indeed, I suppose it will be impossible now to reproduce all the facts as they actually transpired during the first few weeks. But this much is correct. On the first day there were but two students present, James Logan and I. He was several years my senior. I have seen the statement that the academy opened in the old loom-house with some half-dozen young men present the first day, among whom were Daniel and Samuel Lattimer, James Logan, David V. Smock, and young McNutt. But none of them were there on the morning of the opening save Logan.[1] He and I had the distinguished honor of being the pioneer students.

For the academy thus established an act of incorporation was obtained from the legislature December 30, 1828. As there was now every promise of permanent success the Presbytery sought to transfer the school to the supervision of the Synod, and at the fall meeting in 1829 a committee was appointed to effect that object. The committee appeared in Synod in October, and having reported the action of Presbytery it was approved by Synod and the academy was adopted as a Synodical school "provided the trustees of the same will permit the Synod to establish a theological department and appoint the theological professors."[2] The condition named was willingly acceded to, the negotiations were at once completed, and the school became the Synod's property.

Steady progress had from the first been made toward

[1] A little later (July 4, 1877), while suffering severely from the cancerous affection which was soon to terminate his useful life, Mr. Cheever wrote as follows; "The real fact, as nearly as it will probably ever be ascertained in this world is—there were but two at the first recitation, three at the second, and several others dropped in that week, and more the week following. This is probably the order as to their coming: (1) Cheever, (2) Logan, (3) Smock, (4) McNutt, (5) Hanna, (6) Creswell, (7) Daniel Lattimer, (8) Samuel Lattimer, (9) Tilford, (10) Graham, (11) Miller." Mr. Cheever adds: "Perhaps one reason why my memory of those early days ought to be better than that of others is that my father was Dr. Crowe's nearest neighbor and intimate friend. These matters were themes of constant conversation between Dr. Crowe and my father, in my presence. I call up with more ease the recollection of those days than I do the transactions after 1832, when I reëntered and graduated."

[2] "Minutes Synod of Indiana," Vol. I., pp. 101, 102.

the work and position of a college, and in 1833, the legislature having amended its charter, the Hanover Academy was in future to be known as Hanover College. Funds had been diligently collected, buildings had been erected, and the Rev. James Blythe, D.D., of Lexington, Ky., became the first president of the enlarged institution. Of the first board of trustees of the college the Rev. John M. Dickey was president, the Rev. James H. Johnston secretary, and the Hon. Williamson Dunn treasurer. From the first college catalogue it appears that there were already in attendance seven theological, sixty-three collegiate, and one hundred and thirteen preparatory students. Since that early day the college has shared with similar institutions a varied experience of prosperity and gloom, but now, with seventy years of history back of it, has in its faculty, its alumni, its endowments and traditions, a permanent foundation.

The INDIANA THEOLOGICAL SEMINARY was conspicuously a child of providence from the first. Reference has been made to the motive in which it originated, and so imperative did this motive become, as year after year the need of ministers increased, that desire advanced to what looks like desperation, and the audacity of the first efforts gives to this chapter of history the tone of romance. Throughout the church and on the floor of the General Assembly there were already most earnest discussions as to the feasibility of establishing a divinity school in the West. To these debates the little band of pioneers in Indiana listened with unflagging attention, and in the midst of the rivalry between Allegheny Town and Walnut Hills had sufficient assurance to propose as a better location Charlestown, in Clark County! "An overture was presented requesting Synod to consider what exertions ought to be made by this body to secure the location of the Western

Theological Seminary at Charlestown in Indiana."[1] The next day after the presentation of this overture, in accordance with the report of an able committee to which it had been referred, it was resolved :

(1) That Synod approve the resolution of the General Assembly to establish a Western Theological Seminary. (2) That if such seminary is ultimately to become a benefit to the rapidly increasing population west of the mountains, it ought to be at present located in a central situation without much regard to the amount of monies offered by the several places now proposed. (3) That Synod consider Allegheny Town as entirely too far east to be considered even as a western town, and Charlestown as more central than Walnut Hills. (4) That Charlestown is a healthful situation and easy of access, and that the maintenance of students and the salaries of professors will be for many years very far less than at the other places, owing among other things to the comparative plainness of our manners. (5) That the seminary may and probably ought to commence on a small scale, and be gradually enlarged, as the funds and the number of students increase. (6) Synod pledge themselves to use their highest efforts to aid the seminary, if located at Charlestown. (7) A committee should be appointed to address a communication to the General Assembly, stating the reasons which induce the Synod of Indiana to recommend Charlestown as a suitable site for the intended theological seminary, and that this committee be required to ascertain as far as practicable, by communicating with other Synods, and by any other means they may see proper, how much interest may exist in favor of Charlestown, and how large an amount of money may probably be raised for that place, which also shall be stated to the General Assembly.[2]

The committee suggested by the last resolution was appointed — Messrs. Dickey, Hamilton, and Bush, strong and true men all of them. But at this interval it will occasion no surprise that their faith was disappointed, and that Bush, describing the Assembly of 1827 and the triumph of Allegheny Town, confessed that he "did not

[1] "Minutes Synod of Indiana," Vol. I., p. 13.
[2] "Minutes Synod of Indiana," Vol. I., pp. 21-3.

plead hard for Charlestown, which could have stood no chance against the formidable bids of the other two sites."[1]

To Crowe, Dickey, and Johnston and their associates this first "Waterloo defeat," however, only furnished new enthusiasm and better discipline. Promptly turning from the more ambitious design to their own smaller resources, in October, 1827, it was resolved "that a committee of three members of Synod be appointed to consider the expediency of taking preparatory steps for the establishment of a literary and theological seminary, under the care of Synod ; and, should such a course be by them thought expedient, that they be authorized to draw up a plan of such seminary and report on the subject at the next stated meeting of Synod."[2] This committee[3] made report at the subsequent meeting in 1828, when, "after some discussion" the further consideration of it was indefinitely postponed "excepting the item concerning a theological seminary," which was postponed for another year.[4] At Shoal Creek church, Bond County, Ill., October 16, 1829,

the order of the day, namely, the report respecting a theological seminary, was taken up and the following resolution was adopted, viz.:

WHEREAS, Hanover Academy has been incorporated by an act of the legislature of the State of Indiana, according to which act the Board of Trustees of said Academy are permitted, by special provision, to place it under the care of any body of learned men that they may select ; and

WHEREAS, the board, at a late meeting, appointed a committee of their body to make a tender of the institution to the Synod of Indiana, that said Synod might avail themselves of the corporate privileges granted, in founding a theological seminary, in connection with the Academy, therefore,

Resolved, That a committee be appointed, on the part of the

[1] Cf. biographical notice of Rush.
[2] " Minutes Synod of Indiana," Vol. I., p. 53.
[3] The committee were Messrs. Dickey, Crowe, and Johnston.
[4] " Minutes Synod of Indiana," Vol. I., p. 62.

INDIANA PRESBYTERIANS AND EDUCATION. 237

Synod, to confer with the committee of the Trustees of the Academy, and to report on the subject as soon as may be practicable.[1]

The day following the committee reported

that they have conferred with said committee, and have examined the charter of said Academy and inquired into its present prospects, and they believe that the interests of the churches within our bounds would be promoted by taking said Academy under the care of this Synod. They therefore recommend the adoption of the following resolutions, viz.: (1) That this Synod adopt said Academy as a Synodical school, provided the trustees of the same will permit the Synod to establish a theological department and appoint the theological professors. . . . (3) That this Synod appoint a Board of Directors, to superintend the theological department of Hanover Academy. (4) That the Synod at this time appoint a theological professor. (5) That the Synod appoint a committee to prepare a plan of union, to be agreed upon by the trustees of the Academy and the Synod of Indiana, and also a plan for the regulation of the theological department.[2]

The sagacious and prudent men who had had this business in charge did not venture thus far without considering whether for the proposed chair of theology a competent scholar could be obtained. With the Rev. Dr. John Matthews an informal correspondence had been opened, as to the possibility of his coming to Hanover if an invitation should be extended to him. The following reply was addressed to the "Rev. Messrs. J. F. Crow and J. H. Johnston":

SHEPHERDSTOWN, VA., September 23, 1829.

Your joint letter of the 10th inst. was duly received and its suggestions have been the subject of serious consideration. I suppose that consideration is all that can be expected from me, in the present stage of the business to which you refer. Materials which would justify a decision, one way or the other, are not yet

[1] "Minutes Synod of Indiana," Vol. I., pp. 93, 94.

[2] "Minutes Synod of Indiana," Vol. I., pp. 101-3. As the committee here required Messrs. Moreland, Martin, Dickey, Cobb, and Johnston were named.

furnished, nor is it in your power to furnish them, as they would be derived from events yet future, and over which your ageney may have but a limited influence. I wish to feel, as every minister of the gospel ought to feel, devoted to the great Head of the church. This, of course, implies a willingness to labour wherever he may, in his providence, call me. Altho my labours have not been blessed of late years with the same numbers added to the church as formerly, yet I must consider it my duty to remain and labour here, till a call from some other quarter shall reach me. If this call should come, it will then be the subject of consideration with a view to a decision. If the claims of this call are stronger than those arising out of my present location, they will prevail. One thing indispensably necessary would be, the prospect of usefulness;—another would be, a support for my family. I have not for twenty years past attended to anything but the duties of the ministry, have received at no time more than a bare support, and that with the greatest economy. A support is all I expect. My family consists of myself and wife; one daughter grown; four little boys, the oldest ten; and two sons at the Seminary at Princeton, all dependent on my salary; with one or two servants. I am not competent to judge what would answer this purpose in your state, not being acquainted with the expenses of living there. You will see therefore that from the nature of the case I cannot give a decisive answer to your proposition, and must of course leave you, and all who may feel interested in the case, to be influenced by your own views of expediency respecting the interests of your institution, and of the church in your growing state. If inclination alone was to guide me, if about to remove from this region, my views would turn to the West, not on my own individual account so much as on account of my sons, whom I must leave before many years, and leave, too, dependent on their own efforts to gain a subsistence in life. I shall have nothing to leave them that would exempt them from these efforts. An education is all that I can furnish myself the pleasure of giving them. I feel a very deep interest in the progress of religion and literature in your state, and indeed in all the western country. It is all important that there should be both Theological and Literary Institutions of reputable character to exert a favourable influence on the growing population of that section of our country. I shall be pleased to hear from you when you may find it convenient.

This communication gave such encouragement that the

business proceeded without embarrassment in the Synod, and Dr. Matthews was named unanimously for the professorship.[1] The Virginia pastor accepted the call to Indiana and at once began to devote himself to the interests of the divinity school. He wrote from New York, March 15, 1830, to Mr. Johnston, as follows :

You will no doubt be surprised to receive a letter from me, dated in this city; but so it is. I am here as an agent for the Hanover Theological Seminary. My object is to secure, if possible, a moderate salary for a Tutor or Professor of Biblical Literature in the seminary. This proceeds from an earnest desire that the seminary should not commence without an assistant in this department. I have supposed that if it was known that there was such a teacher in the seminary it would give it more importance, and give a pledge that young men could receive a full course of study for the ministry.

The plan proposed is this: to raise five hundred dollars for five years, and I now hope this object will be accomplished. I have already obtained thirteen subscriptions of $25 each for five years. I am encouraged to believe that seven, perhaps ten, more can be obtained. The clergymen of this city, to whom I have mentioned the plan, cordially approve of it, and Dr. Spring is one of the subscribers. If the plan succeeds I shall be much rejoiced. Nor can I suppose that the Synod of Indiana, or any friend of the Seminary will object to it. In addition to the annual subscriptions I will receive some donations, and some books; but to what amount is yet uncertain. I expect to spend a few days in Philadelphia and in Baltimore in the same agency. I find I am a poor agent; but my desire to secure this Assistant induces me to make the effort. A young man can be obtained from Princeton or elsewhere, qualified for this department. I have supposed that the seminary would not commence till next fall, probably after the meeting of your Synod. The subscriptions obtained here are payable in April in each year, and the first payment to be in 1831. This is the time proposed by the subscribers themselves; and I suppose it will answer the purpose, as the subscription may be relied on.

Your letter was received shortly before I left home, which was on the 1st inst. Numerous engagements prevented me from

[1] Cf. " Minutes Indiana Synod," Vol. I., pp. 108, 109.

writing to you before I set out, and besides, I did not know but my agency would be an entire failure. We expect to remove some time in the month of May, but whether in the early or latter part is yet uncertain. We must accomplish the journey, if possible, before the season for steamboat navigation is over. I expect to find a letter from you when I return home, and will then write to you again, and give you the result of my agency, and if possible fix the time when we may be expected in Indiana.

The professors at Princeton gave me their cordial approbation of the seminary and of the object of my agency, in writing; so also did some of the clergy of Philadelphia. Upon the whole I hope the great Head of the church will bless the Hanover Seminary, and I hope its friends will not cease to pray for its prosperity and usefulness.

Still another letter to Mr. Johnston, written from Shepherdstown, April 13, 1830, indicates, as does the entire history, how insignificant were the resources, and how bold and enterprising the faith, by which these projects were advanced:

I hope you received my letter from New York, giving an account of the agency I had undertaken for the Hanover Theological Seminary. The result of that agency has been that $500 annually for five years has been secured, the first payment to be in April, 1831. This is for the special purpose of securing the assistance of a teacher of Biblical Literature in the seminary, and this it is believed will be sufficient for this purpose. In Philadelphia $80 has been, and probably $100 will be secured annually for five years, the first payment in May, 1830. Eighty dollars of this I have received. With this $80, and other donations, after deducting my expenses, there is now in my hands $130 for the seminary. The number of volumes I obtained will probably be about thirty, some of them valuable. . . . We expect to commence our removal early in May—the day is not yet fixed, and will reach Madison, with the favour of God, some time from the 15th to the 20th of the month.[1]

Meanwhile the committee designated for the purpose

[1] These manuscripts of Dr. Matthews all painfully indicate how serious an affliction must have been that "trembling in his hands," referred to by Dr. Woods. Cf. Sprague's "Annals," Vol. IV., p. 294.

was perfecting a plan for uniting the divinity school with the Hanover Academy, and in 1830 the Synod adopted their report. In accordance with this compact the trustees gave to the Synod the supervision of the academy, upon condition "that the Theological Seminary about to be erected by the Synod of Indiana shall be located at Hanover Academy, or its immediate vicinity, in Jefferson County, . . . the seminary being considered the theological department of said academy." The Synod was to have the whole control of the theological department, appointing its directors, choosing the professors, governing the pupils, and managing the funds. The negotiations were completed by the selection of the following gentlemen to constitute the first board of directors of the seminary: *Ministers*, J. F. Crow, J. R. Moreland, William W. Martin, A. Wylie, L. Cobb, James Thomson, B. C. Cressy, Samuel Gregg, William Sickels, S. R. Alexander, Alexander Williamson, S. G. Lowry, J. M. Dickey, J. H. Johnston, C. Butler; *Elders*, Samuel Smock, Jeremiah Sullivan, Victor King, Alexander Walker, Samuel S. Graham, Williamson Dunn, Andrew Wier, Joseph Hart, James H. Thomson, W. B. Laughlin, John Hendricks, James M. Ray, Ebenezer Sharpe, James Scott, and Dr. B. Bradley. A teacher of oriental and biblical literature was at the same time chosen, John W. Cunningham having no competitor. It was understood that he should be permitted, upon his acceptance of the place, to spend six months in further study at Andover. It was also resolved "that the salary of the professor of theology be for the present fixed at six hundred dollars per annum, and that it commence on the first day of May, 1830."

The inauguration of Dr. Matthews as professor of theology occurred June 29, 1831, when he delivered a thoughtful address upon "Ministerial Qualifications."[1]

[1] This discourse, together with the Rev. B. C. Cressy's address on the same occasion, was printed by Arion & Lodge, Madison, 1831.

Financial questions of course at once began to assume a commanding prominence. Even upon the modest scale of prices suggested by the chief professor's salary more money was required than the woods of Indiana could provide. An agent was accordingly appointed to solicit aid in the older states—the Rev. Benjamin C. Cressy, a man of scholarship and discretion. At Boston, December, 1832, he printed an appeal for the seminary. He said:

> The prosperity of this institution has thus far exceeded the most sanguine anticipations of its founders, and for this very reason now labors under the most serious embarrassment. Enlarged accommodations are immediately needed; but to go forward without the prospect of assistance will be presumption, to go back will blast the hopes of thousands. Under these circumstances we appeal to the friends of learning and religion to aid us. Our funds are exhausted, our instructors are to be supported, our library is small, applications for the reception of students are constantly increasing, and yet we have more already than we have room to accommodate. For the want of better accommodations many of our students have been under the necessity of occupying contracted log-cabins. In the midst of difficulties, with a spirit of tireless perseverance and great personal sacrifices, the professors "have labored and have not fainted." The friends of the institution in the vicinity have been liberal, and are ready to do all in their power, but the necessary aid cannot there be obtained. And what shall be done? . . . We believe that He, whose is the silver and the gold, will incline the friends of learning and religion to aid us in sustaining this enterprise.[1]

The anticipations of adequate financial support were not realized. At the Synod in 1831 a subscription paper was circulated, once and again. In 1832 there is mention of one agent at the East, and of another "to enter on his agency shortly," still another being under appointment to visit the churches at home. There is allusion in 1833 to the "arrears in which the seminary is now involved." It

---

[1] "An Appeal in Behalf of the Indiana Theological Seminary Located at South Hanover, Indiana." Boston, 1832.

is attempted in 1834 to unite with Indiana the Synods of Illinois, Kentucky, Cincinnati, and Ohio in the care of the seminary. The following year Dr. Crowe explains a plan to raise twelve thousand dollars in Indiana. Similar laborious methods are perseveringly prosecuted, including assessments upon the Presbyteries and congregations—the difficulties largely increased by the controversies of 1838, until in 1840 the "proposition of Mr. E. Ayres for a change in the plan of the seminary" was adopted, and the institution was transferred to New Albany.

In the new location it was still a burden upon the poverty of this new region; but when there was little money there was more faith, and the self-denying work of professors and directors was rewarded by its undoubted utility. The ability of the faculty was conspicuous and the spirit with which they imbued the students is blessing the church to-day. For nearly twenty years the school held on, always hindered by insufficient financial resources, until in 1859, amidst the commotions preceding the War of the Rebellion, it was committed to the General Assembly and by that body established in the city of Chicago, as the Seminary of the Northwest, later to be known as McCormick Seminary.[1]

JOHN MATTHEWS, who received the first appointment to

[1] The Assembly of 1859 (Old School) held its sessions at Indianapolis. On Monday afternoon, May 23, the order of the day was taken up—"the report of the Standing Committee on Theological Seminaries upon the papers connected with the transfer of the Presbyterian Theological Seminary of the Northwest. The whole report of the committee was read, as also were proposals, from different localities, of gifts of money and land toward the endowment of this institution, and the following resolutions were adopted unanimously, viz.:

"1. *Resolved*, That in accordance with the overtures, emanating from eight Synods, this Assembly does now accept the direction and control of the seminary known by the corporate name and style of the Presbyterian Theological Seminary of the Northwest.

"2. *Resolved*, That this Assembly during its present sessions will decide by a majority of the votes of its members, what place within the limits of these eight Synods be selected as the seat of said Seminary."—" Minutes Assembly of 1859," pp. 516, 517.

The debates affecting the seminary were protracted and noteworthy. Besides the problem as to location were most interesting personal matters, while the jealousy between North and South, everywhere apparent at this period, added to the heat.

the chair of theology in the seminary, was born in Guilford County, N. C., January 19, 1772. His father, who in early life had emigrated from Ireland, was a small farmer. The son, having until he was twenty years of age wrought at various mechanical employments, then began a course of study under the Rev. Dr. David Caldwell, in whose family he for a time resided. He received licensure, March, 1801, from the Presbytery of Orange, and a few months later went as a missionary to Natchez, Miss. Returning in 1803 to North Carolina he became pastor of the Nutbush and Grassy Creek churches. Three years later, resigning this charge, he was installed over the church in Martinsburg, Va., but soon afterward received an urgent call to the pulpit at Shepherdstown, Va., made vacant by the transfer of Dr. Hoge to the presidency of Hampden Sidney College. This church he continued to serve until his removal to Indiana, a period of twenty-four years. During portions of this time he also served the Charlestown and Martinsburg churches, preaching frequently besides at Harper's Ferry. In connection with the seminary he resided at Hanover, and at New Albany, until his death, May 19, 1848.

Dr. Matthews was twice married—December 8, 1803, to Elizabeth, daughter of John Daniel, of Charlotte County, Va.; and in April, 1818, to Elizabeth, daughter of James Wilson of Berkley County, Va. Of his six sons three became clergymen of the Presbyterian Church.

Besides a large number of sermons and addresses, and articles in literary and theological journals, Dr. Matthews was the author of two more extended treatises entitled, "Letters on the Divine Purpose" and "The Influence of the Bible."[1]

---

[1] See Sprague's "Annals," Vol. IV., pp. 292-4. Letters from the Rev. Drs. James Wood, James M. Brown, Samuel B. Wilson, and William C. Matthews are appended to Sprague's biographical sketch.

Born in revolutionary times Dr. Matthews was the contemporary and friend of a body of ministers, including Drs. Alexander, Spence, Waugh, Moses Hoge, John H. Rice, and others, whose solid, scriptural, spiritual theology constituted them almost a distinct school of divines. Dr. Matthews was the peer of any in that honored group ; and it is scarcely extravagant to say that had he and Dr. Archibald Alexander exchanged places, the history of the church had not been materially different. The great characteristic of his mind was simplicity. He defined everything to its ultimate elements. He traced everything through all its history to its remotest possible and logical uses. His mind seemed to be a case of pigeon-holes, where every thought seemed to lie by itself, wrapped in its own proper word, which would rarely, if ever, be changed, and always ready for immediate use. His power of definition was inimitable, and gave him signal and speedy success in controversy. Whoever in debate with him failed to detect mistake or fallacy in definitions might as well concede the whole argument. His sole text-book as professor was the Confession of Faith, out of which he drew an extensive scheme of both didactics and polemics. His course was prefaced by lectures upon mental philosophy and logic, as bearing upon the ministerial office and work. His method was the Socratic, both for instruction and disputation. His observation had been careful, his experience varied, his thinking deliberate and thorough ; so that while never voluble he was always ready to enter at once upon any train of remark or discussion, and always with the right word for every place. His promptitude indeed resembled special preparation.

Another conspicuous trait in the character of Dr. Matthews was his modesty. He shrank from no duty, but he sought no distinction, no fame, and even avoided publicity. His was in eminent degree the power of godliness. The first, last, and deepest impression left upon his students, his friends, and his neighbors, was that he was a holy man, of deep and rare attainment in grace, of rich and ripened fruit of the indwelling spirit of Christ.[1]

Dr. Matthews, was in person spare and tall. While in his last years the infirmities of age manifestly increased he was able to continue active labor to the close of life.

[1] Dr. J. Edwards's address in " Services of the Laying of the Corner-Stone and Addresses at the Dedication of the Chapel and Library of the Presbyterian Theological Seminary of the Northwest." 24 pp.

Only a week before his death he met his students as usual in the lecture room. Submitting, however, to a surgical operation the result was quickly fatal.

ERASMUS DARWIN MACMASTER, who succeeded Dr. Matthews in the chair of theology, was a man of prodigious native force. His individuality of feature and form, of manner and mind, would have commanded attention anywhere. His scholastic attainments were of a high order. Upon the arena of manly conflict his weapons were those of a giant, while in the domestic precinct and in the circles of friendship he had a child's simplicity and a woman's tenderness.[1] Of Scotch Covenanter blood, a son of the Rev. Gilbert MacMaster, long pastor of the Reformed Presbyterian Church, Princeton, Ind., he was born in the year 1806. He graduated from Union College. While pastor at Ballston Spa, N. Y., he attracted the notice of representatives of Hanover College, Indiana, who were attending a meeting of the Synod of New York in search of a president for their institution. The invitation which they extended to him was favorably received, and in 1838 he removed to the West. An agitation for the enlargement of the institution and its transfer to Madison, with a new charter, as Madison University, involved Dr. MacMaster with some of the earliest friends of Hanover who clung to the old place and the old patient methods.[2] In 1844 the transfer was effected; but the lack of support enforced the abandonment of the enterprise after one year of trial. Thereupon Dr. MacMaster was called to the presidency of Miami University and took up his residence at Oxford, Ohio. Upon the death

[1] An old friend recalls the gracious affectionateness with which he unfailingly greeted his sisters on retiring for the night and when he met them in the morning.

[2] See "Speech of Mr. MacMaster in the Synod of Indiana, October 4, 1844, in relation to Madison University," with postscript. Madison, Jones and Lodge, 1844. 39 pp.

of Dr. Matthews, however, the Indiana Seminary looked at once to him, and he came in 1849 to New Albany as teacher of divinity. Here he continued for ten years, and until the institution was established by the Assembly of 1859 in Chicago. That Assembly was an animated one. For the last time, in full force and with undaunted courage, the South came to meet their brethren of the North. In that stormy period everything touched in some way the institution of slavery.[1] When it came to the choice of professors for the reorganized divinity school a man with the well-known progressive sentiments of Dr. MacMaster was sure to be thrust aside. Out of two hundred and seventy-seven votes he received but forty-five for the chair of didactic theology. Thereupon he went into retirement, watching silently the marvelous events of the Civil War, which brought so sudden and complete a vindication.[2] He saw the Presbyterians of the North all facing at last, and many of them facing about, toward his platform. He was no longer in the minority. At St. Louis in 1866 the General Assembly placed him in the chair for which he was so eminently fitted, and he went to Chicago as professor of theology. He had hardly entered upon his duties, however, when death overtook him. After ten days of suffering he expired, December 10, 1866. His death was as remarkable as his life had been. During his illness his mind was constantly upon the Scriptures. He repeated passage after passage, and, it may be said, chapter after chapter, in the original Greek.

[1] See "Speech in the General Assembly of the Presbyterian Church, May 30, 1859, on the Presbyterian Theological Seminary of the Northwest," by E. D. MacMaster. Cincinnati Gazette Co. 1859. With appendix. 40 pp. Also, "The Late General Assembly and the Theological Seminary of the Northwest," by "Alpha." 16 pp. The public press of the time teemed with communications from well-sharpened quills.

[2] Dr. MacMaster was a great admirer of Bacon, whose portrait adorned the wall of his study. Underneath the picture, in the doctor's "horrible chirography," was a sentence from Bacon, in which the philosopher declared his willingness to leave his character to the judgment of posterity.

He had the unshaken and exulting confidence of Paul. In the closing moment his eyes kindled to intense brilliancy, his hands were raised as if in surprise and adoration, and to his brother he said: "I see heaven opened and Jesus standing at the right hand of God." These were his last words.[1]

The Rev. Dr. Edward P. Humphrey, who, as a director of the seminary at New Albany, was brought into close official relations toward him, writes[2] as follows of the subject of this sketch:

Dr. MacMaster had an imposing personality. He was very tall, his hair was thick and white, his countenance open and full of expression, his eyes shining with thought and emotion. In his movements he was deliberate; not graceful but dignified; with a certain magisterial air. He was somewhat reserved, especially among strangers. I doubt whether his most intimate friends would venture to take undue liberty with him. And yet he was polite and affable, and never forgetful of even the minor courtesies of life; always a model Christian gentleman.

His father was an eminent and honored minister of his church—one of the branches of the kirk of Scotland wherein the Presbyterianism was intensified; whose right to be rested on the assumption that it was the best representative in existence of the best type of the pure and unadulterated old faith. The mother was a person of marked clearness of spiritual vision and of great force of character, modified by womanly gentleness. The son closely resembled her in his best qualities.

Dr. MacMaster was not what men call a popular preacher. Those who had often heard him preach expected from him, when they went to hear him again, a sermon full of weighty matter, the substance and the arguments and illustrations taken from the divine word, the whole arranged with the skill of an accomplished logician, the points made with prodigious clearness and force, rarely lighted up with a touch of poetry or fancy; although, when the current of thought became very deep and rapid, imagery

---

[1] The "remarkable spiritual vision" here referred to is vividly remembered by the Rev. Dr. George L. Spining, who was a pupil of Dr. MacMaster's, and who witnessed the final scene.

[2] Louisville, Ky., March 1, 1886.

sometimes came to the surface, clothed with Miltonic grandeur.[1] The power of impassioned exhortation was not among his gifts. He set forth the matter and excellencies of the gospel offer lucidly and earnestly, and then left his hearers to the workings of the spirit of God upon their consciences. I do not remember to have seen him preach a written sermon, or use even brief notes. He had a copious vocabulary at his command and never faltered for a word.

The great work of his life was done in teaching systematic theology in the New Albany Seminary. Few men have been as thoroughly furnished for that great office by knowledge of the divine word, by thorough inward conviction of the agreement of the Presbyterian system of doctrine with that word, and by a gift of teaching every way admirable. His method was his own. The topic for the day had been previously announced; the students were expected to gather, from the Scriptures and from other sources, information as full as possible in regard to the doctrine in hand. Dr. MacMaster took the chair, with no table before him, no printed book or written memorandum in his hand. The students were seated in a semi-circle near by. They were called on, in their order, to answer questions proposed by the teacher—these questions so formed as to elicit the knowledge or the ignorance of the pupil, his difficulties, and his mistakes, arising from confusion of thought or from imperfect definitions. The teacher, too, was ready to be interrogated. An animated conversation was likely to spring up, leading to inquiry and thought and private study. Such a mode of teaching would be a failure in the hands of some men; but Dr. MacMaster was too full of resources to fail, too clear in his conceptions, too ready and patient in his dealing with the quick-witted and the plodding; correcting the over-complacent and encouraging the diffident. His pupils to this day talk about the clearness of his spiritual and intellectual vision, his love of truth, his eagerness in its exposition and defense, his skill in detecting subtle and dangerous errors in religion, and

[1] Dr. MacMaster's public prayers must have had something of the character of the discourses here described by Dr. Humphrey. On a single occasion I had the pleasure of seeing and hearing Dr. MacMaster. A year before his death he was present at a union morning prayer-meeting of the two Synods (Old and New School) of southern Indiana, in the First Presbyterian Church, Madison. He was called upon to offer prayer. Even his name had been previously unknown to me; but the thought and language and tone of the prayer at once enchained attention. It was a body of divinity—deliberate, systematic, progressive, complete. Its intellectuality would have seemed out of place but for the masterful lighting up of Scripture which it embodied, together with a certain awful worshipfulness. I judge that the prayer must have occupied the greater part of an hour.

the exceptionable, stimulating effect of his mode of teaching. When to all this we add testimony to his blameless Christian life, his unstained honor and integrity in the sight of all men, we have before us the image of an eminent servant of God.

JOHN W. CUNNINGHAM, the first professor of sacred rhetoric in the seminary, after a few years sought the more congenial work of the pastorate, continuing it until his death.

GEORGE B. BISHOP was Mr. Cunningham's successor. He was a fine scholar, an admirable teacher, and withal a fearless, pungent preacher. But coming to the professorship with health already impaired by study, his career was short.

JAMES WOOD, another professor in this chair, was more than a professor.

He was an unwearied and successful soliciting agent. He was the careful superintendent of the seminary's property. He kept the refectory. He gave or got assistance for every indigent or troubled student. He was a fair scholar, but was a better theologian and preacher than exegete. He had, too, that kindly tact, that Christian art of "putting things" which enabled him to bear his part in a heated controversy with calmness, firmness, and without bitterness.

THOMAS EBENEZER THOMAS, LEWIS W. GREEN, WILLIAM M. SCOTT, and PHILIP LINDSLEY are all well-known and honored names which belong to a later period of the seminary's history.

WABASH COLLEGE was established a little after the close of the era to which these sketches particularly refer. It would, however, be inappropriate to conclude a chapter relating to Presbyterian education in Indiana without some mention of an institution which has had so successful a career and now stands almost alone in the state as to the fulness of its endowments and the promise of future enlargement.

This college owes its origin to the counsels and efforts of five home missionaries, who early selected the upper Wabash valley as their field of labor. One of the earliest to agitate this subject was Rev. James Thomson, who settled in Crawfordsville, November, 1827, and others connected with Crawfordsville Presbytery, then embracing most of the country of the upper Wabash, who often spoke to each other of the importance of a timely effort to plant an institution of learning, under good religious influence, and after the model of those planted by the fathers in the older portions of the country. It was not, however, till the autumn of 1832 that any definite measures were taken to carry the design into effect. The first meeting on this subject was held at the house of Rev. James Thomson, November 21, 1832. Present at this meeting were Rev. Messrs. James Thomson, James A. Carnahan, John S. Thomson, Edmund O. Hovey, and John M. Ellis, together with Messrs. John Gilliland, Hezekiah Robinson, and John McConnel.

The deliberations of this meeting resulted in the unanimous resolution that efforts should be made without delay to establish at Crawfordsville an institution of learning in connection with manual labor. At that time there was no literary institution, either located or projected, in this state north of Bloomington. Some of the considerations that showed the importance of the measure determined upon at that meeting are stated in the following extract from a letter written afterward by one of the persons who shared in its deliberations: "Being at that time an agent of the American Education Society, I became acquainted with the painful destitution of educated ministers in Indiana, and I learned from the brethren that they had been urging the moral destitutions of the state on the attention of eastern churches and theological seminaries, imploring their aid in sending more laborers into the great field whitening for the harvest. And that for these four years of entreaty, only two additional ministers could be obtained. This was a most depressing demonstration that the East could not be relied on to furnish pastors for the teeming multitudes of this great state. At the same time it was found that there were some twelve or fifteen pious young men, of the best promise, in the churches of the Wabash country, who would study for the ministry could they but have the facilities of education.

This seemed, in those circumstances, the clearest providential indication to found a college for the education of such young men."

A committee, to act temporarily as trustees of the institution, was appointed at this meeting. A liberal subscription was obtained from the citizens of Crawfordsville, a tract of fifteen acres of land was donated by Hon. Williamson Dunn, upon which the trustees, having selected a site for the building in the forest, in the midst of nature's unbroken loneliness, consecrated this enterprise for the furtherance of virtue and knowledge among mankind, to God, and solemnly invoked upon it the divine blessing.

Measures were shortly afterward adopted for the erection of a suitable building for the preparatory department of the institution. The trustees appointed Mr. Caleb Mills, then a theological student at Andover, Mass., as the principal of the preparatory department and Teachers' Seminary, under whose instruction the institution, in this form, went into operation December 3, 1833, with *twelve* students, nine of whom were professed Christians.

In January, 1834, application was made to the state legislature for a charter, which was granted, under the name of "Wabash Manual Labor College and Teachers' Seminary." One feature of this charter—that requiring the trustees to provide manual labor for the students—has, in a subsequent modification of it, been laid aside; the other is retained, and deemed of prime importance.

The enterprise thus commenced was prosecuted with unremitting zeal. By proper efforts at the West and at the East, funds were obtained; as the number of students increased additional teachers were appointed; regular college classes were formed; a president for the institution—Rev. Elihu W. Baldwin, of New York—a man peculiarly fitted for the work to which he was called, was secured; the erection of a large college edifice was entered upon, and, in the fall of 1838, was completed; a library was collected and a philosophical apparatus commenced. Everything promised prosperity; but reverses and trials were at hand. This edifice, just completed, was destroyed by fire, and library and apparatus were consumed with it, causing a loss of not less than $15,000. This loss occurring at a period of great commercial embarrassment, involved the necessity of procuring a loan of $8,000, in addition to all the funds that could be obtained by voluntary contribution. The debt thus incurred was a crushing incubus on the enterprise for eight years. In the mean time, a

INDIANA PRESBYTERIANS AND EDUCATION. 253

loss still more deeply felt was occasioned by the death of the beloved president of the college, which occurred October 15, 1840.

But amid these discouragements, the friends of Wabash College yielded not to despondency. A successor to Dr. Baldwin, in every respect worthy of the position which had been made vacant by his death, was found in Rev. Charles White, D.D., who entered on the duties of president in the fall of 1841, and whose useful and efficient labors for the advancement of the institution were continued for a period of twenty years. The college was also relieved, at length, from the pressure of its pecuniary embarrassments. Through the liberality of individuals, means were furnished, in 1846, for the liquidation of the debt that bore so heavily upon it. Important aid has been received also from the "Society for the Promotion of Collegiate and Theological Education at the West." Liberal donations for founding professorships have recently been made.[1]

Under the administrations of the Rev. Dr. Joseph F. Tuttle, Dr. White's successor, and of the Rev. Dr. George S. Burroughs, now at the head of the institution, the advance has been continuous.[2]

[1] Johnston's "Historical Discourse," pp. 23-6.

[2] See also Hovey's "Historical Sketch of Wabash College," Dr. Tuttle's baccalaureate of 1876, and various similar sketches by Dr. Tuttle.

APPENDIX.

I.

MISSIONARY AGENCIES AT WORK IN INDIANA PREVIOUS TO 1826.

TRANSYLVANIA PRESBYTERY issued the first commission to a missionary to Indiana. This action was taken at Danville, April 14, 1803. (Cf. Chapter III.)

In its care for the "regions beyond" the GENERAL ASSEMBLY was not much behind. An appointment was made in 1805 (see Assembly's minutes) for three months' missionary service "in the Indian (*sic*) Territory," etc. At its first meeting, May 21, 1789, the General Assembly had taken under consideration the work of missions, and each of the four synods was directed to name to the next Assembly two persons qualified to serve as missionaries on the frontier. The Presbyteries were instructed to make collections for the support of the missionaries. In May, 1790, several appointments of missionaries were accordingly made, western New York and Pennsylvania being then on the extreme frontier line. Similar appointments were made by the successive Assemblies until 1802. At that time, the importance and extent of the enterprise having greatly increased, it was resolved "that a committee be chosen annually by the General Assembly, to be denominated 'The Standing Committee of Missions'; that this committee shall consist of seven members, of whom four shall be clergymen and three laymen." To this committee were entrusted the appointment and oversight of missionaries and the general management of missionary work during the recess of the Assembly. The committee continued its labors with great success until 1816, when the Assembly organized "the Board of Missions acting under the authority of the General Assembly of the Presbyterian Church in the United States."

Of the voluntary organizations which sent early aid to the Indiana wilderness the CONNECTICUT MISSIONARY SOCIETY was perhaps the most prominent. The General Association of Connecticut is composed of delegates from each of the local associations in the state and seems to have held its first meeting at Hartford in 1709. Soon after the War of the Revolution great numbers of the people of Connecticut having emigrated westward, attention was directed to their religious wants, and in 1795 the association issued an address to the new settlements making known their purpose to send them "settled ministers, well reputed in the churches, to preach among them the unsearchable riches of Christ, and as occasion might offer to gather and organize churches, to administer sealing ordinances, to instruct their young people, catechize their children, and perform all those ministerial duties which are usually practiced in the churches and congregations of Connecticut." Previous to this period, however, a few missionaries had been sent out, the first apparently in 1788. Until 1798 the General Association conducted directly, during its annual sessions, its missionary enterprises, as the General Assembly of the Presbyterian Church for a time was accustomed to do. But at the meeting in June, 1798, the association organized itself into a missionary society, with a board of trustees empowered to conduct its business. The object of the society was "to Christianize the heathen in North America and to support and promote Christian knowledge in the new settlements within the United States." This organization had from the first a most efficient management, and after more than twenty years of great activity formed an important nucleus of the later national society.

During the early part of the present century, in New England and New York especially, a large number of state, district, county, and city mission societies were founded. Among these was the "YOUNG MEN'S MISSIONARY SOCIETY" of New York City. It had been organized January 23, 1809, as the "Assistant New York Missionary Society," changing its name as above indicated in 1816. This society became tributary to the "United Domestic Missionary Society" of New York, soon after the organization of the latter.

The "UNITED DOMESTIC MISSIONARY SOCIETY" of New York, a combination of a number of smaller societies of different religious denominations, was established in New York City in May, 1822. The fourth and last annual report of the society shows that during the year preceding they had aided 127 missionaries, four of whom were in Indiana. In connection with the meeting of the society May 12, 1826, a convention was held to consider the propriety of associating in a single organization the kindred missionary societies throughout the country, and it was finally resolved "that the recommendation of the convention be adopted, and that the United Domestic Missionary Society now become the AMERICAN HOME MISSIONARY SOCIETY, under the constitution recommended by the convention." The convention was composed of representatives from the states of New Hampshire, Vermont, Massachusetts, Connecticut, New York, New Jersey, Pennsylvania, Ohio, Indiana, Kentucky, South Carolina, Alabama, and Arkansas. Its object was declared to be "to assist congregations that are unable to support the gospel ministry, and to send the gospel to the destitute within the United States."

THE INDIANA MISSIONARY SOCIETY was formed at a meeting of the friends of missions held at Livonia on the first Friday of August, 1822, according to a recommendation of Louisville Presbytery. The organization was tributary to the Assembly's Committee of Missions. Little was done the first year besides the establishment of a few auxiliary associations. During the second year ten weeks of missionary labor were accomplished. The third year the society had in its employ six missionaries resident within its bounds. Afterward its missionaries were found in every part of the state. At the annual meeting in August, 1826, the constitution was so amended as to make the society auxiliary to the American Home Missionary Society; and the missionaries sent by the parent society to Indiana were located by the standing committee of the auxiliary. (See Dickey's "Brief History," pp. 18, 19.) Among the officers of the society were the Rev. Samuel T. Scott, president; Dr. Isaac Coe, the Hon. James Scott, the Hon. William Hendricks, and General Homer Johnston, vice-presidents; the Rev. William W. Martin, recording secretary; and the Rev. Isaac Reed, corresponding secretary. The Rev. John M. Dickey was chairman of the standing committee.

II.

ECCLESIASTICAL RELATIONS OF THE INDIANA CONGREGATIONS PREVIOUS TO 1826.

1. TRANSYLVANIA PRESBYTERY, constituted May 17, 1786, by the Synod of New York and Philadelphia, had no

definite northern limits, but exercised jurisdiction over the Indiana territory.

2. With the consent of the Synod of Virginia Transylvania Presbytery was separated (March 27, 1799) into the three Presbyteries of Transylvania, West Lexington, and Washington. The last-named Presbytery comprised that part of Kentucky lying northeast of Main Licking and *the settlement on the northwest side of the Ohio River*. At this time, as also in 1802 when from these Presbyteries the Synod of Kentucky was constituted, there were no Presbyterian churches in Indiana, and this region was evidently not considered in defining the Presbyterial boundaries.

3. Miami Presbytery was erected in 1810 (from Washington) and in 1815 the General Assembly granted a petition of the Synod of Ohio (constituted in 1814) to make the Ohio River the boundary between the Synods of Kentucky and Ohio. This action placed the Indiana churches within the limits of Miami Presbytery. In 1811 (October 15) the Presbytery of Muhlenburg was, however, permitted to "extend its bounds so as to include Mr. Scott at Vincennes."

4. In 1817 the dividing line between the Synods of Kentucky and Ohio was changed by the Assembly so as to include within the bounds of the latter so much of the former Synod as lay within the state of Indiana, west of a line drawn due north from the mouth of Kentucky River. Most of the Indiana churches thus came under the jurisdiction of Louisville Presbytery (formed from Transylvania in 1814), a few preaching stations like Rising Sun and Lawrenceburgh, east of the line indicated, being still left within the boundaries of Miami.

5. By an act of the Synod of Kentucky, October, 1823, all that part of Indiana previously within the limits of Louisville Presbytery was constituted into the new Presbytery of Salem.

6. In October, 1824, that part of the state of Indiana which lies south and west of the following lines, viz.: beginning opposite the mouth of Green River, running due north twenty miles, thence northwestwardly to the mouth of White River, was attached to Muhlenburg Presbytery. At the same time that part of the state of Illinois belonging to the Synod of Kentucky which lies north of line due west from the mouth of White River was added to Salem Presbytery.

7. By the Synod of Kentucky, October, 1825, two new Presbyteries were formed, Wabash on the west and Madison on the east, and with Salem and Missouri Presbyteries were constituted by the General Assembly, May 29, 1826, into the Synod of Indiana.

III.

Bibliography.

DICKEY, JOHN M.: *Brief History of the Presbyterian Church in the State of Indiana.* Madison, printed by C. P. J. Arion, 1828.

REED, ISAAC: *The Christian Traveller, in five parts, including nine years and eighteen thousand miles.* New York, printed by J. and J. Harper, 82 Cliff St., 1828.

HALL, BAYNARD R.: *The New Purchase; or, Seven and a Half Years in the Far West.* By Robert Carlton, Esq. 2 vols. New York, D. Appleton & Co., 200 Broadway. Philadelphia, George S. Appleton, 148 Chestnut St., 1843. *Second edition*, two volumes in one (with portrait). New Albany, Ind., John R. Nunemacher. Also *third edition*, revised by the author.

BISHOP, ROBERT H.: *An Outline History of the Presbyterian Church in Kentucky, containing the Memoirs of Rev. David Rice.* Lexington, 1824.

HUMPHREY, EDWARD P., AND CLELAND, THOMAS H.: *Memoirs of the Rev. Thomas Cleland, D.D., compiled from his private papers.* Cincinnati, Moore, Wilstach, Keys & Co., printers, 25 West Fourth St., 1859.

STOWE, HARRIET BEECHER: *Men of Our Times.* Hartford Publishing Company, 1868.

BALDRIDGE, SAMUEL C.: *Sketches of the Life and Times of the Rev. Stephen Bliss, A.M., with notices of his co-laborers.* Cincinnati, Elm Street Printing Company, 1870.

MCCLUNG, JOHN ALEXANDER: *Sketches of Western Adventure, containing an Account of the most interesting Incidents connected with the Settlement of the West, from 1755 to 1794.* Also additional *Sketches of Adventure*, and a *Biography of J. A. McClung*, by H. Waller. Covington, 1872.

MORRIS, B. F.: *Review of Ten Years' Service with the Main Street Presbyterian Church and Congregation of Rising Sun, Indiana, from April, 1844, to April, 1854.* Williamson & Doyle, printers. 8 pp.

POST, M. M.: *A Retrospect after Thirty Years' Ministry at Logansport, Indiana.* Logansport, published by T. H. Bringhurst, 1860. 24 pp.

MCCARER, W. H.: *Remembrance of Past Days.* Evansville, Journal Company, 1860. 26 pp.

JOHNSTON, JAMES H.: *A Ministry of Forty Years in Indiana.* Indianapolis, Holloway, Douglass & Co., 1865. 30 pp.

BISHOP, JOHN M.: Ed. *Salem Presbytery Reporter*, Vol. I., No. 1. New Albany, April, 1850. 32 pp.

LAW, JOHN: *The Colonial History of Vincennes, under the French, British and American Governments from its first Settlement down to the Territorial Administration of General W. H. Harrison. Being an Address before the Vincennes Historical and Antiquarian Society, with Additional Notes and Illustrations.* Vincennes, 1858.

WILLIAMS, J. L.: *Historical Sketch of the First Presbyterian Church, Fort Wayne, Indiana, with Early Reminiscences of the Place. A Lecture before the Congregation, March 7, 1860.* John W. Dawson, printer. 27 pp. The same revised, and *read before the Congregation, October 16, 1881*, the semi-centennial of its organization. Daily News Printing House. 28 pp.

CLELAND, P. S.: *A Quarter-Century Discourse, delivered at Greenwood, Indiana, December 18, 1864, at the Twenty-fifth Anniversary of his Ministry to the Presbyterian Church in that place.* Indianapolis, Holloway, Douglass & Co., printers, 1865. 31 pp.

HOVEY, HORACE C.: *The Origin and Growth of Presbyterianism in New Albany* (printed in the *New Albany Ledger*, November 25, 1867).

BANTA, D. D.: *Historical Address delivered in the First Presbyterian Church of Franklin, Indiana, November 30, 1874.* 43 pp.

MONFORT, J. G.: *Historical Sketch of the Presbyterian Church of Greensburg, Indiana.* Cincinnati, Elm Street Printing Company, 1870. 32 pp.

MONFORT, J. G.: *Presbyterianism North of the Ohio, an Historical Discourse delivered in the Second Presby-*

terian Church of Cincinnati April 9, 1872, being the Fiftieth Anniversary of the Presbytery of Cincinnati. Cincinnati, 1872. 12 pp.

EDSON, HANFORD A.: *The Church God's Building, an Historical Discourse delivered December 22, 1867, at the opening of the New Chapel of the Second Presbyterian Church, Indianapolis, Indiana.* Indianapolis, Douglass & Conner, 1868. 18 pp.

GREENE, JAMES : *Semi-Centennial Anniversary of the Establishment of Sunday-schools in Indianapolis,* with *Historical Sketch of the Origin and Progress of the Indianapolis Sabbath-schools.* April 6, 1873. 33 pp.

CONDIT, BLACKFORD : *Historic Discourse delivered at the Quarter-Century Anniversary of the Second Presbyterian Church, Terre Haute, Indiana,* December 27, 1873. Cincinnati, 1874. 23 pp.

CHEEVER, WILLIAM M.: *Anniversary Sermon delivered at the Quarter-Century Anniversary of the Second Presbyterian Church, Terre Haute, Indiana,* December 28, 1873. Cincinnati, 1874. 22 pp.

RANNEY, JOSEPH A.: *History of the Presbyterian Church in Delphi, Carroll County, Indiana, being a discourse preached by the Pastor of the Church, November 28, 1875.* La Fayette, Ind., 1875. 16 pp.

DICKEY, N. S.: *History of the Presbyterian Church in Columbus, Indiana* (printed in the *Columbus Republican,* January 7, 1875).

————— —————: *The Sidney Centennial Jubilee* (containing memorials of the Johnston family), Ann Arbor, 1875.

HUTCHISON, J. M.: *The First Presbyterian Church of Jeffersonville, Indiana, and its history* (printed in the *Louisville Courier-Journal,* July 10, 1876).

NEAL, STEPHEN, AND BISHOP, JOHN M.: *An Address containing the History of Boone County from its Organization to the Present, delivered at Lebanon, Indiana, July 4, 1876; and a Sermon on the History and Growth of Presbyterianism in Boone County, Indiana, delivered in the Presbyterian Church at Lebanon, Indiana, July 2, 1876.* Lebanon, Ind., 1876. 16 pp.

SIMPSON, W. H.: *Historical Sermon, First Presbyterian Church, Madison, Indiana, preached July 16, 1876.* Printed by Bert S. Alling, Amateur Banner Office, Madison, Ind. 10 pp.

SLUTER, GEORGE: *Our Beloved Church: Historical Review, First Presbyterian Church, Shelbyville, Indiana.* Shelbyville, Ind., R. Spicer, printer, 1876. 27 pp.

SLUTER, GEORGE: *History of Shelby County, Indiana, from 1822 to 1876, by a Committee of Citizens.* Shelbyville, Ind., R. Spicer, printer, 1876. 40 pp.

POST, E. H.: *Forty-four Years in the History of the Presbyterian Church of Danville, Indiana. A Centennial Discourse, Sunday, June 4, 1876.* Danville, Union Job Office, 1876. 12 pp.

HOGUE, A. A.: *An Historical Discourse preached in the Presbyterian Church, Lebanon, Kentucky, 1857.* Louisville, Hull & Brother, 1859. 16 pp.

TUTTLE, JOSEPH F.: *Presbyterianism on the Frontiers, reprinted from the Presbyterian Quarterly and Princeton Review, July, 1877.* 25 pp.

BISHOP, JOHN M.: *Life in Indiana at Threescore.* Lebanon, 1879. 17 pp.

WISHARD, S. E.: Ed. *History of the Half-Century Celebration of the First Presbyterian Church, Franklin, Indiana.* Cincinnati, 1874.

BANTA, D. D.: *Making a Neighborhood*, delivered at the Shiloh Reunion, May 26, 1887. Franklin, Ind. 49 pp.

REED, ISAAC: *A Funeral Sermon, occasioned by the Early Death of Mr. John Young, Missionary to Indiana and Illinois in the year 1825, with a Sketch of his Life and the Time and Circumstances of his Death.* Indianapolis, printed by Douglass & Maguire. 13 pp.

BEECHER, HENRY WARD: *The Means of Securing Good Rulers, a Sermon delivered on the occasion of the Death of Noah Noble, late Governor of Indiana.* Indianapolis, printed by E. Chamberlain, 1844. 27 pp.

MAXWELL, GEORGE M.: *A Discourse on the Death of Samuel Merrill, delivered at Indianapolis, August 25, 1855, Indianapolis*, printed by the Indianapolis Journal Company, 1855. 17 pp.

PARVIN, THEOPHILUS: *Address on the Life and Character of Andrew Wylie, D.D.*, late president of the State University of Indiana, delivered before the Alumni of the University, July 14, 1858. Indianapolis, Cameron & M'Neely, 1858. 42 pp.

HOPKINS, T. M.: *Reminiscences of Col. John Ketcham, of Monroe County, Indiana.* Bloomington, Whitaker & Walker, 1866. 22 pp.

——— ———: *In Memoriam. Rev. James Chute, first pastor of the First Presbyterian Church of Fort Wayne, Indiana.* Printed for family use, 1874. 6 pp.

JOHNSTON, JAMES H.: *The Dead who Die in the Lord, Blessed. A Sermon preached in Centre Church, Crawfordsville, Indiana, February 26, 1871, on the Death of Rev. Albert Barnes.* Philadelphia, Wm. F. Murphy & Sons, 1874. 16 pp.

TUTTLE, JOSEPH F.: *Father Carnahan, of Dayton. A Discourse delivered at the Funeral of the Rev. James Aikman Carnahan, at Dayton, Indiana, January 22, 1879.* Review Office, Crawfordsville, Ind. 12 pp.

SCHENCK, WILLIAM E.: *A Memorial Sermon on the Life, Labours and Christian Character of Phineas D. Gurley, D.D.* Washington, D. C., William Ballantyne, 1869. 62 pp.

NEILL, EDWARD D.: *Early Days of the Presbyterian Church in Minnesota; the Substance of a Discourse delivered before the Synod of Minnesota, September 26, 1873.* xxvii. pp.

PATTERSON, R. M., and DAVIDSON, ROBERT: *Historical Sketch of the Synod of Philadelphia, and Biographical Sketches of Distinguished Members of the Synod of Philadelphia.* Philadelphia, Presbyterian Board of Publication. 128 pp.

JOHNSTONE, R. A.: *An Historical Sketch of the Presbytery of Transylvania, Kentucky.* Louisville, printed by Bradley & Gilbert, 1876. 45 pp.

STEWART, D. M.: *Historical Discourse of Whitewater Presbytery*, delivered at Lawrenceburgh, April 12, 1876. Indianapolis, Baker, Schmidlap & Co., 1876. 32 pp.

MOORE, AMBROSE Y.: *History of the Presbytery of Indianapolis.* Indianapolis, J. G. Doughty, printer, 1876. 132 pp.

BISHOP, JOHN M.: Ed. *Crawfordsville Presbytery.* Numbers 1–11. Pp. 1–102.

WHALLON, E. P.: *History of the Presbytery of Vincennes.* Indianapolis, 1888. 52 pp.

MCNARY, W. P.: *A Memorial Sermon of Rev. John McMaster, D.D.* Albion, Ill., 1876. 15 pp.

CRESSY, BENJAMIN C., AND MATTHEWS, JOHN: *A Discourse on Ministerial Qualifications,* delivered at Hanover, Indiana, June 29, 1831, together with an *Address on occasion of the Inauguration of the latter as Professor of Didactic and Polemic Theology in the Indiana Theological Seminary.* Madison, printed by Arion & Lodge, 1831. 30 pp.

CRESSY, B. C.: *An Appeal in behalf of the Indiana Theological Seminary, located at South Hanover, Indiana.* Boston, printed by Peirce & Parker, No. 9 Cornhill, 1832. 16 pp.

MACMASTER, E. D.: *Speech of Mr. MacMaster in the Synod of Indiana, October 4, 1844, in relation to Madison University.* Madison, Jones & Lodge, 1844. 39 pp.

CROWE, JOHN FINLEY: *A Review of Dr. MacMaster's Speech before the Synod of Indiana, October 4, 1844.* Madison, Jones & Lodge, 1845.

——— ———: *A Defence against the late Assaults upon the New Albany Theological Seminary.* By the Trustees. New Albany, Ind., 1853. 35 pp.

MACMASTER, E. D.: *Speech in the General Assembly of the Presbyterian Church, May 30, 1859, on the Presbyterian Theological Seminary of the Northwest.* Cincinnati, Gazette Company, 1859. 39 pp.

——— ———: *The Late General Assembly and the Theological Seminary of the Northwest.* By "Alpha." 1859. 16 pp.

EDWARDS, J.: *Services of the Laying of the Corner-Stone and Addresses at the Dedication of the Chapel and Library of the Presbyterian Theological Seminary of the Northwest* (including *Historical Review*). Birney, Hand & Co., Chicago. 24 pp.

—————— ——————: *Charter of Hanover College*, Hanover, Ind. 4 pp.

HECKMAN, GEORGE C.: *Log College of the West: Hanover College, or Early Christian Education by the Presbyterian Church in Indiana. A Semi-Centennial Sketch.* Courier Print, Madison, Ind. 12 pp.

TUTTLE, JOSEPH F.: *The Origin and Growth of Wabash College.* Logansport, Ind., 1876. 21 pp.

TUTTLE, JOSEPH F.: *Proceedings at the Quarter-Century Anniversary of the Society for the Promotion of Collegiate and Theological Education at the West, held at Marietta, Ohio, Nov. 7-10, 1868.* With an appendix. (Including address: *What has Wabash College Done?*) New York, The Iron & Smith Book Manufacturing Company, 1868. 182 pp.

WYLIE, ANDREW: *Sermon on the Subject of the Union of Christians for the Conversion of the World. Delivered Madison, Ind., April 20, 1834.* Printed by J. Lodge and E. Patrick, Madison, 1834. 17 pp.

SMART, JAMES H.: Ed. *The Indiana Schools and the Men who have Worked in Them.* Cincinnati, 1876.

WOODBURN, JAMES ALBERT: *Higher Education in Indiana.* Washington, Government Printing Office, 1891.

SPALDING, M. J.: *Sketches of the Early Catholic Missions of Kentucky, from their commencement in 1787 to 1826-7.* Louisville, 1844.

EVANS, MADISON: *Biographical Sketches of the Pioneer Preachers of Indiana.* With portraits. J. Challen & Sons, Philadelphia, 1862.

GOODE, W. H.: *Outposts of Zion.* Cincinnati, 1864.

HIBBEN, W. W.: *Rev. James Havens, one of the Heroes of Indiana Methodism.* Indianapolis, 1872.

HOLLIDAY, F. C.: *Indiana Methodism.* Cincinnati, 1873.

DARBY, W. J., AND JENKINS, J. E.: Eds. *Cumberland Presbyterianism in Southern Indiana.* Indianapolis, 1876.

SMITH, J. C.: *Reminiscences of Early Methodism in Indiana. Including sketches of various prominent ministers together with narratives of women eminent for piety, poetry, and song. Also descriptions of remarkable camp-meetings, revivals, incidents and other miscellany. With an appendix containing essays on various theological subjects of practical interest.* Indianapolis, 1879.

SLAUGHTER, P., DASHIELL, T. G., AND OTHERS: *Addresses and Historical Papers before the Centennial Council of the Protestant Episcopal Church in the Diocese of Virginia at its meeting in St. Paul's and St. John's Churches in Richmond, May 20–24, 1885.* New York, Thomas Whittaker.

SPRAGUE, WM. B.: *Annals of the American Pulpit.* New York, 1865–73.

FOOTE, WILLIAM HENRY: *Sketches of North Carolina, historical and biographical.* New York, 1846.

WHEELER, JOHN H.: *Historical Sketches of North Carolina from 1584 to 1851. Compiled from original records, official documents, and traditional statements, with biographical sketches of her distinguished statesmen, jurists, lawyers, soldiers, divines, etc.* Philadelphia, 1851.

FOOTE, WILLIAM HENRY: *Sketches of Virginia, historical and biographical.* Philadelphia, 1850. *Ditto*, second series, Philadelphia, 1855.

DAVIDSON, ROBERT : *History of the Presbyterian Church in the State of Kentucky, with a Preliminary Sketch of the Churches in the Valley of Virginia.* New York, Robert Carter, 1847.

PATTERSON, ROBERT W.: *Early Society in Southern Illinois.* Address before Chicago Historical Society, October 19, 1880. Fergus's Historical Publications, 1881. Illinois Local History, Vol. VI.

NORTON, A. T.: *History of the Presbyterian Church in the State of Illinois.* Vol. I. 735 pp. St. Louis, W. S. Bryan, 1879.

PATTON, JACOB HARRIS : *The Triumph of the Presbytery of Hanover; or, Separation of Church and State in Virginia.* New York, A. D. F. Randolph, 1888.

MEADE, W.: *Old Churches, Ministers, and Families of Virginia.* Philadelphia, 1857.

NEVIN, ALFRED : *Churches of the Valley.*

SMITH, JOSEPH : *Old Redstone, or Historical Sketches of Western Presbyterianism, its Early Ministers, its Perilous Times, and its First Records.* Philadelphia, 1854.

HOTCHKIN, JAMES H.: *A History of the Purchase and Settlement of Western New York and of the Rise, Progress, and Present State of the Presbyterian Church in that Section.* New York, M. W. Dodd, 1848.

WILSON : *Historical Almanac.*

————: *Index Volume of Princeton Review.*

NEVIN, ALFRED : *Encyclopædia of the Presbyterian Church in the United States of America.* Philadelphia, 1884.

HODGE, CHARLES: *The Constitutional History of the Presbyterian Church in the United States of America.* Philadelphia, Presbyterian Board of Publication, 1851.

WEBSTER, RICHARD : *History of the Presbyterian Church in America from its origin until the year 1760, with Biographical Sketches of its Early Ministers.* Philadelphia, 1857.

GILLETT, E. H.: *History of the Presbyterian Church in the United States of America.* 2 vols. Philadelphia Presbyterian Publication Committee, 1864.

BRIGGS, C. A.: *American Presbyterianism, its Origin and Early History.* New York, Charles Scribner's Sons, 1885.

SMITH, HENRY B. : *The Reformed Churches of Europe and America in Relation to General Church History. An Address delivered before the General Assembly May 21, 1855.* Philadelphia, printed by Henry B. Ashmead. 36 pp.

GREEN, ASHBEL : *History of Presbyterian Missions.* 1822.

SMITH, JAMES : *History of the Cumberland Presbyterian Church.*

McDONNOLD, B. W.: *History of the Cumberland Presbyterian Church.* 679 pp. Nashville, 1888.

GALLAGHER, JAMES : *The Western Sketch-Book.* Boston, 1850.

ALEXANDER, ARCHIBALD : *Biographical Sketches of the Founder and Principal Alumni of the Log College.* Philadelphia, 1851.

CLELAND, THOMAS : *The Kentucky Revival.* (Article in *Princeton Review*, Vol. VI.)

ALEXANDER, ARCHIBALD: *Review of Davidson's History.* (Articles in *Princeton Review*, 1847, pp. 141 and 470.)

HALL, JOHN : *History of the First Presbyterian Church, Trenton, New Jersey.*

McGready, James: *Narrative* prefixed to *Posthumous Works.*

Alexander, James W.: *Memoir of Archibald Alexander.*

Alexander, James W.: *Memoir of James Waddel.*

Miller, Samuel: *Life of John Rodgers.* Philadelphia, Presbyterian Board of Publication, 1840.

Spring, Gardiner: *Life of Samuel J. Mills.*

Hatfield, Edwin F.: *A Memoir of Elisha Baldwin, D.D., First President of Wabash College.* New York, 1843.

Schermerhorn, John F., and Mills, Samuel J.: *Communications Relative to the Progress of Bible Societies in the United States addressed to the Bible Society of Philadelphia.* Philadelphia, 1813.

Schermerhorn, John F., and Mills, Samuel J.: *A Correct View of that part of the United States which lies West of the Alleghany Mountains with regard to Religion and Morals.* Hartford, Conn., 1814. 52 pp.

Mills, Samuel J., and Smith, Daniel: *Report of a Missionary Tour through that part of the United States which lies West of the Alleghany Mountains performed under the direction of the Massachusetts Missionary Society.* Andover, 1815.

Morse, Jedediah: *Report to the Secretary of War of the United States on Indian Affairs, comprising a narrative of a tour performed in the summer of 1820.* New Haven, 1822.

McCoy, Isaac: *History of Baptist Indian Missions, embracing Remarks on the Former and Present Condition of the Aboriginal Tribes; their Settlement within the Indian Territory and their Future Prospects.* Washington, 1840.

PETERS, ABSALOM : *A Brief Answer to an Official Reply of the Board of Missions of the General Assembly to Six Letters of the Rev. Absalom Peters, Corresponding Secretary of the American Home Missionary Society, entitled "A Plea for Union in the West." Also, Mr. Peters' Reply to the Rev. Dr. J. L. Wilson's Four Propositions Sustained against the Claims of the American Home Missionary Society.* With an appendix. New York, printed by Clayton & Van Norden, 1831. 48 pp.

BOUTON, NATHANIEL : *History of the Origin of the American Home Missionary Society.* (Article in *The Home Missionary*, 1876.)

HENNEPIN, LOUIS : *Description de la Louisiane.* Utrecht, 1697.

JOUTEL, ———: *A Journal of the Last Voyage Performed by Monsr. de la Sale, to the Gulph of Mexico, to find out the Mouth of the Mississippi River.* London, 1714.

VOLNEY, CONSTANTIN FRANÇOIS : *View of the Climate and Soil of the United States.* London, 1804.

BOUQUET, HENRY : *An Historical Account of his Expedition against the Ohio Indians in 1764, with preface by Francis Parkman, and a translation of Dumas' Life of General Bouquet.* Cincinnati, 1868.

SARGENT, WINTHROP : *Diary of Colonel Winthrop Sargent, Adjutant General of the United States Army during the Campaign of 1791.*

CLARK, GEORGE ROGERS : *Sketch of His Campaign in the Illinois in 1778-9, and an Appendix containing the Public and Private Instructions to Col. Clark; and Major Bowman's Journal of the taking of Post St. Vincents.* Cincinnati, 1869.

SMITH, WILLIAM HENRY: Ed. *The Life and Public Services of Arthur St. Clair, Soldier of the Revolutionary War, etc., with his Correspondence and Papers arranged and annotated.* Cincinnati, 1882.

BURNET, JACOB: *Notes on the Early Settlement of the Northwestern Territory.* Portrait. 1847.

HILDRETH, S. P.: *Pioneer History; An Account of the First Examination of the Ohio Valley and the Early Settlement of the Northwest Territory.* Cincinnati, 1848.

COX, SANDFORD C.: *Recollections of the Early Settlement of the Wabash Valley.* La Fayette, 1860.

DAWSON, MOSES: *A Historical Narrative of the Civil and Military Services of Major-General William Henry Harrison, and a Vindication of his Character and Conduct, with a detail of his Negotiations and Wars with the Indians.* Cincinnati, 1824.

TODD, C. S.: *Civil and Military Services of W. H. Harrison.* Cincinnati, 1847.

SPARKS, JARED: *Life of Anthony Wayne.* New York, 1872.

PARKMAN, FRANCIS: *France and England in North America.* Boston, 1870–84.

PARKMAN, FRANCIS: *La Salle and the Discovery of the Great West.* Eleventh edition. Revised with additions. Boston, 1879.

MARSHALL, H.: *History of Kentucky.* Frankfort, 1824.

KNAPP, H. S.: *History of the Maumee Valley, commencing with its occupation by the French in 1680.* Toledo, Ohio, 1872.

DILLON, JOHN B.: *A History of Indiana, from its Earliest Exploration by Europeans to the close of the Territorial*

Government in 1816; Comprehending a History of the Discovery, Settlement, and Civil and Military Affairs of the Territory of the United States, Northwest of the River Ohio, and a General Review of the Progress of Public Affairs in Indiana, from 1816 to 1856. Map and illustrations. Indianapolis, 1859.

GOODRICH, DEWITT C., AND TUTTLE, CHARLES R.: *Illustrated History of the State of Indiana.* Indianapolis, Richard S. Peale & Co., 1875.

ENGLISH, WM. HAYDEN: *Conquest of the Country N. W. of the River Ohio.* 2 vols. Indianapolis, The Bowen-Merrill Company, 1896.

DUNN, J. P., Jr.: *Indiana, a Redemption from Slavery.* Houghton, Mifflin & Co., 1888.

SMITH, WILLIAM HENRY: *History of the State of Indiana.* 2 vols. The B. L. Blair Company, Indianapolis, 1897.

SMITH, OLIVER H.: *Early Indiana Trials and Sketches.* Cincinnati, 1858.

BRICE, WALLACE A.: *History of Fort Wayne, Indiana, with Biographical Sketches of Anthony Wayne and others.* Illustrated. Fort Wayne, 1868.

BROWN, IGNATIUS: *Indianapolis Directory, 1868–9.* (To which is prefixed, *History of Indianapolis.*) Indianapolis, 1868.

HOLLOWAY, W. R.: *Indianapolis, a Historical and Statistical Sketch.* Indianapolis, 1870.

NOWLAND, J. H. B.: *Early Reminiscences of Indianapolis.* Indianapolis, 1870.

STEWART, JAMES HERVEY: *Recollections of the Early Settlement of Carroll County, Indiana.* Cincinnati, 1872.

YOUNG, ANDREW W.: *History of Wayne County, Indiana.* Illustrated. Cincinnati, 1872.

PACKARD, JASPER: *History of La Porte County, Indiana.* La Porte, 1876.

HOVEY, ALVIN P., AND EDSON, WILLIAM P.: *Centennial Historical Sketch of Posey County, Indiana, and a Centennial Oration by William P. Edson.* Mount Vernon, 1876.

NOWLAND, J. H. B.: *Sketches of Prominent Citizens of Indianapolis.* Indianapolis, 1877.

Reports of Connecticut Missionary Society.

Reports of American Home Missionary Society.

Connecticut Evangelical Magazine, 1793-1820.

New York Missionary Magazine.

Indiana Religious Intelligencer, Madison, 1828-9, Rev. James H. Johnston, editor.

Pandect, Cincinnati, 1828, Rev. Joshua L. Wilson, D.D., editor.

Cincinnati Christian Journal, 1829.

Western Missionary Magazine.

Evangelical and Literary Magazine (Rice).

Van Rensselaer's *Presbyterian Magazine.*

Abolition Intelligencer (Crowe).

Missouri Presbyterian Recorder (Hill, Bullard & Homes).

Western Censor and Emigrants' Guide (Indianapolis).

Indianapolis Gazette.

Minutes of the General Assembly, Synod of Kentucky, Synod of Indiana, Presbytery of Transylvania, West Lexington Presbytery, Salem Presbytery, Madison Presbytery.

INDEX.

A. B. C. F. M., 153.
Abingdon Presbytery, 47, 99.
Alden, Lucius, 75, 206, 207-9.
Alexander, Archibald, 85, 90, 94, 128, 245.
Alexander, Samuel R., 49, 107.
Alexander, Thomas, 107.
Alexander, William A. P., 107.
Allegheny Seminary, 174, 234, 235.
Allouez, Father, 20.
American Bible Society, 183, 193.
American Home Missionary Society, 150, 174, 175, 200, 202, 204, 206, 212, 213, 214, 217, 224, 225, 227, 257.
American Tract Society, 193.
Amherst College, 117.
Anderson, Joseph, 61.
Anderson, Rufus, 153.
Andover Seminary, 129, 206, 207, 224, 227, 241.
Armstrong, John, 38.
Assembly's Committee of Missions, 59, 71, 84, 169, 170, 192, 200, 255.
Ayres, Elias, 243.
Bainbridge, 212.
Balch, Hezekiah, 99.
Balch, Hezekiah James, 99.
Balch, James, 98-100, 109, 123, 155, 169.
Balch, Stephen Bloomer, 99.
Baldridge, Samuel, 46, 47, 48, 49, 50, 51, 79, 169, 228.
Baldridge, Samuel C., 49, 50, 53, 75.
Baldwin, Elihu W., 252, 253.
Banks, Daniel C., 84, 123, 152.
Barnes, Albert, 196, 205.
Barton, William B., 133.
Basye, Lismund, 142.
Baxter, Richard, 96.
Beatty, Charles C., 36, 154, 155, 191.
Bedford, 115.
Bethany church, 112.
Bethlehem, 57.
Bevan, Philip, 75.

Bishop, George B., 250.
Blackburn, Samuel E., 217.
Blair, Robert, 13.
Blake, James, 141, 144, 171.
Bliss, Stephen, 107, 187, 210.
Bloomington, 114, 115, 122, 143, 186, 187, 189, 218, 229, 230.
Bloomington State Seminary, 111, 169, 186, 187.
Blue River congregation, 81, 103.
Blythe, James, 234.
Boardman, George S., 133.
Bono church, 104.
Boone, Daniel, 17.
Booneville, 224.
Bovelle, Stephen, 51, 53.
Breckinridge, John, 94.
Brookville, 119, 134.
Brown, Samuel, 81.
Brown, Tilly H., 167, 169, 187, 200.
Brownstown church, 84, 119.
Burlington, Ind., 151.
Burroughs, George S., 253.
Bush, George, 97, 169-84, 187, 189, 192, 193, 214, 225, 235.
Butler, Calvin, 224-6.
Cæsar Creek, 209.
Cameron, Archibald, 36, 38, 45.
Carnahan, James A., 252.
Carolinas, 11, 13, 28.
Cartwright, Peter, 41.
Centerville, 114.
Charlestown, 41, 45, 51, 53, 55, 64, 95, 120, 155, 168, 174, 234, 235, 236.
Charlestown, Va., 244.
Cheever, Joshua Cushman, 232.
Cheever, William M., 105, 160, 232, 233.
Chute, James, 150.
Cincinnati, 35, 52, 134, 179.
Clark, George Rogers, 23, 27, 28.
Clark grants, 95.
Clark, Marston G., 138.
Cleland, Philip S., 113, 116.

277

Cleland, Thomas, 31, 37, 38, 40, 41, 51, 81, 109, 136, 147.
Cobb, Leander, 225, 226, 227, 237.
Coe, Isaac, 141, 142, 144, 170, 171.
Coligny, Admiral, 11.
Columbus, Ind., 72, 227.
Concord church, 75, 120.
Condict, Lewis, 171, 177.
Connecticut Missionary Association, 82, 83, 101, 133, 142, 146, 206, 256.
Connersville, 134.
Conner, William, 138.
Corydon, 80, 138, 154, 190.
Craighead, Thomas, 19, 93.
Crawford, James, 18, 19.
Crawford, James, of Indiana, 217.
Crawfordsville, 71, 155, 196, 202, 203, 205, 210, 225, 227, 251, 252.
Cressy, Benjamin C., 103, 241, 242.
Crowe, John Finley, 79, 97, 156, 157-61, 162, 171, 174, 200, 205, 231, 232, 236, 237.
Crozier, John, 106.
Cumberland church, 34.
Cumberland controversy, 37.
Cumberland Presbytery, 99.
Cunningham, John W., 250.
Curtis, Harvey, 75.
Dablon, Claude, 20.
Danville, Ky., 110, 157, 185.
Dartmouth College, 136, 146, 170.
Davies, Samuel, 16, 17, 19, 85, 86, 87, 89, 92, 96.
Davies, Samuel, 13.
Day, Ezra H., 97, 145, 152, 153, 167, 169.
Delphi, 190.
Derrow, Nathan B., 75, 83.
De Soto, 20.
Dickerson, Henry L., 210.
Dickey, James H., 45, 53.
Dickey, John McElroy, 40, 54, 61-79, 97, 101, 109, 136, 152, 158, 162, 171, 200, 205, 219, 228, 231, 234, 235, 236, 237.
Dickey, Ninian S., 67, 97.
Dickey, William, 63, 84.
Dillsborough, 50, 208.
Doak, Samuel, 46, 47, 51.
Domestic Missionary Society, 193, 197.
Dufour, 27.
Dunbar, 11.
Duncan, James, 217.
Dunlapsville, 134.
Dunn, Williamson, 119, 189, 234 252.

Eagle Creek church, 96.
Ebenezer church, 154.
Edwards, Jonathan, 86, 87.
Eliot, John, 11.
Ellis, John M., 251.
Evansville, 84, 224.
Fall River, Mass., 124, 125.
Finley, Samuel, 56, 158.
Florida, 11.
Foote, Obed, 170.
Fort Wayne (Kekionga), 20, 22, 24, 26, 28, 29, 52, 148, 149, 150.
Fowler, Orin, 75, 97, 101, 116, 117-27, 152.
Franklin, 72, 104, 135, 136.
Frazer, Alexander, 171.
Fulton, Samuel, 36.
Gaines, Ludwell G., 142.
General Assembly, 61, 101, 110, 128, 129, 131, 133, 148, 156, 171, 174, 200, 210, 218, 234, 235, 243, 247, 255, 256, 260.
Gilliland, John, 251.
Goodell, William, 75, 97, 153, 154.
Graham church, 83.
Granville, Ohio, 110.
Gray, Daniel, 61.
Graysville, 100.
Green, Lewis W., 250.
Greensburgh, 212.
Greenville College, 99.
Greenwood, 98.
Gregg, Samuel, 210.
Hall, Baynard R., 110, 114, 169, 184-90, 193, 218, 229.
Hall, Nathan H., 63.
Hamilton College, 196, 198.
Hamilton, James, 13.
Hamilton, John T., 167, 168, 169, 235.
Hampton, John, 13.
Hanna, Samuel, 149.
Hanover Academy, 201, 234, 236, 237, 241.
Hanover College, 79, 159, 230, 234, 246.
Hanover, Ind., 50, 57, 115, 136, 159, 232, 239, 244.
Hanover Theological Seminary, 240, 241.
Hanover, Va., 14, 16, 18, 19, 87, 90.
Harmar, 28.
Harney, John H., 229.
Harris, Thompson S., 133
Harrison, Ohio, 118.
Harrison, William Henry, 23, 28, 39, 41, 80.
Hawley, Ransom, 116.

INDEX. 279

Henderson, Alexander, 13.
Henderson, William, 227.
Hickman, Clement, 84, 169.
Hobart, Peter, 11.
Hoge, Samuel D., 170.
Holland, 134.
Holt, Samuel, 30.
Honey Creek church, 49.
Hopewell church (Turman's Creek), 100.
Hovey, Edmund O., 251.
Howe, John, 64.
Humphrey, Edward P., 248.
Indiana Missionary Society, 72, 193, 200, 201, 209, 224, 225, 231, 258.
Indiana Religious Intelligencer, 202.
Indianapolis, 104, 138-47, 155, 170, 174, 178, 186, 187, 189, 191, 192, 214.
Indiana, Synod of, 161, 210, 216, 219-24, 236, 260.
Indiana Theological Seminary, 159, 174, 234, 242, 247.
Jacob, Henry, 12.
Jefferson church, 121.
Jeffersonville, 55, 217.
Jenks, Ahab, 133.
Johnston, James H., 72, 79, 151, 159, 192, 193, 194-205, 224, 231, 234, 236, 237, 239, 240.
Joutel, 21, 22.
Kemper, James, 35, 36, 53.
Kentucky, 14, 17, 18, 19, 28, 29, 30, 31, 32, 35, 38, 39, 40, 41, 46, 47, 53, 60, 82, 93, 96, 109, 110, 111, 146, 147, 154, 158.
Kentucky, Synod of, 131, 162, 218, 259
Ketcham, John, 25, 122.
Kingston, 135, 212.
Knox County, 42, 45.
La Fayette (Ouiatenon), 22, 24, 26, 189.
Laggan Presbytery, 12, 13.
Lancaster Presbytery, 48.
Lapsley, Joseph B., 51, 53, 81.
La Salle, 21.
Law, John, 28.
Lawrenceburgh, 46, 47, 48, 50, 53, 55, 134, 228, 259.
Lexington, 42, 51, 68.
Lindsley, Philip, 250.
Little, Henry, 74, 115, 190, 202, 210.
Livingston, Robert, 11, 12.
Livonia, 82, 103, 104, 106, 145.
Londonderry, 13.
Long Island Presbytery, 108.

Louisville, 39, 95, 123, 168.
Louisville Presbytery, 155, 168, 217, 259.
Lowry, Samuel G., 155, 212-3.
Lowry, William, 117, 227.
Lyle, John, 102.
MacMaster, Erasmus Darwin, 246-50.
MacMaster, Gilbert, 246.
Madison, 57, 58, 59, 72, 109, 119, 124, 128, 136, 156, 168, 192, 198, 199, 200, 202, 203.
Madison Presbytery, 58, 210, 212, 217, 218, 232.
Madison University, 246.
Makemie Francis, 12, 13, 14, 18.
Marest, Father, 22.
Marquette, 20, 21.
Martin, Claudius B. H., 107.
Martin, Samuel N. D., 107.
Martin, William A. P., 107.
Martin, William W., 79, 97, 101, 102-7, 109, 119, 120, 144, 158, 162, 170, 205, 219, 226, 228, 231, 237.
Massachusetts Missionary Society, 54, 55.
Matthews, John, 174, 205, 237, 239, 241, 243-6.
McCalla, Daniel, 91.
McClelland, John, 13.
McClung, John A., 95.
McClure, Andrew, 19.
McClure, D., 109.
McCormick Theological Seminary, 243.
McCoy, Isaac, 148.
McFarland, Francis, 133.
McGready, James, 31, 32, 33, 34, 35, 41, 43, 53, 81, 84, 100.
McLeod, Lewis, 209.
McNemar, Richard, 134.
McNish, George, 13.
Mecklenburgh Declaration, 11, 99.
Merrill, Samuel, 76.
Miami Presbytery, 48, 52, 56, 134, 259.
Miami University, 246.
Middlebury College, 150.
Milligan, Thomas S., 68, 73, 213.
Mills, Caleb, 252.
Mills, Samuel J., 35, 40, 54, 55, 56, 61, 75.
Missouri, 129, 133, 142.
Missouri Presbytery, 218.
Monfort, David, 133-5, 136.
Moore, James, 91, 94.
Moreland, John R., 178, 237.
Moriah, N. Y., 114.
Morris Reading House, 15.

Mount Carmel, 134.
Mount Pleasant, 120.
Muhlenburg Presbytery, 65, 167, 259, 260.
Nelson, Samuel K., 110.
Nesbit, William, 210.
New Albany, 55, 84, 109, 110, 145, 151, 152, 167, 168, 243, 247, 249.
New Brunswick Presbytery, 86, 170, 210.
New Castle Presbytery, 52.
New Hope church, 49, 75.
New Lexington church, 68, 71, 121.
New Providence church, 50, 72, 98.
New Winchester, 212.
New York, 109.
North Carolina, 32, 33, 34.
Northwestern Territory, 23.
Noyes, James, 11.
Ogden, Isaac A., 218.
Ohio, 30, 35.
Ohio, Falls of the, 55.
Ohio, Synod of, 149, 259.
Oneida Female Missionary Society, 108.
Orleans, 103, 104.
Oxford, Ohio, 118.
Palestine church, 104.
Palmyra church, 45, 53, 64.
Paoli, 103, 104, 119, 226.
Paris, Ky., 102.
Parker, Thomas, 11.
Parkersburgh, 212.
Peaks of Otter, 18, 19.
Pennsylvania, 13, 32, 102.
Perrin, Truman, 216.
Pisgah church, 68, 71, 75, 81.
Pittinger, Nicholas, 156.
Pittsburg Missionary Society, 61.
Platt, Adams W., 133.
Posey, Thomas, 80, 138, 151.
Post, Martin M., 73, 79.
Princeton College, 17, 85, 89, 129, 170, 185.
Princeton, Ind., 84, 103, 104, 224, 226, 246.
Princeton, N. J., 19, 93, 158, 169, 174, 179, 192, 193, 196, 197, 217, 227, 239.
Princeton Seminary, 111, 128, 129, 134, 136, 150, 158, 170, 196, 209.
Proctor, David Choate, 142, 143, 145, 146, 147, 154, 169, 170.
Putnamville, 115.
Rankin, Adam, 18, 19.
Rankin, Arthur T., 47.
Rankin, John, 47, 150.
Rannels, Samuel, 31, 41, 102.

Ray, James M., 141, 142, 144, 171, 217.
Redstone Presbytery, 33.
Reed, Isaac, 97, 101, 107-16, 119, 123, 136, 142, 144, 152, 162, 170, 171, 187, 189, 192, 228.
Rice, David, 17, 18, 19, 36, 38, 85, 90.
Richmond, Ind., 150, 169.
Ripley, Ohio, 150.
Rising Sun, 36, 75, 209, 259.
Rivet, Father, 228.
Roan, John, 16.
Robertson, Samuel B., 31, 41, 45, 53.
Robinson, Charles Stebbins, 129, 130.
Robinson, Hezekiah, 251.
Robinson, Joseph, 218.
Robinson, William, of Indiana, 48, 51, 54, 56, 57, 59, 60, 65, 79, 101, 109, 122, 136, 162, 169, 228.
Robinson, William, of Virginia, 15, 16.
Rockville, 212.
Rodgers, Ravaud K., 101, 123, 127, 128, 129, 155.
Ross, John, 73, 75, 148, 149, 150, 151, 153, 169.
Salem church, 82, 103, 119, 120.
Salem Presbytery, 113, 155, 162-6, 167, 169, 187, 200, 210, 217, 218, 226, 231, 232, 259, 260.
Schermerhorn, John F., 54.
Scott, Samuel Thornton, 40, 42, 43, 44, 51, 53, 54, 64, 65, 79, 101, 109, 154, 162, 169, 192, 193, 205, 226, 228, 259.
Scott, William M., 250.
Scribner, Joel, 151.
Scudder, Caleb, 141, 143, 171.
Searle, Thomas C., 136, 137, 156, 169.
Shannon, Samuel, 81.
Shelby, Colonel, 39.
Shelbyville, 98.
Shiloh church, 154.
Small, Colonel, 41.
Smith, Daniel, 54, 55.
South Carolina, 161.
South Marion church, 96, 98.
Spencer, 189.
Sprague, William B., 117.
Spring, Gardiner, 239.
St. Clair, Arthur, 23, 28.
Stevens, Thomas, 79.
Stevens, William, 12.
Stewart, James, 210.
Stowe, Harriet Beecher, 78.

INDEX. 281

Sullivan, Jeremiah, 138, 183.
Taylor, Nathaniel, 13.
Taylor, Samuel, 169.
Templin, Terah, 18.
Tennents, 16.
Tennessee, 28, 35, 47, 83, 133.
Terre Haute, 52, 134, 155, 226.
Thomas, Thomas Ebenezer, 250.
Thomson, James, 227, 251.
Thomson, John, 134.
Thomson, John S., 251.
Thornton, John, 91.
Tipton, 151.
Todd, Henry G., 96.
Todd, John, Colonel, 91.
Todd, John, of Indiana, 79, 84-98, 101, 109, 162, 228.
Todd, John, of Virginia, 17, 85-92.
Transylvania Academy, 42.
Transylvania Presbytery, 19, 31, 36, 37, 45, 51, 56, 61, 93, 94, 99, 109, 255, 258, 259.
Transylvania University, 134.
Trimble, Joseph, 156, 169, 198.
Turman's Creek, 100, 155.
Tuttle, Joseph F., 204, 253.
Union College, 185, 192, 246.
United Domestic Missionary Society, 112, 132, 170, 207, 209, 257.
Vance, James, 36, 45, 53.
Vancourt, John, 133.
Velona, 120.
Vermont University, 170.
Vernon church, 136.
Versailles, 115.
Vevay, 119.
Vincennes, 23, 24, 25, 26, 28, 31, 32, 36, 37, 39, 40, 41, 44, 45, 51, 53, 57, 64, 71, 104, 122, 123, 124, 138, 154, 155, 187, 192, 211, 216, 218, 219, 228, 259.
Vincennes University, 229, 230.
Virginia, 13, 18, 23, 27, 28, 31, 35, 46, 83, 92, 98.

Virginia, Synod of, 259.
Volney, C. F. C., 25, 26.
Wabash College, 88, 212, 227, 250.
Wabash Presbytery, 178, 218.
Waddel, James, 85, 91, 92, 101.
Wallace, Matthew G., 48, 52, 53, 148.
Walnut Hills, 174, 234, 235.
Washington Academy, 93.
Washington church, 54, 65, 212, 224, 226.
Washington College, 47, 190, 229.
Washington, George, 14, 27.
Washington Presbytery, 48, 259.
Waveland, 212.
Wayne, Anthony, 24, 27.
Welsh, James, 48, 61.
West Lexington Presbytery, 31, 42, 93, 102, 259.
West Salem church, 104.
Whitaker, Alexander, 11.
White, Charles, 253.
Whitefield, George, 88.
Whitewater, 139.
Wick, William W., 171.
Williams College, 54, 116, 129.
Williams, Jesse L., 52.
Williamson, Alexander, 169, 187, 190, 191, 193, 200.
Williamson, Thomas, 30.
Wilson, Joshua L., 48.
Wilson, Peter, 52.
Wirt, William, 101.
Wood, James, 250.
Woolsey, Theodore D., 203, 204.
Wylie, Andrew, 189, 229.
Wylie, William, 81.
Yale College, 117, 203.
Yandes, Daniel, 170.
Young, John, 169, 193, 195, 194, 198, 199.
Young Men's Missionary Society (N. Y.), 136, 257.

www.ingramcontent.com/pod-product-compliance
Lightning Source LLC
Chambersburg PA
CBHW031250250426
43672CB00029BA/1736